IDENTITY CRISIS

HEALTH CARE BRANDING'S HIDDEN PROBLEMS AND PROVEN STRATEGIES TO SOLVE THEM

VINCE PARRY

PARRY BRANDING GROUP

Identity Crisis: Healthcare Branding's Hidden Problems and Proven Strategies to Solve Them

For information about this title or to order other books and/or electronic media, contact the publisher:

Parry Branding Group, Inc.
parrybrandinggroup.com/contact
vparry@parrybranding.com

ISBNs: 978-0-9978574-1-2 (paperback)
978-0-9978574-0-5 (ebook)

Printed in the United States of America
Cover and interior design: 1106 Design

PRAISE FOR *IDENTITY CRISIS*

"Good marketing is good storytelling. And the healthcare category could use a heavy dose of this advice. Vince Parry certainly brings this kind of thinking to an industry that needs it."

—Jack Trout, Global Marketing Expert and Author

"The patron saint of all good, common-sense brand builders.

In *Identity Crisis*, what Vince Parry knows about healthcare branding and positioning is all anyone will ever need to know. He is a combination of that one wise professor everyone on campus wants to take and James Randi, the magician who debunks the charlatans of his industry."

—Martin Mannion, Chief Strategy Officer, Guidemark Health

"A landmark book.

Identity Crisis reveals keen insights on healthcare brands of all kind, including how companies can best harness the power of their corporate and portfolio brand assets. Essential reading for pharmaceutical, biotech and device clients looking to secure an edge in the market."

—R. Blane Walter, Partner, Talisman Capital; Former CEO, inVentiv Health

"Required reading for students moving forward.

Finally! The book that takes a look into the mind of a veteran healthcare branding expert. *Identity Crisis* is a must read for anyone who wants to understand branding in the healthcare industry and beyond."

—Pete Marchisini, COO Alamo Pharma Services; Faculty, Rutgers Business School, Pharmaceutical MBA Program.

"Advance your healthcare brand and career armed with these insights.

Identity Crisis demonstrates why 'consumer' branding approaches don't work for our unique customers, lifecycles, and market dynamics in healthcare, and more importantly, which proven strategic approaches do."

—Suzanne Goss, Director of Strategy, UNIFIED, an Omnicom Agency

"*Identity Crisis* is a bold creative act of its own.

Vince Parry's entire approach to healthcare branding delivers imaginative insights and processes that drive creative teams to achieve their best work. The author makes branding not only enlightening, but fun as well."

—Tina Fascetti, Chief Creative Officer, Guidemark Health

"Whether you are a patient or a doctor, this book will prove both enlightening and enjoyable.

As both a physician and a consumer, *Identity Crisis* has opened my eyes to the marketing and branding processes surrounding the products and medications I use most commonly. The book has taught me how my choices are guided by Mr. Parry's industry and, more importantly, how it influences the decisions we make for patients."

—Julie A. Foont, M.D.

In memory of my father,
Dr. Vincent C. Parry

That I would be good
if I got and stayed sick

—Alanis Morissette
"*That I would be good*"

TABLE OF CONTENTS

Acknowledgments

Throughout this book I have referred to "my colleagues" or "our team" or aspects of identity deliverables (e.g., logos) that I don't have the acumen to produce myself. I wish to acknowledge openly these great talents and thank them generously. I could have never written this book without having known and worked with them.

The greatest single influence on my work and on my thinking without a doubt has been Joe Paumi, my creative partner for 13 years while he and I were Co-Creative Directors and good friends at Sudler & Hennessey. Joe taught me the value of not overthinking what we do, the importance of laughter as a job requirement, and the difference between working hard and working smart. Joe is one of the industry's top designers and creative talents, and the man behind many of the logos discussed in this book, including Lipitor, Vioxx, Zestril, Tamiflu and others. But much more than this, he has always been the id to my ego.

I must sincerely thank the strategists who came to work for me at Y Brand (a former company of inVentiv Health) and took the brave chance of making brand identity the sole focus of their careers. A smarter, more loyal group of people one could ever hope to meet in the business world, they are: Suzanne Goss, who is so gifted, knowledgeable, and forever one step ahead of me that she earned the reputation as "Vince's

Brain" among us all; Martin Mannion, a force of nature that took the branding world and made it his own fun party with wit, insight, and fierce dedication; Rodney Sexton, who brought the disciplines of education into the branding process to create his own brand of brilliant thinking; Chetan Vijayvergiya, our neuroscience PhD who helped us create a branding of the science platform that had few rivals; Miles West, who used his background and training as a Creative Director of Art to challenge the design team in ways that truly brought out the essence of the brand strategy; and Clare Carroll, whose leadership and loyalty created the space I needed to be as effective as I could in performing the multitude of tasks for which I was responsible as Chief Branding Officer of inVentiv Health.

I have had the great fortune of working with some of the top designers who I managed to lure from the more evolved, more refined consumer world of graphic design to help pull healthcare branding design out of the dark ages kicking and screaming. As previously noted, from 2002 to 2012, I ran inVentiv Health's branding capability from a unit called Y Brand, one of the most satisfying enterprises of my entire career. I wish to acknowledge and thank the paragon talents of Raphael Holguin, Fernando Fernandez, Diane DePaolis and, ultimately, Tiphaine Guillemet, who continues to help me deliver stellar graphic design and creative leadership for Parry Branding Group. Many of the observations in this book regarding the principles of graphic design and its proper role in branding I learned from them, and for that I give thanks every day.

Over the years, I have learned the humility to know what I don't know and to listen and learn from those who do. One such person is Blane Walter. I met Blane when he was recruiting a replacement for Chris Snell, the Chief Creative Officer of his flagship agency at the time, Gerbig Snell and Weisheimer (now GWS Worldwide). Back then Blane, by his own admission, knew very little about either the agency or healthcare businesses, and I knew very little about building companies. By virtue of being quick studies and good listeners, we forged an understanding that allowed each of us to flourish in new ways. Blane is an intuitive genius about people. He would invest in talent, not merely hire it. Instead of shoehorning people into prescribed roles, Blane would assess a candidates' strengths and potential and then create a job description around these aspects. He took a 250-person organization and helped expand it into the global powerhouse that is inVentiv Health, and I am thankful to have played a part in an exchange of learning and knowledge that was truly transformational.

I have too many other mentors to count, but will try not to leave anyone out. From the Sudler & Hennessey days: Robert (Bob) Gouterman, the former EVP of the Marketing, Medical, and Media Department, who taught me the fundamentals of healthcare marketing; the late Harold Grossman, also part of Bob's group, who taught me how to think about data and apply it in new and insightful ways; Ted Lawrence, the Managing Director, who revealed to me just how savvy one could be in bridging the frequent divide between creative and account services, and who never shied away from imparting sage advice whether solicited or not, thank goodness; Robin Davenport, a Creative Director under Joe and me at S&H, who understood that her brilliant concepts must first serve the brand identity; and Tina Fascetti, an Associate Creative Director at S&H, who has deservedly risen to the top of her field and who taught me the art of collaboration, as well as just how high my expectations could go when creating ideas together.

Aside from Blane Walter at inVentiv, I would be remiss if I did not also acknowledge two other great influences on me at this company: Guy Mastrion, one of the founders of Palio (an inVentiv Health agency) and its Chief Creative Officer (and now leading his own agency, Brandforming), who was the most creative person in the entire inVentiv organization and yet such a humble, humane presence in an often demanding world; and Brian Heffernan, the Chief Growth Officer and storyteller *par excellence*, who re-invented the ways and means by which we pitched and won new business.

As for clients, while I have had fun and learned from the best of them, the one who remains at the top of my list is Charlotte O. McKines, the former VP Global Marketing Communications and Channel Strategies of Merck, whose emotional toughness and fierce intelligence are magically wedded to a heart of gold and an unwavering loyalty that continue to enhance our friendship.

Having been a writer all my life but having no clue about how to write and publish a book, I must thank B.G. Dilworth, agent and advisor, who steadfastly took me through every step of the process and helped me find the best aspects of my voice.

And last but first in my heart, I must thank my wife, Carolyn, for her support and great patience while I spent the better part of my days and nights writing this book when I could have been out and about enjoying her company as I always do.

You are all going to branding heaven.

PREFACE

A few years ago, while I was teaching a seminar on healthcare branding at Rutgers, one of the MBA students raised his hand and asked if I could recommend any good books on healthcare branding. I couldn't. I was ashamed. Surely there must be some seminal texts that exist of which I was embarrassingly unaware. I apologized, took his card, and promised to get back to him with a good answer as quickly as possible.

As a former Chief Creative Officer and Chief Branding Officer in healthcare communications over the course of my career, I would always require my staff to have a working knowledge of fundamental branding texts:

- *Positioning: The Battle for Your Mind* by Al Ries and Jack Trout
- *Building Strong Brands* by David A. Aaker

and also the seminal books that contain timeless lessons on research, promotion fundamentals, and brand planning:

- *Confessions of An Ad Man* by David Ogilvy
- *Truth, Lies and Advertising: The Art of Account Planning* by Jon Steel

While these are great books—books everyone in the commercial arts of branding, marketing, advertising, and communications should own—they really don't deal with the unique subject of what I and many others in my field do for a living each day: branding health and wellness concepts, including companies, franchises, products, services, technologies, and illnesses.

The next day, I searched all the top book-selling sites on the Internet, seeking to uncover a half dozen or so gems that I could read and pass on to my students so I wouldn't be derelict in my professorial responsibilities (I was a guest lecturer, to be honest). I found books written by the heads of branding firms and other experts about healthcare. But these used the term "branding" so broadly that it might as well have been called "the kitchen sink of healthcare marketing." Where were the texts that told the stories of being in the trenches, like me? Where were the texts that revealed the many ways in which healthcare brand identity development and cultivation differed from the consumer goods world of Ries, Trout, Ogilvy, Aaker, and Steel? Where were the rigorous case studies of why healthcare branding is so behind the curve and wrong-headed as my colleagues and I know firsthand? Where were the tomes of wisdom that showed the way to resolve the hidden branding problems in healthcare by employing the proven processes my colleagues and I had invented or co-opted from health psychology and used in our daily interactions with clients to keep them on track? I was shocked to find that there were none. Zip. Zero.

Don't get me wrong. There are many books on healthcare marketing. But healthcare marketing—versus healthcare brand identity development and cultivation—are topics as different as TV repair and show business. The first is an academic study on the nuts and bolts of, essentially, pharmaceutical product management, while the second is about our healthcare ethos: the characteristic spirit of our healthcare-oriented culture as manifested in its beliefs, fallacies, shortcomings, and aspirations.

So I decided to write one myself.

I have always been a writer by discipline. I have a Master's degree in English. I have always been fascinated with storytelling. Up until my late 20s, I'd never even considered a career as a promotional writer, crafting copy for ads and sales brochures that weaved persuasive narratives about products or services or anything, for that matter, that had to do with advertising. It seemed industrial, foreign, and impure to my writerly ambitions. Even though I had grown up in the eye of the healthcare hurricane and watched the magnificence and tragedy swirl at such close range, it took me years to realize that I had a perspective that could help tell better stories about wellness and illness as an insider. My father was a Marcus Welby-era family physician. My mother worked as a receptionist at hospitals while my father went to medical school. As a teenager, I—like my friends—got part-time jobs through our respective fathers. So while my friends were stocking shelves at their fathers' stores or working as assistants in their dads' offices, I was given the opportunity to clerk at hospital and retail pharmacies. My father's office was in our home. Patients would enter and exit from a side door. My father's friends were all doctors. My brother became a doctor and took over my father's practice in that same home. And over the years, in my interactions with patients and healthcare providers and staff, and observing how diabetes, arthritis, irritable bowel syndrome, multiple sclerosis, heart disease, and cancer compromised and ultimately felled those around me, I knew I had to go into the field of healthcare brand identity because so many of the lives I witnessed were identified with wellness and illness.

I soon discovered that I was not alone. Many of my colleagues have a passion for trying to take the great mysteries of illness and its insidious calculations and promoting the very health remedies over the past three decades that ultimately rendered such illnesses less onerous. These colleagues had had brushes with serious illness, whether in their families or with themselves, and found, like me, that their own identities were wound together in a double helix with the identities of those illnesses. The pathologies had come to define our experience in some essential ways. And then there were others—natural creative talents or ad men and women—whose failed novels or unsold paintings or leadership yearnings had driven them into the commercial arts. However, they, too, balked at the vocation of selling the next soft drink, snow tire, or cat food and chose, instead, to apply themselves in ways that had more meaning for them. While they couldn't point to a household brand name SUV or laundry detergent and tell their friends, "Hey, I did that one," they opted for the satisfaction of operating behind the scenes, keeping the dark birds of illness at bay with true stories about new therapies, and smiling whenever the rates of cancer or heart disease declined. (Of course, our industry has its fair share of jerks, too. What enterprise doesn't?)

Things have changed radically over the past many years. It was once a quaint notion that health was the opposite of sickness, but today health is so much a part of our lives that it defines our own identities in ways that have accelerated faster than our ability to assimilate them. Healthcare isn't just a big business now; it also plays a fundamental role in how we face the world every day and make brand choices. Our healthcare technology—our state of the science—has grown so acutely effective that it creates a mandate to lead a healthy life or else betray one's own identity. The truth of our self-evaluation as health-minded individuals has activated the population to seek out brands that reflect who we aspire to be. The purposeful hunt for which cereal or which activity wrist calculator to buy is ready evidence at hand. However, nowhere is our dance with health and wellness more engaged and engaging than when our identities are compromised by illness and we spiral into the existential limbo of becoming a patient in the hopes that we'll come out the other end, whole once again.

Why has no one offered an inside critique that is honest and helpful and not just another cynical, clichéd hack at the healthcare industry?

How do illness and wellness alter who we are in our own minds and affect how we buy healthcare brands? Why do doctors become the different specialists they become? What does it say about them and their desire to use healthcare brands to define their own brand of practice? Why do healthcare companies feel the need to treat many of our life-altering drugs as if they were consumer goods brands, with laughable TV commercials and stuffed-animal illness icons parading across our screens, urging you to visit your doctor and see if whatever is right for you? Why do we all pretend that doctors are emotionless automatons, affected only by hard data when selecting the therapies they prescribe? And why do so many of our healthcare brands pander to this wide-eyed view of healthcare with logos that feature heavy-handed design and cartoon patients with arms raised in celebration of the wonder of it all? There are a multitude of hidden problems in healthcare branding, and it has created an identity crisis both for the brands and the people who help make such brands a flattering reflection of themselves as healthy individuals.

The answers to these questions and how to address these problems constitute the story I set out to tell with this book. I have witnessed it all from the front lines, launched brand identities for some of the most successful healthcare brands over the last few decades, and have created or evolved many of the strategic practices associated with crafting effective healthcare brand identities from research through to design. For those of you who, like my inquisitive grad student, wish to learn more about your trade, this book can serve as a means of sharpening your skills and avoiding the pitfalls of past mistakes. For others fascinated by the thoughts my questions raise, this book will hopefully illuminate and intrigue on a societal level. But whoever you are, I promise that you will get a front-row seat to healthcare branding's hidden problems—the Identity Crises that have plagued so much of the industry for years—and proven strategies for how to solve them.

1

What Healthcare Branding Wants To Be If It Grows Up

Something is amiss with healthcare branding. Everyone is uncomfortable with it but can't figure out exactly why. And it's not anything so isolated as a brand name that defies pronunciation or a TV campaign that asks you to believe people genuinely love their laxative. The problem is more insidious and pervasive than this, and it hides in plain sight. Healthcare branding has an identity crisis: a foundational uncertainty and confusion about its expected purpose and role in society. Should the branding of a treatment for psoriasis or diabetes or blood pressure avail itself of the proven processes used to brand beer, SUVs and mobile phones? Or should healthcare branding behave like a clinical bulletin from the front lines, detached from passion and sticking to the facts, ma'am, just the facts?

The truth is, healthcare branding doesn't know what it wants to be because the ideas about health, illness and wellness in our culture have evolved faster and more dramatically than we have assimilated them. More to the point, how we embrace ideas of health, illness and wellness as inalienable elements of our own identities—how we define who *we* are—has not quite caught up with our willingness to be honest with ourselves. The very brands that extend and improve all of our lives are at once lionized as miracles of modern technology and demonized as the wolves of big business preying on the sheep of our citizenry. The loudest voices declaiming healthcare as some type of entitlement guaranteed under the Constitution are the same voices protesting at the polls against government interfering with our capitalistic way of life. And the same self-appointed consumer advocates who raise the specter of Big Pharma's supposed exploitation of patient fears seem oblivious to the irony that they, too, are stoking paranoia and profiting off of those same fears with bestselling books. All parties—companies, critics, doctors, patients and insurance companies, heck, even the FDA—are all contributories to the healthcare identity crisis and the way it affects the transaction of services and healthcare brands. It seems the American people want to have their cake, eat it too, and then heckle the cake maker for baking something so sweet and essential to our needs yet not giving it away for free. We are conflicted and uncertain about healthcare, and as a result healthcare branding is a reflection of our own identity crisis regarding health, illness and wellness, always wondering what it wants to be if it ever grows up and bears responsibility for being true to itself.

[It seems the American people want to have their cake, eat it too, and then heckle the cake maker for baking something so sweet and essential to our needs yet not giving it away for free.]

Many healthcare brands—companies, products and services—do manage to discover who they really are and thrive in the world. But far too many healthcare brands lose their way and assume one bad identity after another in failed pursuits of understanding their place in our lives. I have worked in healthcare branding for more than 30 years and have seen both types of healthcare brand identities, the lost and the found. And I promise to tell you all that I know in this book about how to avoid an identity crisis for your brand by pursuing proven best practices in every step of the branding process. However, before we begin, we must first take a look into the deep, dark truthful mirror and learn how we have come to struggle with aspects of health and wellness as they relate to the very core of our own personal identities.

Wellness in America has always been homogenously viewed as a synonym for normalcy, a pristine landscape in which we all thrive happily save for the occasional journey into uncharted territory, where illness bullies us for brief bouts until we find our way back home. Fifty years ago, America observed its hospitals and medical professionals through the weekly prism of television's *Dr. Kildare* or *Ben Casey* in much the same way we view dramas about Navy Seal teams today: important men (yes, always men back then) waging battle against forces dark enough to give us chills, but so far away that we knew it would never touch our lives. TV doctors waged war, just not on our shores. And real doctors, the ones people went to, were of the type found on *Marcus Welby, MD*: wise, kind demi gods ever ready to lay on hands, mend a wound, or make a house call as long as their advice was never questioned. (I know firsthand, because my father was such a doctor for more than 40 years. At his wake, a hundred patients in the community showed up to pay their respects.)

Illness was the great exception to the rule of wellness back then, or so it clearly seemed. Vaccination had all but eliminated the deadliest plagues of the past. The pre-Internet Era cloistered the population's perspective on health statistics. Social networks were the size of hair salons. Many of the health conditions that are today's household words had yet to be acknowledged or given medical names, thereby reducing the dialogue about illness to its lowest common denominators. "Quit whining." "Walk it off." Or my grandmother's favorite, "It's all in your head." (To her credit, my grandmother lived to be 91 and died peacefully in her sleep.)

American optimism in the '50s and '60s cleaved the concept of illness into two categories: *annoying, acute maladies* which we easily accepted and from which we easily recovered, such as a cold, a broken arm, or indigestion; and *terrifying mysteries* such as cancer or heart disease for which there had yet to be effective treatments, so why risk even talking about them?

"Did you hear what happened to Mr. Simon who lived down the block?" a neighbor would say in a low whisper. "He had the Big C."

Like Lord Voldemort in the *Harry Potter* series, cancer could not even be mentioned by name lest it conjure an evil fate for the utterer.

This perfect storm of ignorance, popular disinterest in enlightenment, and the gung-ho fallacy of American post-war fortitude made the question of how to think about illness and wellness seem as pointless as a contemplation of air or water. It's just there. What's to think about?

Hence, people didn't get what we now know to be a form of arthritis; they got "gout" because they consumed alcohol and food excessively. *That can't be taken seriously, because it's their own damn fault.* They didn't get what we now call overactive bladder; they grew feeble and weak with age and were "incontinent." *Nothing you can do. People get old.* They didn't get multiple sclerosis; they became hysterical because, *You know how women can get* (unless, of course, you remove the hysteria with a hysterectomy). If it wasn't fatal, illness was a normal part of life to be accepted as one would accept pain with childbirth or losing one's hair.

Happily, things have changed since the dark ages of the 1960s, when I was taken out of grade school for weeks because my infected tonsils were mischaracterized as "blood cancer." Part of this change has come with the advent of modern medicine—the brilliant therapeutic discoveries of chemists, biologists and engineers working for pharmaceutical and biotech companies. There have also been advances in diagnostic devices that have illuminated the blind darkness of pathogenesis. And then there's the Age of Information, ushered in by the worldwide web and the technological prowess of Silicon Valley, breathing fresh air into an ongoing dialogue about health and wellness. There are numerous authoritative sites, such as WebMD and MayoClinic.org, where one can get expert, factual information, or get pointed in the right direction for additional resources. (And there's also a lot of misinformation, admittedly. Quite a lot.)

Such change agents as technology and the information age have been written about and awarded and put up on entertainment screens big and small. Each alone has evolved behaviors dramatically, and taken together along with other factors such as whole-food consciousness, nutraceuticals and the fitness craze, a revolution has taken place. Health is no longer just a quaint notion of normalcy measured by the spring in our grandparents' step. Nor is it just one of the driving industries of our economy. It is also one of the primary ways we define who we are in our daily lives. For in order to have changed behaviors on such a magnitude, one must first have had to change our culture's beliefs about health on an equally large scale. And along with those changing beliefs comes a new way of relating to our well-being, one that implies a public awareness of the difference between normal, age-appropriate pains and conditions, and the signs and symptoms that something might be really wrong, warranting a doctor's intervention and treatment.

Far from being the big bad wolf taking advantage of helpless sheep, healthcare marketing is in good part responsible for this transformational public awareness and intense interest in personal health and well-being. How do people now generally know that chronic heartburn isn't the result of too much pizza, but instead a condition called gastroesophageal reflux disorder, or GERD? Why do 40- to 50-year-old women no longer puzzle over hot flashes or mood swings, chalking it up to something called perimenopause? Why do the brand names Viagra, Lipitor, and Botox share close company with Coca-Cola, Google, and Tiffany in the nightly monologues of talk-show hosts? I submit that the public's understanding of all of these branded entities and their ilk is due to the work done by me and other marketers like me. For the past 30 years, my colleagues and I have been instrumental in discovering, strategizing, and creating healthcare branding for products, companies, services, illnesses and the scientific concepts underlying health, wellness and illness.

Industry critics perceive as antagonistic and contentious the reality that our ideas about health, wellness and illness have been shaped by the discipline of branding. To the contrary, by bringing greater clarity to what ails us, giving the conditions and diseases that torment us helpful names that unite us against them, and elevating the dialogue between patients and their gate-keeper physicians about which treatment approaches to take (or not), we have delivered the American public from the primitive past. Unlike many cultures co-existing on the planet with us today, we no longer think of illness and wellness as quaint, mysterious concepts or regard them as evidence of divine punishment and reward. People no longer have to suffer in silence, wondering why they feel the strange way they do, alone and ashamed and at the mercy of ignorance.

There's another reason why branding healthcare concepts is so vital to our collective consciousness. We do not see health as it is; we see health as *we* are.

> [WELLNESS AND ILLNESS ARE AMONG THE PRIMARY DRIVERS OF OUR OWN IDENTITIES—OF HOW WE SUBJECTIVELY DEFINE OURSELVES IN RELATION TO THE WORLD.]

Today, wellness has left behind its reputation as merely the converse of illness. Health is now perceived by people—each in their own fashion—as an aspirational state of being where one is at one's best. It has moral as well as physical implications. The guilt one feels biting into a cupcake. The runner's high. The righteous burn in pursuit of a personal duty. "I'm going to be good today," many of us have thought, because to betray one's health rituals is a betrayal of self.

One great influence behind this sea change is the ready availability of therapies that make it hard not to comply. How can any reasonable person say "no" to one pill once a day for many conditions that used to cause serious morbidity and compromise our longevity? Heart disease, diabetes, depression, even AIDS can all be medically well managed with less effort than ever before. This has helped create an imperative to embrace health as a self-defining value. The simpler it is to achieve health goals, the more people want to set them. Wear a pedometer and make your steps goal for the day. Track your sleep habits. It's both a psychic and physical reward.

Because medical and technological advances now put an idealized state of health within easier reach, we have become the kind of people who feel that we are not being true to ourselves if we neglect to grab hold of it. Pharmaceutical companies are not the only active force in the dynamic. People implore healthcare manufacturers to help them boost whatever they feel is holding them back from their idealized healthy selves, whether it is a disease or just normal signs of an aging body. Wrinkles, pregnancy and baldness may not be pathological conditions, but that doesn't stop people from insisting on Botox (botulinium toxin), oral contraceptives, and Propecia (finasteride) respectively. And they do insist on them, not because healthcare manufacturers have brainwashed the country into becoming "patients," but rather because people now more than ever demand greater control over their bodies, and the technology exists to empower them.

Today health and wellness extend into all aspects of life beyond therapies and Big Pharma. Walking down the cereal aisle in the grocery store, you would think you entered a clinic of sorts as you read how Cheerios and other whole-grain products are part of a heart-healthy regimen. When I was young, we used to choose cereal by the prize being offered inside, not its health benefits. Chairs and car seats are now ergonomically designed so that the alignment of your spine mirrors the alignment with your self-perceptions about doing right by your body. Spas issue a siren's call to all whose mental well-being craves care and feeding. Fitbit, Jawbone, and other accessories keep us in touch with how far we've walked or biked or how deeply we've slept. Dating sites demand that we declare if we are "drug and disease free." From cosmetics to clothing to sunglasses to emotional-support animals, there is hardly a product or service that doesn't strive to appeal to how we use health and wellness to define ourselves.

Like every other brand choice people make about what car to buy, or which coffee to prefer, or which sports franchise to root for, the consuming of health products and services helps us define who we are or who we wish to be. However, unlike non-healthcare consumer brands, the products and services in question are not something that people necessarily *want* to buy, but rather things they *need* to buy. Nobody *wants* to buy insulin. You buy insulin (or your insurance company does it for you) because you need it to live a longer, healthier life.

People make consumer brand choices to craft (albeit, often unconsciously) a public image of what makes them uniquely them (even if it's what the great majority is also doing).

"Hey, I'm cool, I've got the newest iPhone! Wanna see?"

This is far from a secret, as my counterparts in the consumer goods world have expounded upon it for decades.

In contrast, people do not consume healthcare brands to celebrate who they are. Rarely, if ever, do people gain social status or improved personal image from showing off the new medicine they're taking or medical device they now use.

"Hey, I'm cool, I've got the newest continuous positive airway pressure machine! Wanna see?"

Rather, people make brand choices about healthcare to *protect* their image from crashing down. The same person who proudly wears Prada suits, reads *Fortune* magazine, drives a hybrid sports car, and subscribes to a posh gym doesn't want anyone to suspect he or she has herpes, depression, or any other condition that would otherwise mar their polished façade.

When creating healthcare brand identities, I often counsel clients that the best thing their brand can promise people is that no one will know that they have the condition being treated. I can see the disappointment bloom on their faces when they grow to accept that the subject of their careers—while very helpful or even essential—has the potential to turn people off. But this is an essential truth about healthcare branding that makes it different from consumer brand marketing.

I scratch my head when I see healthcare brands promoted by companies that completely ignore this truth (and waste millions of dollars in the process). Take, for instance, the long-running national advertising campaign for a prominent prescription brand of pain reliever. Do septuagenarians really stroll the beach with their golden retriever, hold hands, twirl, and expound on how much they adore their arthritis medication? Have the marketers behind this campaign even talked meaningfully with senior citizens? There are not enough pain relievers in the world to make them happy about going up a flight of stairs, let alone playing fetch with a dog on a beach. And who in the world, as one current campaign showcases, openly loves their laxative? This is shallow, wishful thinking on the part of marketers who are either too lazy to do their homework, or, worse, truly believe that patients are as obsessed with the brands they market as are the marketers whose careers depend upon the brands' success.

This is a great example of what I call *The Celebration Fallacy*: a type of magical thinking whereby healthcare manufacturers and their agencies imagine their brands will be received by the masses as heroes, thereby putting forth identities where the healthcare brands are the celebrated saviors of sick peoples' normal lives.

The Celebration Fallacy is one of the predominant drivers of identity crisis in healthcare branding today. The conceit goes something like this:

all brands help you be you—in too many ways to count—and brand success is achieved only when people celebrate the brand as a hero in fitting tribute—by worshipping it, shouting about it, showing it off to others, fighting over it, and wrapping themselves in it like a flag. This conceit may actually hold true for some consumer brands. For instance, Apple brand identities are held up as beauty queens on a runway. Are you worth it?

Budweiser is "the king of beers," and as such, enjoys some nice snuggling by its loyal subjects.

This "brand as hero" approach is actually a holdover from marketing's adolescent past, as seen on the next page in a now-forbidden print ad of a man so enthralled by his brand of cigarette that he'd resort to violence rather than have it taken from him.

But this "celebration" conceit turns to fallacy when applied to healthcare brands. Like consumer brands, healthcare brands help you be you: doctor, patient, healthcare manufacturer, and award-seeking agency. However, healthcare brand success is not hero worship at all. Healthcare brands—in real life—elicit no celebrations, no shouting from the mountain tops, no fistfights. Instead, successful healthcare brands operate intentionally behind the scenes to protect the self's desire to maintain normalcy, however "normal" is defined by the subject. Physicians identify as healers. Patients want to think of themselves as really all right, just like everyone else. And pharma, biotech, device companies, and their healthcare brands aspire to be heroic and applauded for all the good work they do.

But the cold, hard truth is that sick people don't want anyone to know about their illnesses or treatments. They keep it to themselves. Physicians understand that people aren't happy to see them under most circumstances and derive an extra measure of satisfaction in knowing they are fighting the good fight even when patients don't appreciate them. And healthcare manufacturers are viewed—very unfairly in my opinion—not as the purveyors of modern miracles, but rather as a necessary evil. It's the nature of health and wellness and therefore a natural dynamic of the health and wellness business when building brand identities.

As branding professionals working in health and wellness industries, we must be vigilant to avoid The Celebration Fallacy and always keep in mind our brand's underlying imperative to protect normalcy and incorporate it into our basic assumptions about what we do. As an illustration of this point, let's take a look at a different pain reliever, ibuprofen. Back in the mid-1980s, the FDA approved the then popularly prescribed pain reliever ibuprofen for sale over the counter (OTC, i.e., no longer as a prescription medication). Two large, experienced healthcare companies received licenses from the current manufacturer (the now defunct Upjohn Pharmaceuticals) to market branded versions: Advil, from American Home Products, and Nuprin, from Bristol Myers Squibb.

The two brands started out on equal footing. The drug and dosage contained in Advil and Nuprin were identical, the promotional budgets for the two brands comparable. Yet after a year on the market, Advil had grossed $500 million and Nuprin only $50 million. So, what happened? The answer is that they were pursuing different brand identities, and the Nuprin brand identity was built on a celebration of the brand instead of conveying how the brand protects its customers' normalcy and self-values.

I remember my colleagues and I entering the Nuprin product manager's office one day. On the desk were images of the Nuprin print campaign. They featured huge, full-color photos of the spokes-couple—Jimmy Connors and Chris Evert, at the time top-seeded tennis champions who were American darlings, formerly engaged to each other in the 1970s, one of the closest things America had to royalty. Their TV spots for Nuprin also featured this beloved tennis couple arguing jocularly with one another on whose pain was worse. Nuprin, of course, was right for both of them. The folks at Nuprin were in love with this campaign and didn't understand how Advil was outselling them ten-to-one. After all, it was the same drug, and they were spending the same amount on advertising as Advil.

It was our job as marketing consultants to analyze the situation and provide the client with a solution for getting Nuprin back in the race.

In the end, we advised them that their problem was less a matter of advertising and more a matter of brand identity. That is, it wasn't about taking different or better photos of Connors and Evert happily claiming that Nuprin made their hard work on the court possible. It was that the Nuprin brand identity was seen as not taking *ordinary* people's pain seriously. Consumers did not see a reflection of their situation in the Nuprin brand. Connors and Evert were attractive, wealthy superstars. "What the hell do they know about my pain?" you might hear a patient exclaim in market research.

Unfortunately, the Nuprin marketers refused to heed our advice and understand that they had made a fatal error in judgment by ignoring how people relate their identities to illness and wellness. Nuprin continued to throw good money after bad until finally the brand was pulled off the shelves for poor sales. I hate to say we told them so, but I truly believe Nuprin would still be around today if the decision makers there had listened to our advice and adjusted the product's identity to reflect genuine customers' self-values.

A few years later, I was hired by Sudler & Hennessey, which had the Advil account. Those old enough to recall will remember that the Advil brand identity leveraged the dull, serious—but highly relevant—image that ibuprofen was the product of extensive medical research and the revolutionary standard bearer of OTC pain relievers that had preceded it. "First there was aspirin. Then there was Tylenol. Now, there's Advil," read the straightforward tag line. The smart folks at American Home Products (and our agency) understood that people didn't think that their pain was fun to talk about. The values that they built into the Advil brand identity—clinical, innovative, reliable—accurately reflected what people expected from their pain reliever. *Just make the pain go away.* It is no accident that these are the same values people expect from their physicians. When people peered into the Advil brand identity, they saw a doctor helping their pain go away, not some celebrity couple.

There is a research exercise that I sometimes perform to help understand just how a particular illness is incorporated into customers' self-image. I ask each research participant to jot down the different roles they play in life. For example, mother, wife, Catholic, real estate agent and good friend are not uncommon, to name but a few. What I inevitably find is that some chronic health conditions have become an integral part of the self-definition. Mother, wife, Catholic, hemophiliac. Or cancer survivor. Or diabetic.

Likewise, I invited a neighbor over for dinner and asked if it was OK to serve red meat. "Not really," he sheepishly replied. "My wife's a cardiac."

Today, more so than ever, understanding how people think about illness and wellness as they relate to their personal identities is the first essential step in properly developing a healthcare brand. Healthcare brands must acknowledge how much people's identities are defined by their relative states of well-being, and to what extent people who are not 100% well define themselves by their health issues, such as being an insomniac, an obsessive-compulsive worrier, or a breast cancer survivor. Miss this connection, and your brand runs the risk of ending up like poor Nuprin (alas, we knew him well).

Delving further into the healthcare identity crisis, I've discovered that, unlike the world of consumer goods branding, healthcare branding must cope with people's sense of entitlement. Most people today consider health a moral imperative. It is the way life should be. Illness is an aberration, an assault. It is a crime against our inalienable right to be healthy and happy. Illness makes people feel persecuted. Look around, and you can find tales of oppression on social media, outrage in best-selling books at the costs associated with getting and staying healthy, and resentment of the fantasies perpetrated by some healthcare brands offering pretty promises to maintain and restore our idealized state of wellness. My late mother, who passed away from complications of multiple sclerosis, sums up the incongruity more eloquently and humorously than I ever could.

"I'd give my right arm for good health," she would say, fully conscious of the paradox.

This issue of understanding how health and wellness drive our identity is true not only for patients but also for another key audience vital to a successful healthcare brand identity: healthcare professionals. We must take physicians and allied health professionals into account when developing a healthcare brand identity, or we run the risk of killing our brand. More on this in a later chapter. However, the fact that all prescription medicines require a written document from an expert (the doctor) to the actual end user (the patient) makes healthcare branding infinitely more complex than most consumer goods brands, which require no middleman/woman expert to obtain. Healthcare practitioners—while they don't necessarily consume the prescribed drug—consume the values associated with advocating for the drug with a trusting patient. Good healthcare practitioners pride themselves on being compassionate, savvy advocates for those in their care. They understand that they are (still today) a patient's most trusted source for health advice. They need to feel responsible, informed, and self-satisfied with their role in the regulated healthcare transaction model. They seek approval from their patients as evidence of their own accomplishments. In the end, what a doctor wants most from prescribing a drug or device is to feel that they have done the best job they could have, honored the training and heritage of their profession, and maintained their esteem in the eyes of their patients and colleagues as paragons of their science and art.

Ironically, most healthcare industry brands neglect the psychological basis for brand choices by healthcare providers and choose, instead, to bank on the functional (but essential) facts about the drug brand to win doctors' approval. This reliance on functional attributes as the starting point for brand choices among healthcare practitioners stems from the old-fashioned idea that doctors are hyper-rational beings, impervious to any ideas but the science behind a brand. This is another symptom of the identity crisis in our industry, this one manifesting itself with physicians: they act as though they are impervious to emotional brand choices in order to define their self-image as clinical and detached. And healthcare manufacturers and patients play along because no one, including doctors themselves, dares to admit that doctors are subjective beings like the rest of us, a form of cultural denial that helps maintain our illusion of how health and wellness shape our own identities.

The truth is that I and my colleagues have many times personally witnessed healthcare providers being influenced by the same practical and emotional connections in healthcare brand choices that we see at work with consumers. Beyond my own observations, research with hundreds of thousands of healthcare providers shows that their desire to fulfill the image of themselves as masters of benevolent care compel them to behave humanly (vs. as an automaton), as we all do, about their brand preferences.

The three most common values underlying the brand choices made by healthcare providers show us the human-nature underpinnings of their profession:

- The Popular Choice ("If everyone else is using it, then the chances of me losing a lawsuit if something goes wrong is lessened, because I'm part of the rule rather the exception.")
- The Smart Choice ("I'm on the cutting edge; I think progressively.")
- The Reliable Choice ("I've been using it for years, and it has never betrayed me or my standards.").

I'll be getting into more detail in Chapter 5 about what drives doctors' allegiances to brands. Suffice it to say at this point that healthcare brands must appeal to both advocate and user, or the buying transaction doesn't happen. Nothing destroys a healthcare brand identity faster than misaligning a brand promise with the realities of how people on both sides of the healthcare equation think about illness and wellness.

> WE CAN EFFECTIVELY CREATE HEALTHCARE BRANDS ONLY BY APPRECIATING AND HONORING HOW EVERYONE'S IDENTITY IS DEFINED BY HEALTH AND HOW THEY THINK ABOUT HEALTH FROM THEIR PERSPECTIVE.

Over the course of this book, I intend to answer many of the questions brought about by attempts to effectively avoid identity crises for healthcare brands. These include: Have we branded the illnesses and conditions in ways that remove barriers to discussing them and pursuing clear, resolvable solutions? Have we captured how the remedies and services provide a branded experience that allows caregivers and care-receivers to each see a flattering reflection of themselves in advocating or consuming such remedies respectively? Have we taken into account on behalf of healthcare brands what people believe about themselves when they get ill or what professionals believe about themselves in restoring wellness, or at least "a new normal," in the minds of patients?

By examining the complex aspects of healthcare branding, identifying the acts and processes that produce an identity crisis, we can pursue the proven best practices that enlighten our collective appreciation of illness and wellness as drivers of identity, and put forth successfully branded concepts from which all can benefit.

Let's get started.

2

Branding Is Poorly Branded

Another hidden problem that clouds any productive conversation about branding is the rampant misuse of the term "branding" itself. "Brand" and "branding" are often used as catchalls for whatever activities a given marketer or ad agency is undertaking to get the word out about their product or service. I've participated in dozens of healthcare advertising award ceremonies over the years, and I'm continually struck by how many of the winning campaigns communicate no sense of brand identity beyond the logo featured in its usual place, the lower right hand corner of the medium. Yet if you asked any of the ad agencies accepting the awards if they felt that they were building the brand, they would unanimously say, "Of course. We're really good at branding."

Where is the disconnect? It lies in the very term itself. Branding is poorly branded. If you Google the term "branding," you'll get a diversity of definitions that evoke the parable of the blind men and the elephant. Depending on one's orientation, the elephant is a "'pillar" (leg), "snake" (tail), "fan" (ear) and so on. And after reading all of the definitions out there, the only thing that gets defined is a sense of confusion.

Here are some random definitions I ran across after Googling the term "branding":

- The over-simplified definition: A brand is a promise. (A colleague of mine improves upon this by adding 'well kept' at the end.)
- The can't-make up-one's-mind definition: A brand is derived from who you are, who you want to be, and who people perceive you to be.
- The achingly precious definition: Branding is convincing that voice in someone's head to be on your side. (This is just one of many in this category.)
- And, of course, the kitchen-sink definition: Branding is the ratio between leadership, vision, communication, culture and user experience. (Speaking of definitions, *Webster's* defines a ratio as a relationship between two things, not five).

So it is not surprising, then, that marketers and agencies consider anything done on behalf of a product to be branding. It's a big mistake to assume that all advertising campaigns are branding, all web sites are branding, all broadcast spots are branding, and all sales materials are branding. In and of themselves, they're not. They are tactics that are used on behalf of the brand, which may or (more typically) may not advance the brand's identity in a concerted way.

Using our ibuprofen example in the previous chapter, the marketing and advertising efforts behind Advil succeeded in selling the product and establishing its identity as the go-to OTC pain reliever of its time. Similar expenditures on marketing and advertising efforts behind Nuprin failed to establish an identity for the product that related to its target buyers, and this failure eventually drove Nuprin out of the marketplace. Placing a logo on a promotional piece or using one of the approved brand colors are fairly empty gestures toward truly delivering the full experience of a brand's identity.

> BRANDING IS THE DISCIPLINE AND ART OF TAKING WHAT CUSTOMERS VALUE ABOUT THEMSELVES AND TRANSFERRING THESE TO A PRODUCT, COMPANY OR SERVICE IN A WAY THAT CUSTOMERS SEE A FLATTERING SELF-REFLECTION IN THE BRAND'S IDENTITY.

The conversation around branding can take on meaning only by . . . well, *rebranding* the discourse around the term *identity*. If we reframed the question to the proud acceptors of advertising awards to "Do you feel that your campaign is true to the brand's identity?" we may get very different answers than just the reflexive affirmative. The question may evoke more questions: "Aren't identity and branding the same thing?" Or it may provoke a defensive response: "We didn't do the logo. We do the more important work of promoting the brand." Or it may just not register: "What do you mean? Our campaign *is* the identity." (This last is a verbatim statement from a creative director at a top-10 healthcare advertising agency.)

This is not merely a semantic issue, but goes to the very heart of what we do and why I'm writing this book. If we ask three people what business they're in, and they all answer "television," they haven't really told us much about what they do for a living. A camera operator, actor, and screenplay writer all technically work in television, but their contributions to the business—the vastly different roles they play—make their answer so broad that it becomes empty of any real meaning. Similarly, the term "branding" differs significantly based on the ways that individual healthcare marketers and communications personnel see their roles and responsibilities—in other words, their own identities.

Often, what ad agencies and their clients perceive as a successful campaign will turn out to be counterproductive to building brand identity. Promotional campaigns are commonly considered successful if they do a good job building awareness, getting customers to remain engaged for measurable periods of time, and creating customer recall after the promotional exposure—all important aspects of good communications. It would be common sense to believe, then, that all successful ad campaigns naturally advance the brand's identity and equity. But this simply isn't true.

Brand identities can be successful only if they create a flattering reflection of the customer's own beliefs and values . . . the customer's own identity. Brand success is measured by brand equity research and customer loyalty over time. These are two very different benchmarks than those used to judge the success of an ad campaign—awareness and memorability—which do not necessarily equate to reflecting a customer's beliefs about him- or herself. To judge branding success, one must carefully examine not just the fact that customers engage with brands, but more importantly, *why* they engage.

A case in point: the top-10 pharmaceutical company that used to be known simply as Abbott Laboratories (now AbbVie) once promoted a brand of the antibiotic clarithromycin called Biaxin. At one point, Biaxin was among the company's top-selling brands. Abbott hired a leading Chicago healthcare agency to promote Biaxin. This agency specifically fancies itself as an expert in building brand identities, in part because they are perennial winners of advertising industry awards for most creative agency and also because of an iconic style they appear to have appropriated from another Chicago-based agency, Leo Burnett. Leo Burnett used to specialize in creating lovable characters to embody his client's brands, such as The Pillsbury Doughboy, Tony the Tiger, The Jolly Green Giant, and Charlie the Tuna, among many others.

For Biaxin, this Burnett-styled healthcare ad agency came up with a campaign that featured a friendly bulldog as the metaphorical mascot for Biaxin, and headlines such as "Tough not ruff," referring to the drug's ability to be tough on infections but not 'ruff' (rough, get it?) on one's digestive tract (some antibiotics can cause stomach upset and nausea). The campaign got off to a great start, and doctors prescribed Biaxin for a variety of common upper and lower respiratory conditions. They loved the drug, and it appeared that they also loved the brand, until sales leveled off after the first 18 months and then began to decline.

At the time, I was the Chief Branding Officer for inVentiv Health, a top healthcare marketing, sales, and communication company. While we didn't have the Biaxin account, some of the Abbott brand managers attended a healthcare marketing summit and saw a talk I gave called "Memorably Wrong: Are you fostering a false brand identity?" After hearing my talk, they came to me and my team to help determine why sales of Biaxin were going in the wrong direction.

"We can't figure it out," one of the Abbott executives said. "We keep spending more than our competition. Our advertising campaign has 99% awareness and 98% unaided brand recall."

As with the Nuprin example I cited in the previous chapter, we suspected that Biaxin's problem wasn't the advertising campaign, but rather an identity crisis. I and my team went to work on the Biaxin account and conducted several Brand Insight Groups, a proprietary research methodology discussed in Chapter 7, and one that is specifically designed to capture a customer's relationship to the brand identity, not the advertising campaign.

Some of our key findings related to the kind of doctors who were the leading prescribers of the brand. They were family medicine doctors, or general practitioners, as they used to be called. They had chosen general medicine (vs. a distinctive specialty) because they wanted to work across a broad range of health conditions without getting too niched into one. Also, they aspired to be a respected mentor to families, growing with them as they aged in close, ongoing relationships. They are people who embrace a routine of daily care and are very loyal to a set of medical brands with which they are reliably familiar. Using antibiotics was a common resort for them to treat a variety of respiratory infections effectively. They described the Biaxin brand as a comfortable, trusted choice that helped them get the job done without fuss or problems. We discovered that, in using Biaxin, these doctors hoped to project their own values to their patients, such as comfort, reassurance and reliability. It was their go-to choice because it created a flattering reflection of their own brand of care. In one research exercise that asked them to cite an article of clothing that best described the brand, they compared Biaxin to their favorite pair of well-worn blue jeans.

Then I exposed the same doctors to the bulldog campaign and asked them how they felt about it. Just as advertising research had shown, they remembered the campaign very well. However, they saw no connection between Biaxin, the reliable, trusted antibiotic, and the "Tough not ruff" bulldog campaign.

"Biaxin's not a dog," one doctor said. "It's not stubborn or lethargic like a bulldog. And it's not cute. It's serious and responsible, like me."

"When I give my patients Biaxin," another doctor added, "I feel like I can put my feet up at the end of the day knowing I've done right by my patients, that they're on the road to a problem-free recovery."

Just as I had laid out in my summit talk that engaged the Biaxin brand managers, the bulldog advertising campaign was Memorably Wrong. It made a lot of customers aware of Biaxin and got them to try it . . . but for the wrong reasons—a threat to an effective, enduring brand identity. The campaign won promotional awards at big industry ceremonies, but it did not reflect the practical and emotional identity that made Biaxin uniquely Biaxin in the minds of prescribing doctors.

> THERE IS GREAT PRIDE IN FIELDING A CAMPAIGN THAT DOES ITS JOB OF ENGAGING CUSTOMERS. BUT THERE IS DISHONOR IN WILLFULLY DOING IT WITHOUT ADVANCING THE IDENTITY OF THE BRAND.

To quote David Ogilvy, a self-declared "ad man," "A good advertisement is one that sells the product without drawing attention to itself."

Going for award-winning recognition at the expense of the brand will set in motion the brand identity's inevitable destruction. You can imagine how unhappy and resentful Biaxin's ad agency was with our findings. While the Biaxin brand managers were thrilled that they had found a way to get their brand out of its identity crisis, some of the agency's personnel seemed more concerned that their award-winning campaign was exposed for what it was: great advertising with bad branding. However, given the chance to redeem themselves, the Chicago healthcare agency came up with a successful new campaign that was a flattering reflection of customer self-values found in our branding research. The visual presented a doctor in his fuchsia-colored office, sitting in a chair with his hands behind his head and feet up on the desk. The headline read, "Dr. Peterson has no second thoughts about prescribing once-daily BIAXIN XL (unlike his decision to paint the waiting room fuchsia)." And the tag line, "Tough, not ruff," was changed to "Rest assured." It is no coincidence that both the image and the copy came directly from our branding research, and that the "waiting room" color is Biaxin fuchsia. Good advertising and effective branding helped Biaxin's sales get back on a winning track.

> MARKETERS AND AGENCIES IN HEALTHCARE HABITUALLY CONFUSE PROMOTION WITH BRANDING, EVEN THINKING THAT THEY ARE ONE AND THE SAME, A FREQUENT CAUSE OF IDENTITY CRISIS.

It is hard to lay blame on any one individual in the healthcare marketing field for misunderstanding a brand's identity in the course of its life. It's a systemic problem, as I've argued in the first chapter. The professional healthcare culture (i.e., the industry tasked with marketing prescription medicines, devices, and health services) isn't even consciously aware a problem exists, never mind that its basic assumptions and current best practices are to blame.

Why is that? Again, we need to look at the history of how healthcare brands have been presented to the public, especially to physicians. First, the professional healthcare industry suffers from a long-standing habit: pharmaceutical and device companies have principally pursued a sales model over a branding model. That is, the lion's share of promotional activity, up until recently, has been focused on sales representatives and short-term sales measures.

There is sound rational thinking behind this sales model. The limited patent life of a prescription healthcare brand creates urgency around fast and steady sales at the expense of examining and nurturing why customers are buying over the long term. As stated in the last chapter, many prescription brands are entities that people don't *want* to buy, but rather *need* to buy. So as long as demand remains high, the proper cultivation of brand identity becomes a secondary goal at best. (Ironically, like the professionals in charge of Biaxin, clients often revisit branding precisely when demand falls off, rather than addressing it at the outset to ensure healthy loyalty and esteem for the brand.)

Another sign that the professional healthcare culture misunderstands branding is the way it focuses on logos and colors and ignores the essential behavioral and experiential aspects that form brand identity and why customers engage with brands.

Yet another contributing factor to the industry disconnect with robust branding practices is found in the structure and staffing of the companies involved. With healthcare brands in general, there is no one person or team responsible for creating and maintaining brand equity as there is with consumer brands like Coca Cola, American Express and Dove, to name but a few. Professional healthcare Brand Directors are charged with all aspects of launching or running a brand: the size and shape of the pill, how much it should cost, how much money should be spent on education, promotion, and sales, what the key markets around the world should be, how to get it on the formularies of governments and insurance companies, how the competition will react, and so on. It's no wonder that when it comes time to address the all-important question of brand identity—*why* customers would engage with the brand—the task is treated like one more functional box to tick on an overwhelming list.

Without a seasoned branding expert or internal team fully dedicated to helping the Brand Director understand the value and developmental protocols essential to creating a unique and dimensional brand identity, pharmaceutical, biotech, and device companies default to the lowest driver of brand identity: what it looks like on paper, specifically, the logo and symbol, a.k.a. the brandmark (which will be discussed in Chapter 9). And since the brandmark most traditionally appears on things like advertisements, websites, social media, and sales brochures, Brand Directors almost invariably give this assignment not to a branding agency—which would have a very different philosophy and approach to the creation of brand identity—but rather to the general healthcare advertising agencies, the primary interest of which is to sell advertising and promotional materials. Their entire business model is usually based on churning out promotion at an hourly rate, which ironically benefits them in the event of needing to re-do campaigns plagued with bad branding. They know very little about brand identity cultivation in the firmest sense of the term. (This also holds true for service brands such as hospitals and practice management organizations, which I will explore further in the next chapter.)

The symbiosis of this relationship between professional healthcare marketers and general healthcare agencies has produced vast sums of money on both sides over the decades, but sadly, very few iconic brand identities. For every household-name healthcare brand, there are hundreds of consumer stars. Try this: cover over the logo of different healthcare brands you see in magazines, and see if you can tell which ad is for which brand. I'll lay 10 to 1 you can't tell one from the other. Aside from maybe a person in the ad or TV spot wearing one of the brand colors, it's all happy, smiling people engaged with friends or family, or ill souls now able to pursue their art career, hike and barbeque, or go on vacation to fabulous places enabled by the drug or device or health service. (Doesn't anyone have a job to go to?) Try covering up the logo of an ad for Coca-Cola or Apple. You'll see what I mean about staying true to the brand identity.

Of course, within the existing dynamic discussed here, there are certain pharmaceutical, biotech, device, and service companies in healthcare that follow best-practice principles for building brand identities. However, even they do it as an exception rather than as a rule.

So how should one think about brand identity? Answer: as simply and meaningfully as possible. One doesn't need to get imaginative about defining a concept that's already imaginative by nature. First, start with identity:

Identity is a distinguishing set of essential values or ideas.

Simple enough. From there, I suggest it follows that:

Brand identity is a distinguishing set of essential values or ideas for a product, company, or service as perceived by the customer.

It is our job as branding experts to understand the ideas or values that customers embrace about themselves (either actually or aspirationally) and then connect customers with how the brand reflects those ideas or values.

It is important to realize that not all identities are great or even very good. Most, by definition, are completely ordinary. Similarly, not all branding is great or even very good, as I have been illustrating through examples. For the sake of expediency, when I talk about brand identity, I am referring to paragon behavior and best practices and how to achieve them.

> THE MOST PROFOUND MISTAKE IN HEALTHCARE BRANDING IS TO BELIEVE THAT THE PROCESS STARTS WITH THE PRODUCT, SERVICE, OR COMPANY. IT DOESN'T. IT STARTS WITH THE CUSTOMER.

Just because patients need to buy healthcare brands doesn't mean that they are a captive audience for product-centric brand identities. Quite the opposite. Healthcare brand managers go to work every day and think about one thing: their product, service, or company. Whereas doctors and patients go to work and live their lives, never thinking about the marketing manager's healthcare brand until they absolutely must. It occupies a fraction of a fraction of their attention. Trying to build a brand identity starting with the product, service, or company is like trying to engage people by shouting at them from outer space. Yet the problem is rampant and hidden in plain sight. And how can you blame them?

You can easily imagine them proclaiming, "Look at what this product can do!"

Or, "Look at how wonderful our maternity ward is!"

Or, "Look at the data and facts! We're not talking about snow tires or watery beer, here. We're talking significant care for a serious medical condition. Everyone should feel as excited about this discovery as we do."

And so it starts. The research and strategizing and tactical plan get produced, and all the forces at work to make the healthcare brand a success try to shoe-horn the brand into the lives of doctors, who are besieged with managing their practices, or patients, who would rather not think about their illness, and perhaps resent having to see a doctor and buy therapies regardless of the great good they might do.

We must flip this entire protocol on its head if we are to think successfully about brand identity. Branding, as I've said, is the discipline and art of truly owning a set of distinctive values and ideas on behalf of a product, service, or company identity. So where do those values and ideas come from? If not the product, then where? Travel back in time with me to see how I learned where brand values and ideas come from.

In the late 1980s, I first arrived at Sudler & Hennessey, Young & Rubicam's flagship healthcare agency and the top global agency of its kind at the time. Like all budding executives, I had to attend a series of training initiatives to transfer many of Y&R's great branding lessons into my own creative process. (Every day, I give thanks for this education.) Our classes were groups of 12 sourced from different communications disciplines across Y&R's global enterprise (advertising, public relations, brand identity, and so on). In one exercise, six of us were given a lemon and asked to sell that lemon to as many of the other six as we could in a two-minute time period. As you might imagine, the group of young, cocky ad men and women—myself whole-heartedly included—went quickly to work explaining why each of our lemons was superior to all others.

"This lemon is an heirloom lemon, bred for perfection over generations."

"This lemon is the cheapest lemon; better buy it before someone else does."

"This lemon is from Jerusalem, and if Jesus were alive today, he'd want to buy this lemon."

None of us sold a single lemon. The other six then went, and they met the same fate. The instructor, a man who was then my age now, and no doubt a veteran creator of many iconic brand identities, grabbed one of the lemons, sat on the front of his desk and began asking us questions.

"It's the end of summer, the hottest of days. What are all of you going to do this weekend?"

We volunteered a variety of answers: go to the beach, have friends over for dinner, watch a sporting event, and so on.

He continued: "Will you be consuming any beverages? Will you be eating any food?"

Of course, we all replied: beer, iced tea, soda, grilled shrimp, salads.

"I bet that iced tea would taste really good with a little lemon," he said. "What do you think about a few drops of lemon on that shrimp and salad? Brings out the flavor—am I right?"

How could we disagree? We all bought his lemon. And what did we buy? The acid content? The ripeness? The pedigree? No. We bought an enhancement of the lives we were already living at the beach, ballpark, and back yard. Our instructor was building a brand identity not based on what he was selling, but rather on *why* we were buying. The values he imparted to the lemon—refreshing, fun, exciting—were our values, a flattering reflection of what we thought about ourselves. And because none of us had taken his approach, his lemon owned those values in our minds, and won our esteem and loyalty.

Brand identity development is successful when we impart values and ideas that customers prize about themselves to a product, service, or institution. It is not based on how products are sold, but rather on *why* customers buy. (The healthcare branding division I created at inVentiv Health was called Y Brand for this very reason.) Additionally, a brand's identity is less about how it appears (its branding hallmarks, such as logo, symbol, color, type, etc.) and significantly more about how it behaves. For a healthcare brand, this is a combination of its clinical acumen and the experience it creates in any brand encounter with customers, such as in-person transactions, sponsorships, online media presence, and other aspects of customer engagement.

So why is this important then? Why should professional healthcare marketers and their agencies rethink the practices and change the dynamics of how brand identities are created and governed throughout their life cycles? Two vital reasons:

1. To create an unstoppable momentum for success; and
2. To better manage time and money.

Let's take the first: creating an unstoppable momentum for success. Our agency team at Sudler & Hennessey launched the global brand identity for Lipitor (atorvastatin). Lipitor is in a class of "statins," drugs that work primarily in the liver to rid the body of cholesterol, thereby keeping fatty "plaques" from forming in vessels and blocking them, preventing heart attacks and strokes. Parke-Davis, the maker of the drug, and its parent brand, Warner-Lambert, were long-standing clients of ours. At the time, the market was dominated by Merck's Zocor (simvastatin) and its forebear Mevacor (lovastatin)—two brands that had trounced Parke-Davis' former market leader, Lopid (gemfibrozil), in the lipid-management category in the years preceding Lipitor's launch. Lipitor was the means to reconquering the category for Parke-Davis. As history has shown since, Lipitor went on to become the best-selling cholesterol reducer in the world, earning around $13 billion a year at peak sales. But the seeds of its success were sown well before it came to market. The driver of its success was its brand identity.

At the time, Zocor had conducted longer-term clinical trials to demonstrate that patients using their brand had significant reductions in heart attacks, strokes, and congestive heart failure. These trials are very difficult and very expensive to conduct because a) a sizable patient sample is needed for practical relevance; and b) the patients must be tracked vigilantly over the course of many years to eliminate other factors that could bias the results, such as diet and exercise. This research allowed Zocor to claim "primary prevention" of life-altering coronary events. A no-brainer. Lipitor, of course, had no such data yet. Further, the guidelines issued by the American College of Cardiology (ACC) and the American Heart Association (AHA) set treatment levels for elevated LDL (bad cholesterol) at between 250 and 300 mg/dl of blood, based mostly on the Zocor research.

Lipitor promised to double Zocor's reductions. However, the quandary was this: why go any lower if you don't have to? It's like buying loudspeakers for your audio system that emit frequencies inaudible to the human ear. Ironically, Lipitor seemed like over-kill. Why would it matter as a new drug on the market? Our job was to find a legitimate way for the Lipitor brand identity to make it matter.

We conducted customer insight research and ran into a pervasive truth that was powerful yet taboo:

Doctor/patient relationships are often informed by self-deception and/or conscious truth avoidance.

That's right: as a matter of course doctors and patients often lie to themselves and to each other. Here's a typical illustration of this point:

Doctor: "How many units of alcohol do you drink per week?"
Patient: "Eight to ten," (knowingly underestimating by at least 50%).
Doctor: "Fine, fine," (knowing the true number is likely higher, since patients often under-report alcohol consumption).

In the case of Zocor, the drug's success had been built, in part, on a similar kind of complicit self-deception between doctors and patients.

All the clinical study subjects in all the trials for Zocor had been on a low-cholesterol diet. And the conditional language around the ACC/AHA guidelines for treatment was predicated on using Zocor only after diet and exercise alone had failed. Out in the real world, physicians in all of the customer research to date insisted that they strictly followed the guidelines and would give their patients Zocor only if those patients were on a low-cholesterol diet and performed moderate exercise. Likewise, the patients volunteered that they willingly complied with their doctors' advice. Human nature being what it is, it would take quite a suspension of disbelief to assume that doctors and patients were all, or even mostly, adhering to the required guidelines. The folks behind Zocor either didn't know or didn't care. Why would they? They were the market leader.

In order to verify our hunch about the doctor/patient self-deception built into Zocor's success, our research asked a different set of questions about the drug. In one exercise, we asked physicians to estimate what percent of patients they suspected of ignoring their advice in different disease categories related to heart disease. The results were what we expected: a true picture of their thinking rather than the canned answers they gave previously to burnish their own identities about upholding high practice standards.

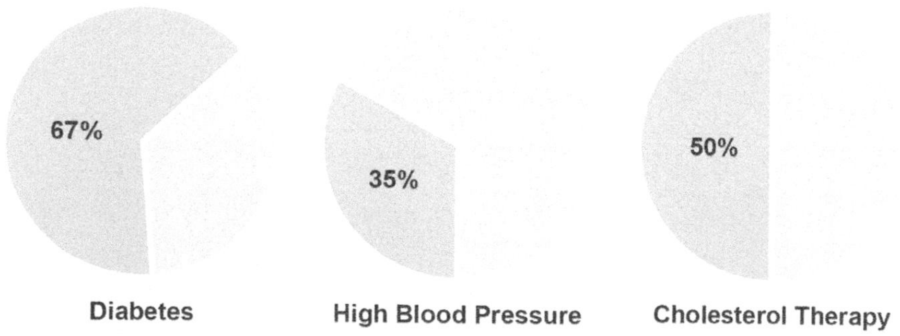

Similarly, we asked patients what percent of the time they followed their doctors' advice on lifestyle modifications for these same disease states. We suspected that their answers skewed lower than reality, but still they weren't completely dishonest.

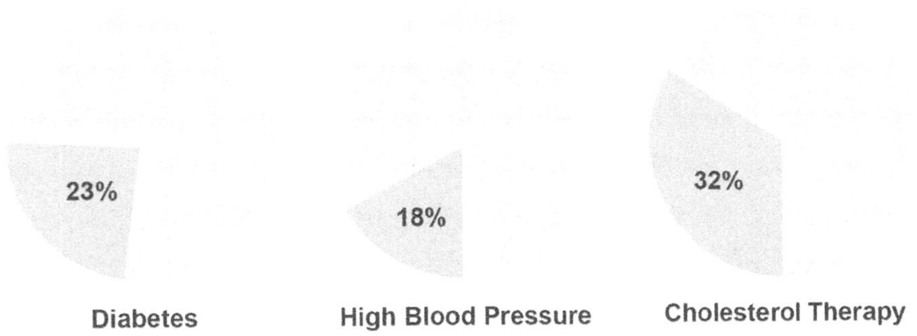

The reality is that everybody cheats. The reality is that life is simply too sweet not to cheat. Zocor's competitors weren't the other medications in the category; Zocor's competitors were the La-Z-Boy lounge chair and the cheeseburger. So if everybody secretly knows that cheating is going on in cholesterol-reduction therapy, then doctors and their patients needed an even more powerful statin to counteract the cheating. They needed "cheating insurance." And that became the Lipitor brand identity: your best cholesterol insurance policy for the real world.

Even without the clinical studies that proved lower cholesterol is better (these would come many years after Lipitor's long-term clinical trials in primary prevention were completed), Lipitor rapidly eclipsed Zocor in sales despite the established drug's head start and proprietary clinical data. In study after study, the Lipitor brand identity snowballed down the mountain, obliterating the competition. Over the decades, Lipitor patients had even greater reductions in mortality and morbidity than patients taking Zocor's highest dose. Based on Lipitor's superior ability to lower bad cholesterol, the ACC/AHA have revised their guidelines several times, with their 2013 targets for therapy significantly lower at around 130 mg/dl even for patients without additional risks, such as diabetes and high blood pressure.

Shortly after our launch, Pfizer acquired Warner-Lambert and its prized asset, Lipitor. Pfizer subsequently awarded the Lipitor promotion to one of their roster agencies, which inherited a brand identity that created an unstoppable momentum for success, fending off new competition and new perspectives on cholesterol management beyond the mere treatment of LDL. Millions of people, myself included, owe longer, disease-free lives to the Lipitor brand, even when a pizza and the prospects of a comfy couch are too sweet to resist. Who wouldn't want that kind of life insurance?

This takes us to the second reason that more healthcare brands should make their brand identity more of a priority: it saves them time and money. Remember the way that Absolut vodka first came to our attention in 1979? Many of you will be too young to remember, but I was struck at the time by how Absolut's brand identity was perfectly captured in its name and personality: the ultimate in cocktail style. The bottle was designed to resemble more of a fine wine than a fairly pedestrian spirit (until Absolut came along, vodka lacked the sophisticated image that was the purview of single-malt scotch and cognac). And that bottle was featured in promotion that said very little, which helped the brand identity speak volumes.

So enduring was the brand identity that the mere mention of it conjured images of fun, coolness, and a guaranteed good time. It's maker, Pernod Ricard, didn't have to alter its approach to the market for many years, thereby saving the time and money it normally takes to field new campaigns, hire and bring new agencies onboard, and orient new employees. They just doubled-down on the brand identity and won the hearts of cocktail fanciers for years.

I'm fortunate to count myself among the many who worked on the only healthcare brand that employed a similar approach to brand identity, the injectable antibiotic Rocephin (ceftriaxone) from Hoffmann-La Roche. Injectable antibiotics are used almost exclusively in hospitals to treat very serious, even life-threatening conditions. Further, hospitals purchase several different injectable antibiotics because the little bugs are crafty and may outsmart one or two antibiotics and then succumb to a third.

Like its competition, Rocephin was a broad-spectrum antibiotic, making it a favorable choice for a variety of infections. And unlike its competition, which had to be injected two or three times daily, Rocephin was dosed only once daily. Believe it or not, this was considered a drawback at the time as physicians—despite the data—were afraid that Rocephin's effects would poop out over 24 hours before the next dose, and leave patients vulnerable to toxic pathogens, and their hospitals vulnerable to costly lawsuits.

The brand identities of the competition were based on Kill Power and used scary photographs of open, infected wounds or blown-up images of microscopic pathogens, as seen on the next page. We nicknamed the style of the time as "beds, bellies and bugs."

We took the Rocephin brand identity in a different direction. Rather than fight head-to-head on which brand killed bugs better, we focused on the daily challenge that hospitals faced keeping patients alive and well, until—hopefully—they went home quickly. Rocephin's brand identity was: Essential To Everyday Wellness. Evoking the folksy adage that "an

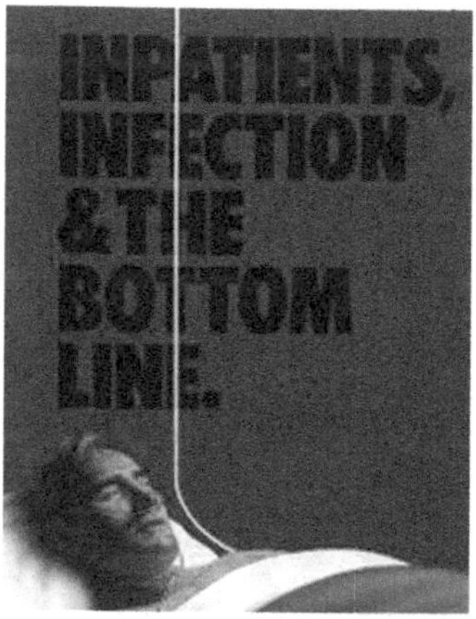

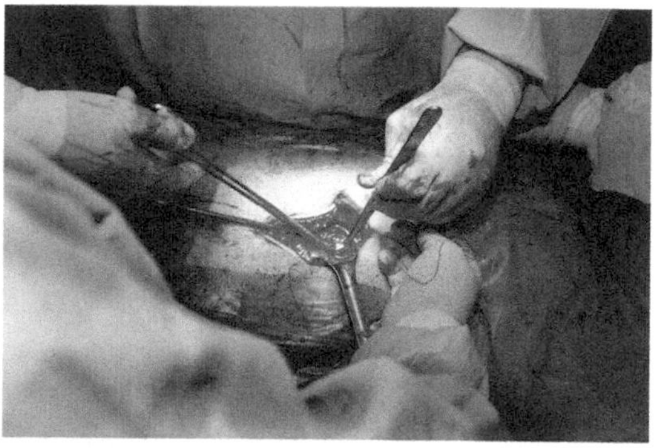

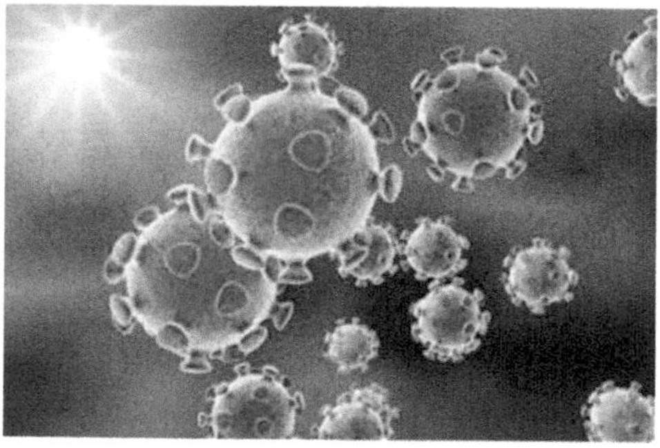

apple a day keeps the doctor away," we let the brand identity do all the work that was needed with this idea:

It was the essence of simplicity. The brand identity was unencumbered by a rational argument, and it resonated with the identities of hospital personnel. Rocephin owned the idea of wellness, not serious problems. And as we saw with the Absolut brand identity, it took very little time and money to win and keep the hearts and minds of our hospital customers, whether they were surgeons, pharmacists, supply and procurement specialists, or department heads.

Along the way, as economic pressures and managed care compelled hospitals to limit the duration of hospital stays, Rocephin's brand identity enabled it to be ready when opportunity knocked. With once-daily dosing, patients could be treated on an outpatient basis and return the next day for another injection without a hospital stay. The phrase "Treat and Street" saluted the brand known for Essential To Everyday Wellness. Today, ceftriaxone is on the World Health Organization's List of Essential Medicines, a list of the most important medications needed in a basic health system.

Like Rocephin, many healthcare brands spend a considerable amount of time and money researching and developing a brand strategy and branding hallmarks—the design elements—that set the brand on its journey out into the market. However, for the overwhelming majority of healthcare brands, that's where the identity work stops. Pharma, biotech, device, and service companies don't conduct—as a rule—annual brand equity studies to see how customers relate to the brand's aspirational values. They allow different educational and promotional agencies to fracture the brand identity in pursuit of creative awards or just out of simple indifference to or ignorance of brand identity guidelines. They opt for ventures that yield short-term sales over long-term brand building. And there is minimal coordination between how the marketing team promotes the brand and how the sales team sells it to healthcare providers. (In most pharma and biotech companies, these two job functions, so crucial to a brand identity's integrity, don't even report up to a common manager.)

It's no surprise that when a company doesn't invest in its brand identity, sooner or later the brand suffers an identity crisis. That's usually when I get called in. Sometimes, I can get the brand back on course using proven, best-practice processes. Other times, the damage is too long-standing or requires a costly makeover, both of which could easily have been avoided. Instead of the current practice of wishing and hoping that one's healthcare brand identity will not grow unhealthy, healthcare marketers need to focus from the outset on creating an unstoppable momentum for lifetime success, just as Rocephin did. Not doing so is a costly long-term mistake.

> [BRANDS THAT DON'T BUILD AND CULTIVATE THEIR IDENTITIES RIGHT FROM THE START ARE DOOMED TO KEEP PAYING FOR IT OVER AND OVER AGAIN.]

A coordinated team effort across promotional platforms is key to nurturing a coherent brand identity and avoiding a crisis. Unfortunately, the healthcare industry violates this rule all the time, and in one sense it's easy to understand why. There are more media channels now than ever before. As pharma, biotech, device, and service brands scramble to reach customers in new and better ways, they hire more and more agencies, each often confined to its own silo, or respective area of expertise: print promotion, education, scientific platforms, broadcast, convention space, digital, social, direct, outdoor, and on and on. These respective silos compete with each other to show better customer numbers and justify the renewal of their budgets. (I was part of a team that worked on a breakthrough therapy for hepatitis C a few years ago, and the fledgling pharma company used six agencies (including ours), none of which connected with each other until I lobbied aggressively for it by pointing out that there were six different brand identities being readied for launch.) This industry-wide bad habit inevitably creates brand identity crises, with brands acting and sounding one way in print, and slightly different in, say, a podcast, and different still in an on-line engagement program, and so on. Instead of creating a brand identity that gains momentum and snowballs as it propels through its lifecycle, many healthcare brands never notice the identity crisis taking place right under their noses. Silo to silo, fundamental values of a brand's identity are suppressed or erased or exaggerated or replaced to suit the whims of an agency campaign.

Healthcare companies save time and money by working first with knowledgeable branding agencies (identity specialists) to create a brand identity for their product, service, or company.

There are two principal reasons for this. First, redundancies are avoided. These days, a company with a new healthcare product coming to market typically hires a scientific agency early on. The agency conducts an industry-wide review of competitive assets, creates a scientific strategy, and then creates visual and verbal nomenclature—*all without creating a brand identity.*

Next, the company hires a general agency as launch approaches. The general agency conducts an industry-wide review of competitive campaigns, creates a promotional strategy, and then creates a promotional campaign while developing a logo, symbol and color palette—*again, all without creating a brand identity.*

The company pays to repeat these efforts again and again with digital agencies, PR agencies, consumer agencies, and so on. They keep paying over and over again for brand "visions" at odds with each other, rather than creating one vision from the outset, and coordinating a series of tactical executions of it.

BRAND IMPLEMENTATION
PARRY BRANDING GROUP MODEL

- Begin with the end in mind
- Involve agencies in decisions, if possible
- Pay once and use it over and over again

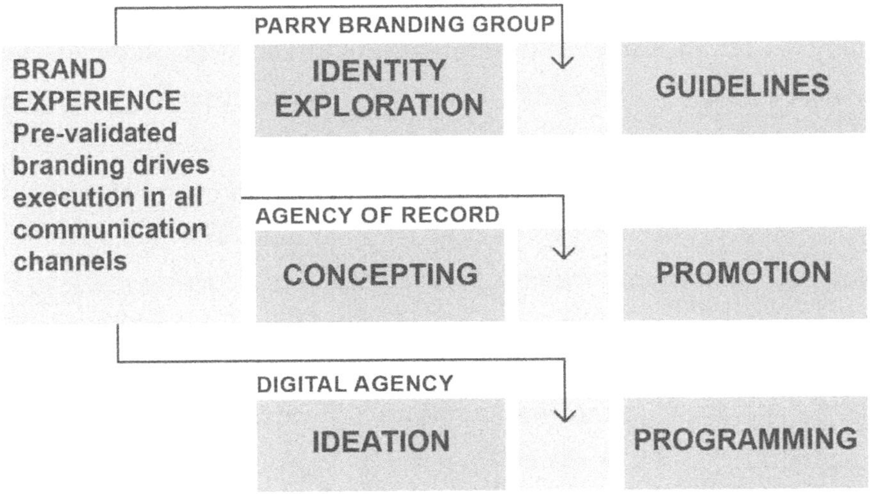

Second, in addition to avoiding redundancies, a branding agency will instill—at the outset—the critical brand values and behaviors that account for situations that most likely will occur well after launch. Without these forecast brand values and behaviors, redundancies are bound to occur. For example, a client wishes to attend a major convention, say, the American Society of Clinical Oncology (ASCO). The brand manager turns to his promotional agency and asks: "What should we do at our booth?"

The agency goes away, brainstorms a number of activities and promotional ideas, and then returns to present them to the client brand team. They present mock-ups of video walls, interactive kiosks, and sales representatives armed with iPads, all of which are designed to talk about the brand's facts, figures, and successes. "It'll make the brand look cutting edge and really compel doctors to interact," one of the agency people might say. The cost is estimated in the six-figure range.

Standard operating procedure, right? Yes, unfortunately, and that's what makes it all the more horrifying. Had the brand been nurtured correctly from the outset, the question—"What should we do at our booth?"—would have been addressed when the brand identity was developed before launch. A branding agency knows that brands will host events and find itself in different venues, sometimes playing a leading role, and sometimes being part of a team of brands. An effective brand experience strategy should be ready and waiting so that when a brand director faces a seeming emergency, he or she can break the glass and retrieve the ready strategy to guide the ad agency purposefully on a consistent course of branding integrity. Instead, the brand director is forced to throw large amounts of cash away taking a blind stab at what an agency says will make them look good. There are other lessons to be drawn here, but I'll save them for a later chapter.

I started off this chapter illustrating just how poorly general agencies—and their clients—understand or even appreciate the difference between a brand identity and a promotional campaign. While I can sympathize with their desire to put their stamp on the brand, I find it unacceptable that that desire extends to ignoring the investment a client has already made in the identity for which the brand stands. (Truth be told, healthcare ad agencies dabble in the creation of brand identities. It constitutes less than five percent of their income. It's no wonder that they instill such planned obsolescence in pursuit of many, different, and potentially award-winning campaigns.)

Here's a test for brand managers: the next time your agency fields a campaign, no matter how much it pleases you in the moment, ask them this: "How is this idea furthering the experience customers have with the brand, and how is it building on the brand's identity?" If they fail to give an answer that respects the investment already made in a brand identity (or worse, no answer at all), fire them. You shouldn't be paying someone good money to advance their own causes over those of the brand, and the buck has to stop with you.

As an identity specialist, my job is to do one thing—brand identity—and to know more than general ad agencies about what works, what doesn't, and why. Identity specialists establish the full range of customer-validated visual and verbal assets, as well as experiential guidance on how the brand should behave toward customers. That is, at the outset, creating the brand identity governs every brand encounter, from the early, scientific assets to the comprehensive and well-integrated promotional assets and brand behaviors. These are captured in a Brand Experience Guideline (discussed in Chapter 9) and form the basis for the various agencies cited above to coordinate tactics that create an unstoppable momentum for success, also eliminating redundancies and saving time and money.

Beginning with the end in mind insures that the brand identity is not made up, *ad hoc*, as one goes along. The idea is not to abandon timely opportunities the brand might have, but rather to be prepared to respond to them in ways that also stay true to the brand's identity. The result is a greater chance for long-term success for your brand, while reducing agency-work redundancy and saving money.

In the next chapter, let's examine how healthcare branding is radically different from consumer-goods branding—another contributing factor to healthcare branding's identity crisis.

3

Medicines Aren't Soft Drinks. Hospitals Aren't Hotels.

Now that we've covered some of the systemic reasons why the creation of brand identity is often ignored and misunderstood by marketing and agency personnel promoting healthcare products, let's turn our attention to another widespread hidden cause of healthcare branding identity crises: the delusion that there is little difference between creating healthcare brands and creating consumer brands.

Sometimes I find myself in competition with consumer branding shops for a prescription drug client. On the surface, this seems like business as usual. The client wants a broad range of experience from which to choose. Into the mix of healthcare branding shops, why not add a perspective from the agencies that brought you brand identities for nationally recognized SUVs, soft drinks, and smart phones? It happens all the time, and it's a HUGE first step on the path to an identity crisis because a consumer branding shop generates success in ways that cannot serve, and in fact can harm, a healthcare client's brands.

One of the biggest reasons for this is the kind of people working in the respective fields of healthcare and consumer goods branding. People go into consumer branding not only because it's fun and cool, but more specifically because it makes for a more impressive-looking portfolio. Consumer goods branding can involve huge budgets, with perhaps the additional kicker of a photo shoot in Fiji. It is a liberated field where the brands can pretty much do or say anything that seems clever or catchy or will earn admiration and applause when those brands strut their stuff on TV and other media.

So people who go into consumer goods branding are seeking a fun job, with the chance to work on household name brands; learn the tricks of the trade for launching that fascinating new brand of nutritional water or that sexy new brand of yoga pants; and generate a stunning portfolio to shop around and get better-paying jobs of the same kind.

People don't go into healthcare branding because it's cool. And hardly any colleagues or clients I know have gone into it by accident. People go into healthcare branding for very specific, often personal reasons. Perhaps their parents or siblings have held healthcare-related jobs, and they wish to follow their family's lead. Or perhaps their life or the life of a loved one has been forever changed by illness, and they wish to devote their career to making sure that doesn't happen to other people. Or they believe, as I do, that healthcare brands represent true innovations (versus, say, yet another brand of lipstick or wine opener) that advance the cause of making life significantly more livable. (To be fair, it's a business that also pays well and is pretty secure. But so is investment banking. Or being a lawyer. Or a systems analyst. You get the point.)

Compared to working with consumer products, healthcare branding doesn't seem impressive to friends and family, because they've rarely heard of the product or don't want to know about the unsexy disease it treats. Healthcare brands operate with much smaller budgets and much more conservative clients. And healthcare branding rarely involves celebrities, unless it's a sports star whose health has been compromised by a punishing career or a movie actress whose child had an unfortunate condition and who wants to raise awareness.

But to the people who actively choose to work in the field, healthcare branding is fun, and it is important for the same reasons consumer branders might find it boring and restrictive. Simply put, healthcare branding is significantly more complex and challenging than consumer branding. It is chess to consumer branding's checkers. The Sunday *Times'* crossword puzzle to consumer branding's Sudoku. Unlike the branding for most consumer goods, healthcare branding operates with extreme restrictions that one must study and master, not just in rendering the design, but also in addressing the entire healthcare transaction model, which I will explain shortly.

As far as the "important" and "impressive" aspects go, those in healthcare branding would rather play a greater role behind the scenes in a more serious production than in the limelight of, say, a popular sitcom. To give you a real-world idea of what I'm talking about, I once joined some of my healthcare colleagues who had formerly worked in the consumer goods world. It was an exploratory assignment from Procter & Gamble and Hallmark, owner of Crayola. The exercise was to brainstorm how to integrate the product offerings of the companies' brands into a "movement" campaign. That is, how to link the brands to some world cause in such a way that people would flock to the movement, creating a win-win-win for the cause, the consumer brands, and the customers. For example, kids could enter a contest to craft a line of Hallmark cards using Crayola crayons and have them sent, along with care packages of P&G products, to our troops overseas through donations by citizens to the cause.

After we completed the exercise over the course of several days, one of the former consumer creative directors said, "Gee, it's great to work once again on such big brands." While the product brand she usually worked on, Zyprexa (olanzapine), one of the world's leading anti-psychotic medications, earned more in one year than all of Hallmark's and Crayola's brands combined, her comment was not about the bottom line, but rather about working in the limelight of public brand awareness. I knew what she meant, though I thought otherwise: Crayons and greeting cards have their place, but healthcare branding is important to people's lives in ways that consumer branding can never be. The two are simply different animals.

> YOU WILL PRECIPITATE AN IDENTITY CRISIS IF YOU APPLY CONSUMER GOODS BRANDING PRACTICES TO HEALTHCARE BRANDS.

While consumer-branding companies excel with clients like Burger King, Chevrolet, and Chanel, they are ill equipped to call themselves experts in healthcare branding. Here are eight reasons why:

1. **Healthcare customers are not consumers.** It stands to reason that a consumer agency would have quite a significant expertise on branding healthcare products and services to consumers. After all, connecting consumers with brands is their bread and butter. They understand what motivates consumers in different demographics, and they also have a wealth of experience about what makes consumers tick.

However, when people get sick, they change their orientation to the world. "I'm not myself, today," goes the old phrase. Their perspectives morph from being giddy consumers of products through which they celebrate their life to unhappy, afraid, and angry souls who need to retreat from the world until they can regain their true selves or discover a new way to live with how illness has changed them. There are books and even a branch of science—health psychology—dedicated to what's called "illness behavior" and "sick behavior," yet this important discipline is ignored to the detriment of the client by branding agencies who use the usual consumer behavior model to attempt to brand healthcare products. (I'll deal with this in more detail in the next chapter.)

2. **There is no free speech.** While it may be well known, it bears acknowledging that every single word and image used to create a healthcare brand is scrutinized by the manufacturer's own internal legal and regulatory divisions and monitored by governmental regulatory agencies such as the FDA in the U.S. and the EMEA in Europe. Here's what they're looking for: If there is a claim either overtly stated or tacitly suggested in the brand name, brand symbol, or brand tag line, then either it cannot be used, or, instead, it must be supported by two well-controlled clinical trials, plus the full prescribing information (the "fair balance" pages of dosing, warnings, and disclaimers that regulatory agencies require for prescription brands) must be presented. All this just for showing a brandmark and tag line that are found to make claims about the brand.

For example, when Rogaine, a hair-loss remedy on which I worked, was first launched as a prescription therapy, it was called Regaine and had a symbol representing a healthy head of hair. Nope, not allowed. Regaine, the FDA determined, was an overt claim that the drug would help you regain the hair you had before. (FDA scrutiny is one of the reasons so many drug names are neologisms.) And the symbol of a full head of hair was visually suggesting that Regaine did its job without question. Hence the name was altered to Rogaine, and the symbol had to show an existing hair follicle that was being "nourished" by the topical therapy. (Rogaine is actually better at keeping hair from falling out, rather than growing new hair.)

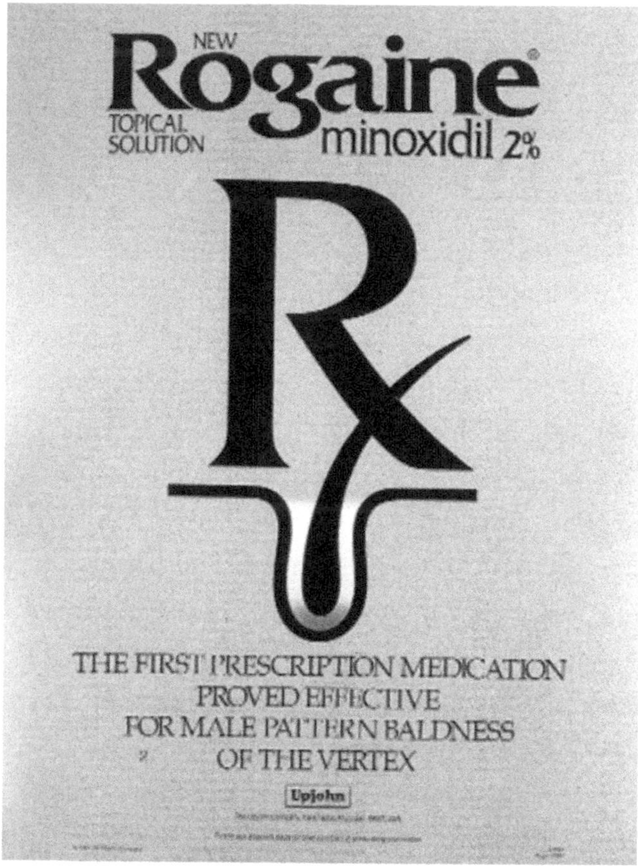

Imagine if the fashion house, Calvin Klein, were told to get rid of their fragrance name, Euphoria, because it constituted a claim that wearing it would lead to ecstatic pleasure? Or Coca-Cola were admonished and pulled from the shelves for overtly stating that to crack a can of its flagship beverage is in no way a means to "open happiness?" Or Energizer, the battery brand, were called on the carpet for featuring their drum-beating bunny symbol, which clearly suggests that their products never lose power or die?

There are voluminous rules and international regulations governing healthcare branding design and nomenclature. Here's just one: the FDA and EMEA each have their own rules for the relative size of the brand name to the generic name of the ingredients, which must appear in close proximity to the brand name in the brandmark. (A few years ago, I worked on a vaccine brand where the generic name was 21 words long. You should have seen the look on my designer's face when she had to find an elegant graphic solution for that.) Such branding requires a working knowledge of all these rules to navigate a branding assignment responsibly in healthcare. Most consumer agencies barely know them, or in some cases, are unaware that they exist.

3. **The healthcare transaction model is completely different from a consumer goods transaction model.** With consumer goods, the customer can see or learn about the brand, walk into a store or go online and make a direct purchase. With regulated healthcare brands, the customer has to admit that maybe he/she has a problem, research it online, and then go to a doctor, who confirms the problem or diagnoses another one. Then, the doctor writes a prescription for the healthcare brand, and the customer has to go to a pharmacist—who may substitute for the brand based on an insurance company's policies—and only then can the customer receive the goods. I'm exhausted just outlining it. The point is that a consumer goods brand identity needs to focus on only one customer—the end user—whereas a regulated healthcare brand must focus on every link in the chain. In addition to appealing to the end user, or patient, the brand has to appeal to the doctor as a reflection of that doctor's practicing identity. If allied health professionals such as nurses or Physician Assistants (PAs) are critical to the process of care for a particular disease or practice, the brand identity must appeal to them as well. Further, the pharmacist must be on board so he/she can endorse the doctor's advice. (More and more, packaging is influencing the ease with which pharmacists can dispense a branded form of the prescribed drug. Think oral

contraceptives.) And lastly, the brand has to be vetted by insurance company representatives so they feel that they are providing the best value for the money.

When you are working in regulated healthcare, brand identities must be created that reflect an entire community of individuals. This means that healthcare brands must be researched differently, strategized differently, and have their brand experiences designed differently than their consumer goods' counterparts. Quite often, consumer goods agencies manage to develop healthcare identities that appeal to their key constituency, consumers. However, because the rest of the customers in the transaction chain have not been factored in, the brand identity risks failure at every turn.

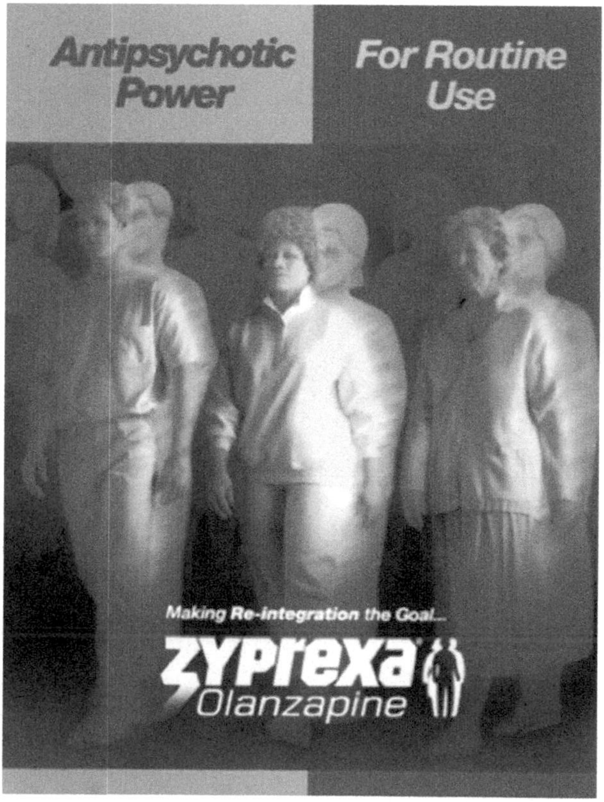

Earlier, I mentioned the antipsychotic drug Zyprexa (olanzapine). Its original brand identity was launched by the sister agency of a very large global consumer shop. The symbol that was part of the brandmark featured the outline of a person, and within it, a similar, smaller outline (see the example on page 54).

It was intended to suggest an "inner true self" emerging from the straightjacket of psychosis, such as schizophrenia or manic depression. Research no doubt showed that such a concept was highly appealing to consumers and their families. So far, so good. But what about the psychiatrists who were asked to prescribe it? After the brand identity had launched, market research revealed that the icon was viewed as a patient getting fatter and fatter, because one side effect of the drug is weight gain. Oops. Time for an expensive rebrand.

4. **Every medical condition is different from every other one.** For the sake of expediency, many of us like to think of a doctor visit as a predictable, homogenous experience. You make an appointment. Present your insurance information when you arrive. Sit in the waiting room and read the outdated magazines. Get ushered into an exam room and then eventually get seen by the doctor.

However universal the doctor-visit experience, the notion that every medical condition or disease is similar to every other one is a reductive fallacy. The patient's journey with each disease, especially those that are chronic and debilitating, doesn't begin or end in the doctor's office and is characterized by its own unique dynamics.

Our team was called in by Biogen (now Biogen Idec) many years ago to help them rebrand their flagship multiple sclerosis (MS) brand Avonex (interferon beta-1a). This was before the advent of some newer, oral therapies. (Avonex is injected once weekly.) Part of the branding research surrounded how neurologists bring up the subject of an MS diagnosis and how the discussion proceeds with patients, leading to the selection of a therapy (or not).

For those of you who are unfamiliar with MS, it is an autoimmune disorder where the body attacks itself, specifically the sheaths of nerve cells in the brain and spinal cord. It is chronic (if you get it, you always have it) and frequently progressive (it gets worse over time). But there are no definitive tests to provide a specific prognosis (brain scans do not always correlate with symptomatology). And while we know that the onset of the disease is usually seen in people aged 20-35 (mostly women), we don't know what causes it, when or if it will flare up again, or how it will impair one's ability to move, walk, and function normally.

Add into the mix drugs like Avonex. They must be taken on a regular basis . . . for life. And they can cause side effects such as flu-like symptoms. And because of the difficulties associated with testing them over a lifetime in clinical trials, such drugs can show only limited data—a few years—in preventing the recurrence of the disease.

So let's look at the journey of an MS patient to see what a brand identity in healthcare must deal with. The patient may decide to dismiss the first symptomatic episode. ("It's just a tingling in my arm.") For others, say, with symptoms of temporary blindness, most will go to a doctor. But they might first see (or be compelled by their health insurance plan to see) a family doctor, who won't be able to diagnose it, or maybe think it's something else. After a few guesses with no visible results, the family doctor may refer the patient to an ophthalmologist, who will conduct an examination, not find any eye-related pathology, and then send the patient back to the family doctor. At this point, the family doctor refers the patient to a neurologist, who does an examination, suspects MS and orders a brain scan. Then this conversation occurs (obviously, I paraphrase):

Neurologist: "I think you have MS. [Explains the condition.] Here are the available therapies. They're all about the same, some more convenient than others. You should decide what's best for you."
Patient: "What? I stopped listening after you said I may have MS."
Patient's spouse/friend/parent who came with them: "We're getting another opinion."

This, we learn from extensive branding research, is one of perhaps four or five conversations between the parties before a therapy is ever prescribed. Confusion. Denial. Anger. Frustration. These are some of the feelings all parties volunteered in the research. And one can see why. It's a Hobson's choice for all parties. For patients: go on a lifelong series of regular self-injections that may or may not prevent the disease from worsening and feel like you have the flu for several weeks in the process? For caregivers (family members or friends who might escort the patient to the visit): take a chance on advocating something intangible and unpredictable and possibly ruin my relationship as a friend/family member? And for neurologists: prescribe a particular brand of therapy that's not really that different from others, cause the patient to feel sick, and then cross his/her fingers that the drug works for this particular patient?

One patient we interviewed in our study called the Avonex brand "elephant repellant." "So if I use it, and I don't see any elephants around, does that mean the drug is keeping them away, too?" he asked.

I use the example of MS because of its complex illness/treatment dynamics, but I could easily use any number of diseases that present the same issues, including diabetes, depression, ulcerative colitis, and many others.

How can a brand define itself under such circumstances so that all involved can see something positive in it among all the negative? That is frequently the challenge in healthcare branding, and it should not be left to someone who thinks it's just like the pickup truck they branded the month before. A customer seeking a remedy for, say, psoriasis, has emotions and motivations and concerns that have nothing in common with a customer seeking to lower his/her cholesterol, for example. In the former case, the customer must deal with the stigma of the condition, the fact that everyone can see that they have it (i.e., lesions on the arms and legs), and the fact that there are no easy therapies available that are both safe and effective. In the latter case, there is no stigma, it is a symptomless (i.e., invisible) condition, and there are many effective and safe therapies from which to choose. The intricacies of understanding how each customer deals with each different condition are possible to master only when healthcare branding is 100% of an agency's focus.

5. **Every physician specialty has a different core psyche.** The flip side to reason number four concerns the party who needs to advocate for a healthcare brand: the doctor. And just as patients with different conditions undergo a different brand experience from one another, so, too, do physicians undergo a different journey from their colleagues to becoming the kind of doctor they are. While doctors have many things in common—a desire to work in the healthcare field, a college education, a medical school degree—the reasons they became the kind of doctor they are vary immensely. What compels people to go into the field of Plastic Surgery has nothing to do with their colleagues who choose Urology. Even physicians who are in family practice or general medicine have different motivators and self-dynamics that must be considered in order to create a healthcare brand with which they can identify.

I'm not just talking about the demographic data—the percentages of people who go into different specialties, whether they work in solo or group practices, annual income statistics, or other such readily available information that agencies often trot out as evidence of healthcare branding expertise. I'm referring to the psychographic profiles that my colleagues and I have developed over decades of interviewing and working with healthcare providers. We know, for instance, that Ob/Gyns enter the field primarily because they treasure the joy of helping their patients bring healthy babies into the world. Yet often they find themselves serving as a woman's only primary care physician. It can make them feel less than thrilled or even inadequate if they are confronting illnesses they didn't sign up for when they chose their specialty. I've done quite a bit of brand identity development in women's care, and no matter how wonderful a brand of birth control might be, it can never get Ob/Gyns too excited. Why? Because it prevents the main love of which they went into the specialty: babies.

In a different scenario, we have Pediatricians, who went into Pediatrics because they wanted to be a family caregiver, but they hate the idea of working with adults and their health issues. That's right. Branding research has shown that Peds cannot stand the chronic lifestyle conditions that adults bring upon themselves by eating and drinking unhealthy things, failing to exercise, and then lying to themselves and their doctors about it all. ("Children are the only patients who don't lie," one Ped confessed.) They love children, lovc watching them grow up, and do everything in their power to *prevent* them from getting sick. (Pediatrics is one of the rare specialties that actually focuses on prevention rather than treatment). What's thrilling to them? Vaccines! They feel that vaccines are the embodiment of their practice ideals. As much as Ob/Gyns tolerate their patients' requests for contraceptive brands, Peds couldn't care more about vaccine brands.

The list goes on, but the point is hopefully clear: when building healthcare brand identities, it takes years of experience to understand the psyche associated with each different type of healthcare provider, so we can create a brand identity that reflects their core values.

As with healthcare products, applying consumer branding techniques to healthcare services will likewise result in an identity crisis. Many types of healthcare services exist. There are hospitals and other point-of-care practices such as walk-in clinics, practice management groups, medication distribution services, and health insurance companies. Let's use hospital service brands as a surrogate for them all, as they provide the most typical example of what's true about all healthcare service brands. As with healthcare products, the brand identity for healthcare services must account for the ways that people think about health and wellness.

Here are the reasons healthcare services branding differs significantly from branding for consumer services:

6. **Nobody wants to jump on the bandwagon**. Service brands—brands that perform a task or deliver things like care and access rather than tangible goods one can hold in one's hand—have a unique opportunity to engage customers on many sensory levels.

Think of a hotel chain such as Ritz Carlton. The brand identity promises to make you feel like you "have arrived" both psychically and physically. They situate their hotels in the most picturesque locales (in New York City, there is one with a front-row seat to the Statue of Liberty and New York harbor, and one overlooking Central Park). When you look out the window of your room, you behold a view reserved primarily for millionaires, if only for a night. Ritz Carlton guest rooms and lobbies are appointed to provide the same privileged experience, with luxurious fabrics to the touch, colorful and soaring floral arrangements to reward sight and smell, and a hushed atmosphere that suggests they've been waiting for you and you only.

You get the idea. Brilliantly rendered service brands are brands you want to join, where you can steep yourself in a world that reflects the person you wish to be. You can visit and revisit this world knowing that the brand experience starts with a rush of anticipation, submerges you in a 360° flattery bath, and endures long after you leave.

Now think of a hospital. No matter which one comes to mind, it's not a brand you wish to join. You will go only if you absolutely must or are carried there in a screaming ambulance. The lights are harsh. The smell is inorganic. You are surrounded by sick people who, like you, don't wish to be there, and by a staff that is overworked and primarily concerned with filling out the correct paperwork so that you are effectively logged into the system. Despite the brave efforts that hospitals make to put forth a brand identity that is caring, competent, and up to the challenge of making you feel like yourself again, the reality—the brand behavior—can never create a brand experience that people want to join. In fact, quite the opposite is true: hospital brands are successful when they become a place that comfortably keeps you there for the absolute minimum amount of time necessary.

It's no wonder that alternative centers for care are becoming an increasingly popular option. Walk-in clinics, outpatient service centers, and even certain chain pharmacies are creating a service experience that truly leverages what people feel about themselves when thinking about health and wellness. That is, a) fit into my life; be located near the same places where I grocery shop or pick up the dry cleaning; b) respect my time; I want to get in without an appointment, get seen, and then get out without feeling like I'm being detained in a gulag; and c) don't make me sicker than when I came in.

It is clinically proven that a sure way to become ill is be around a lot of ill people. If your hospital visit is for one ailment, it is a poor service brand that puts you in contact with other ailments you might bring home. For this reason, surgery centers are quickly becoming a sound alternative brand of service over hospital operating rooms. They do one thing and have to staff and stock supplies for only that one thing.

Further, most surgeries are for conditions that aren't contagious. Low exposure to illness, surgery on your time schedule, and an expedited same-day discharge make people almost not hate being serviced by a surgery center brand.

> TO BE CLEAR, THE GOAL OF BRANDING A HEALTHCARE SERVICE FOLLOWS THE SAME PRIMARY PRINCIPLE OF MEDICINE ITSELF: FIRST, DO NO HARM.

Rather than trying to brook the notion that healthcare service brands can become an idealized experience of modern medicine, the most successful service brand identities in healthcare embrace the idea that you won't be any worse off for engaging with them than not. A low bar, indeed, but a reality that most consumer agencies fail to accept.

Take the scenario I just laid out, and then overlay it with the identities resulting from a consumer branding campaign. Patients—or actors playing patients—appeal to you as a "person" who put themselves and their woes into the hands of a hospital brand. Cue the harp or soft piano music. The tales unfold of lives regained, knees rejuvenated or daughters' weddings attended. Does anybody who has ever been to a hospital buy these fantasies? Hardly.

7. **Healthcare service can never be good enough**. In the absence of proper advice, healthcare service brands make the same common mistake as healthcare product brands: they start with the service first and then try to sell it to customers (remember the Nuprin example?). It becomes a fill-in-the blank exercise:

"OK, what do we do well? We can say our brand is the best ____________." (fill in the blank)

You've all witnessed this. The best doctors. The best department of oncology, or cardiology, or maternity, etc. The best, most advanced equipment. While such aspirations are commendable from both a branding and care-giving discipline, they are doomed to fail over time, because of the nature of delivering a healthcare service. That is, by nature, things go wrong, even under the best of circumstances. Sickness and disease are unpredictable. Doctors are only human, and, as such, fallible. People will die unexpectedly. Even if 99% of the time the healthcare service brand succeeds in fulfilling its identity as, say, having the best maternity ward, it will be that 1% wildcard variable—that inexplicable delivery gone wrong—that will threaten to bring down the brand. There are no do-overs in a situation like this, no way to appease the grieving parents with a complimentary next stay or a bottle of wine sent to their room.

In truth, no consumer service has to contend with such a high bar of perceptual success. Even FedEx, arguably one of the premier package delivery services, loses track of a package once in a while. But because it is not a life-or-death matter, people accept that these things happen to the best of us. Not so with healthcare service brands. There is no forgiving mistakes when it comes to health and wellness.

Aside from setting the hospital up for sure failure, the fill-in-the blank branding approach creates an echo chamber that prohibits much-needed differentiation between hospitals. There's a reason people believe that most hospitals have decent doctors, decent departments, and basically the same level of care as every other brand: no one has bothered to show them otherwise.

Around 2010, I was brought in as part of a team to help a very fine hospital build a better identity. The hospital is Maimonides Medical Center, one of the top facilities in the nation, yet it was struggling at the time to win hearts and minds in New York City, where four of the other best hospitals in the nation happen to be located. Here are some properties of the Maimonides brand I identified:

- It is a center of excellence for cardiology, oncology and surgery.
- It delivers more babies each year than any other hospital in New York State.
- It is an academic teaching center, which means that it provides residency and fellowship training for new doctors.
- It is situated in Borough Park, Brooklyn.

Of all the good things about Maimonides, this last item had caused the majority of the brand's difficulties in getting recognized as a top New York City hospital. Branding research showed that the most esteemed hospital brands in New York City were in the borough of Manhattan, regardless of the hard statistics about good care. One patient in our research group reported having a heart attack and then taking a 40-minute taxi ride into Manhattan for treatment at Columbia-Presbyterian, even though he lived in Brooklyn, just a couple of minutes from Maimonides. So great was the brand equity of Columbia-Presbyterian—an Ivy-League-affiliated teaching hospital in Manhattan—that this man literally risked his life to be treated at an institution on a parity with a safer choice hospital in his own back yard. The good people at Maimonides had tried to build their brand identity on the "best" properties of which every other institution in New York City availed itself. Yet there was no overcoming the fact that Maimonides is located in Brooklyn, and that Brooklyn at the time was considered second best to Manhattan in all things.

Our advice was to build the brand from the outside in: find out what people prize most about being a Brooklynite and then transfer that equity to the Maimonides brand. In our research, we discovered there are 40% more people in Brooklyn than in Manhattan. That's 40% more lives for which to care. (Hospitals and insurance companies often express their value by "lives" in their care.) We also discovered a pride in being a Brooklynite that was unique to that borough of the city. The values of tough under pressure, no nonsense, a fighting spirit, and a melting pot unequalled in New York resonated with potential Brooklyn patients. These were also the values that were credible and relevant for the Maimonides staff and brand of service. Manhattan hospitals, by contrast, were seen by Brooklynites as bureaucratic, elitist, and disingenuous, promising medical experts at the top of their field, but making them available to only select patients.

We wanted to make Maimonides Brooklyn's brand of hospital. That year, the New Jersey Nets basketball franchise moved to Downtown Brooklyn and became the Brooklyn Nets. Maimonides took advantage of the opportunity and signed up as the Official Hospital of the Brooklyn Nets, securing an even greater association with the borough. The branding in our promotional campaign appealed to what Brooklynites wanted in their hospital: a pride of place. (It even used the colloquial spelling for the borough, Bklyn, which all locals use.) Over the past decade, Brooklyn has taken on vital positive equity in the arts, dining, and housing industries, and Maimonides was among the first brands to tap into the electricity. They still have excellent doctors and facilities, but for a healthcare service brand, which can never be good enough because of the life-or-death dynamic inherent in the practice, Maimonides accepted that reality and found a way to thrive by faithfully reflecting the values of their customers instead of selling the quality of their service.

8. **Healthcare services do not have the luxury of refined customer targeting.** Unlike Ritz Carlton, which can afford to focus on only those key customer segments that seek out its brand of luxury, healthcare service brands must take on all comers. No matter if you are a lawyer or a plumber, an atheist or an Orthodox Jew, a descendant of the Mayflower or a newly arrived immigrant, when you become sick and in need of a healthcare service, you join the grumpy fraternity of the unwell and require the same assistance as everyone else. Consumer service brands have the luxury of deciding if they wish to target a specific gender (the spa for women), a specific income range (the tennis club for the upper class), or a specific nationality (the Irish Bar Association).

Any such segregation for a healthcare service is not tolerated and seen as an attempt to restrict a basic human right. It is an inalienable property of a healthcare service brand that it be egalitarian. Admittedly, this is a generalization with some exceptions, such as those private rooms for the wealthy one hears about in certain hospitals, the "red blanket" patients who are singled out for special treatment, or the Platinum-grade insurance plans available to those with greater discretionary lucre than most others. Usually, these aspects do not make it into the brand identity, but rather exist as an unadvertised secret. For the most part, though, universal appeal is a reality that must be accounted for when branding healthcare services.

This creates a unique challenge. When targeting a particular segment of the population as do consumer service brands, it is much easier to create a homogenized set of values that are held dear by a specific group of people. For example, a spa that targets women only will create a brand identity based on values that women most esteem, which translate into a brand promise, branding hallmarks (logo, color, tag line) and other aspects of the brand experience that reflect women's sense of self.

But healthcare brands must try to be all things to all people, and this is a formula that fails more often than it succeeds. A brand identity is most successful when it stands for one thing. Revisiting the consumer package-delivery business, FedEx owns the idea of certainty—the best odds that your package will be delivered when they promise it will. DHL owns the idea of global access—there are many different rules in many different countries, and DHL knows how to navigate those circumstances. The United States Postal Service (USPS) owns the idea of frugality—it will deliver your package for less than the other carriers, but generally as a trade-off for certainty and/or speed.

For healthcare services, trying to be all things to all people often results in an identity crisis. How often have you seen a hospital service brand try to be about its doctors, its technology, its rankings, its departments, its nurses, its location, its celebrity customers, and so on, separately or all at once? Forced to be egalitarian by the dynamic in which it exists, a healthcare service brand all too often will try on different brand identities that may attract opportunistic buyers in the short term, but lose traction with everyone else over the long term. Imagine a restaurant that starts out wanting to identify itself as Northern Italian, and then puts lasagna and ziti (southern Italian dishes) on the menu to cater to a few patrons who seek that. And then the restaurant continues to add cuisines from India, the American southwest, and Japan as more requests come in. After a while, the brand stands for everything, which means it stands for nothing in particular.

About 10 years ago, my team and I were invited to consult on brand identity for the Ohio State University Medical Center (OSUMC). By far the most comprehensive and prestigious hospital brand in the city of Columbus, Ohio, OSUMC was losing business to several local-area hospitals and facing an imminent competitive threat from a large hospital group, OhioHealth, which was buying up the competition and consolidating them. We fielded audits of the branded materials of OSUMC and the other hospitals, and we conducted site visits. Each hospital that we visited for the competition had consistently branded experiences that helped differentiate them from each other: a focus, say, on children, or a Catholic sponsorship, or a particular department (such as cardiology), or a particular location. (One hospital, Riverside Methodist, is situated on a well-trafficked thoroughfare and can also be seen clearly from Route 71, the central artery that divides the city. It was a billboard for itself, a lovely white structure in a nice neighborhood that is easily top-of-mind for all who drive by.)

OSUMC, by contrast, is a grouping of hospitals and centers spread out over different parts of the city. As we toured through the different OSUMC hospital buildings, we observed a different brand experience being put forth in each one, none of them consistent with the other. Here is a sample of the values being promoted that we encountered:

- A highly ranked national institution
- A good percentage of great local doctors
- Magnet accredited (a certified recognition for nursing excellence)
- The only academic teaching center in central Ohio
- Great technology
- Great original research
- Over one million lives under care annually
- Charitable support for the community
- The state-of-the-art James Cancer Center

Even to non-branding experts, it quickly becomes obvious that it is hard to be esteemed for one thing when you are trying to stand for nine. Further, a tour of the main buildings on the Ohio State University campus revealed that the brand on greatest display throughout was not that of the hospital, but rather the powerhouse football team, the OSU Buckeyes. (In case you don't follow college football, the Bucks are perennial champions and a fanatical religion in Columbus. They draw 100,000 fans live for each game, more than most professional franchises.)

One can understand why the hospital would love to align its brand identity with that of a legendary football brand, but it ignores reason number five in the previous section above: when football fans get sick, they stop behaving like football fans. We did find branding for the OSU Medical Center here and there . . . on the rugs and garbage bins. One additional observation: all of the things that OSUMC was putting forth were not about the patients or potential customers, but more about themselves.

Qualitative research with the heterogeneous Columbus customers yielded a brand equity evaluation that was resoundingly homogeneous. Nearly every research subject, regardless of demographics, found the brand cold, self-congratulatory, and too big to care about their little problems. Ouch! (My intention here is not to malign the wonderful institution of OSUMC and the great accomplishments of which they deserve to be very proud. I merely wish to show that given an embarrassing wealth of assets, even the best healthcare service brand can easily find itself in an identity crisis by trying to be all things to all people.)

In addition to focusing on why customers would prefer to buy from OSUMC, the solution to their fractured brand issue would have been to find an esteemed value common to the great majority of its constituency, as we did with Maimonides. (I never got the chance with OSUMC. I think my blunt observation of their branding being only on rugs and garbage bins blew the deal for me.)

This chapter is the beginning discussion on the misperceptions surrounding the differences between consumer buying mindsets and healthcare buying mindsets. The next chapter takes us deeper into this topic. Suffice it to say for now that when thinking about healthcare branding, we must appreciate and understand it as a separate and distinct discipline from consumer branding models. Healthcare branding agencies understand that their task is to play tennis with a higher net than their consumer counterparts. A healthcare brand experience must account for—and even overcome—the forces at work that can undermine all the good a healthcare brand can do for customers on all sides of the buying transaction. A healthcare brand experience must find the silver lining that lies somewhere in the dark cloud between illness and wellness, where no matter how good it gets, it can never be good enough.

The path to launching and nurturing a successful healthcare brand identity is tricky; it's our job to avoid the missteps that could plunge the brand into an identity crisis. The next chapter deals with another unspoken problem affecting healthcare branding: oversimplifying customer identity.

4

The Hidden Problem of Customer Identity

In the last chapter, I touched on the problems that can arise when consumer goods marketers and branding shops treat healthcare customers and brands like consumer-goods customers and brands. But the healthcare industry itself has its own set of unspoken problems. One large problem hiding in plain sight is the fact that many health and wellness clients operate with misconceptions about the identity of their customers, marketing direct-to-consumer (DTC) to those suffering with a health issue in the same way consumer goods are marketed. (Recently some pharma companies have re-branded patients as Heathcare Consumers, or HCCs, but the renaming is more cosmetic than actual as their consideration of this customer segment is still often mischaracterized.)

Regarding the DTC or HCC segment, healthcare branding seems to have come down with a case of Multiple Personality Disorder, with healthcare clients suffering brand disintegration due to incorrectly dividing their customers into two groups: "patient" and "consumer." In this scenario, one is either not well and under a doctor's care (i.e., a patient), or one is well, for now, but will come under a doctor's care sooner or later (i.e., a consumer). While cleaving the group into the sick and the sick-to-be may seem like a logical and easy way to partition resources, it misidentifies customer behavior and thereby creates significant barriers to connecting these audiences effectively with healthcare brands. I'll demonstrate how as we move through this chapter.

As discussed in the previous chapter, a common misconception argues that consumers should be engaged in the same way whether the brand is a snow tire or a pain medication. As such, when creating a consumer brand experience (as they see it, separate and distinct from a "patient" brand experience), healthcare clients often bypass experts in healthcare branding, preferring instead to hire consumer agencies. Their reasoning: part of our goal is to reach consumers; consumer agencies know consumers; *ergo,* they are the best source to align the values of consumers with the values of our healthcare brand.

Let's crack open this chestnut.

As previously mentioned, a consumer-branding model operates from the idea that brands are a celebration of self. That is, people with active, healthy lives are looking to acquire brands that provide a flattering reflection of aspirational self-values. "Look, I got a new Dior bag! A new Zegna suit! A new Foo Fighters CD!" "The Yankees won!" (meaning "I won," because that's what a sports franchise brand means to consumers). When applied to health and wellness brands, a consumer goods branding model needs to assume that consumers always stay consumers throughout their lives, temporarily sidelined by illness, in which case they become temporary "patients" from time to time. Then, after the illness is resolved and has been absorbed into their lives, they return to the consumer buying mindset that they had before they became ill. The illustration of this simplistic behavior model would look something like this:

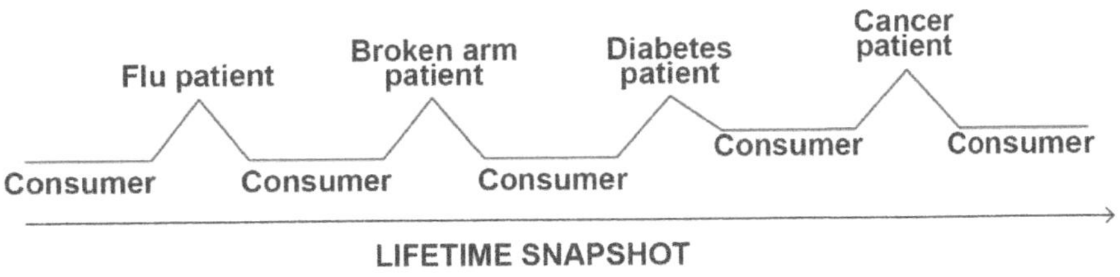

In some instances of short-lived illness, such as the flu, this model might actually be the case for some people, but I believe that in chronic conditions it fosters an identity problem that's at the heart of why many healthcare brands fail to connect with customers.

Let's consider another way of looking at this dynamic that more accurately describes the reality of how illness affects people's lives. When consumers get sick, they become someone different. As I mentioned in the last chapter, they might even say, "I'm not myself today." People do not celebrate the buying process when they become ill. They are now forced to buy brands that they don't want, but rather *need*. When faced with the prospect of, say, herpes, overactive bladder, or depression, consumers experience an alteration to their identity that affects the way they relate to brands in general, and healthcare brands specifically. Healthcare brands are about a *protection* of self, not a celebration like consumer brands. The best someone with an illness can hope for is a return to normalcy. In the case of mild illness, like a rash, normal can be relatively easy to achieve. But in the case of more chronic conditions, like diabetes or psoriasis, people's identities must adjust to accommodate a new, if unwanted, self-characterization: a former self that is now routinely interrupted or altered forever by an Illness that is, respectively, chronically acute or chronic. When people become chronically ill, they seek the "new normal." That is, what is *now* normal considering that illness is a part of one's everyday life? The pursuit of the new normal is an essential mindset to consider when creating relevant and engaging healthcare brands and one that is ignored by the DTC consumer-branding model illustrated above.

Take a recent campaign from the laxative MiraLAX. MiraLAX is in a category referred to as an oral "osmotic." (Milk of Magnesia is another example.) That is, it works by drawing water from the body tissues surrounding the colon (osmosis) thereby preventing constipation by keeping stools a little more watery. The consumer agency working on the campaign went with a wrongly familiar strategy in the category: promoting the celebratory feeling customers will get using the brand. (I know firsthand because years earlier, against our advice, the marketing team of Senokot—another laxative brand—used the same unsuccessful strategy. Its promotion featured elated Senokot patients uninhibitedly dancing to the James Brown song, *I Feel Good (I Knew That I Would.)* MiraLAX pushed the strategy even more over the top with its campaign "Love your lax" / "I love my lax."

In the DTC consumer-branding model, MiraLAX shows people celebrating their lives and their love of MiraLAX. So proud to declare their love, one hypothetical person has it crocheted on a couch pillow, and another on a backpack: I [heart] my lax. Does anyone really buy this conceit? Laxative as hero? Laxative as a bumper sticker about which one wants to shout out to the world?

For comparison, let's take a look at a healthcare branding model in the same laxative category, the success of which results from recognizing the true values and identity of the customer. Benefiber, also an oral agent, works through a bulk-forming action, relieving constipation by using fiber to integrate with the stool and keep it soft. (Citrucel and Metamucil are other examples.) Below is a recent ad for Benefiber.

As stated earlier, the healthcare branding model isn't a celebration of self, but rather a protection of self. What does a constipated person want? Two things: not to let anyone know that they have constipation, for starters, and also to live the normal life they wish to live without being compromised by a bowel irregularity. Benefiber's strategy is to slip itself modestly into an already ongoing activity: managing one's diet.

Relief from constipation is a natural outcome of this strategy. (Remember the lemon example from Chapter 2?) Benefiber knows that it's not the star of the show, but MiraLAX is clueless about how healthcare brands actually fit into the lives of patients. No one really celebrates—much less loves—their laxative. But people do look for ways to manage their diets. Benefiber offers a flattering reflection of the customer by being discreet (no mention of constipation), and also honoring the customer's pride in being a smart eater. Protection of self achieved!

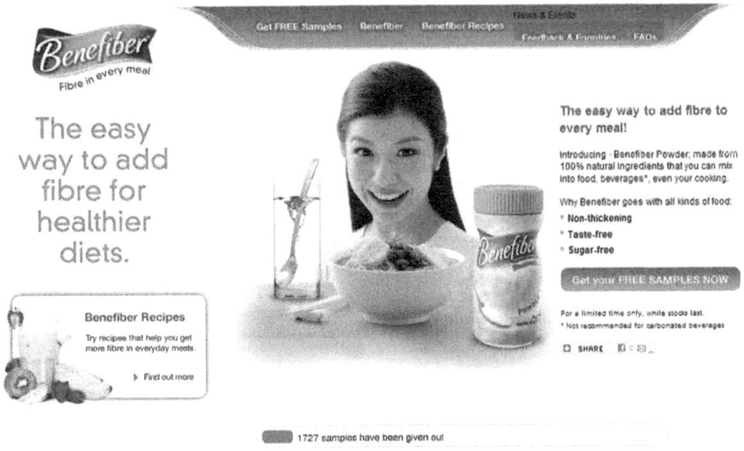

At the root of the identity crisis generated by relegating customers to the dual personalities of "consumer behavior" and "patient behavior" are the terms "consumer" and "patient," which are themselves poorly branded, woefully inadequate, and even antagonistic in today's world. For instance, while the label "consumer" may be happily used to identify all manner of customers in the vast world of consumer goods, the idea of a "healthcare consumer" earns resentment from many who feel the term conjures up an unethical financial scheme where sick people are compelled to "consume" medicine in a conspiracy rigged to maximize greedy corporate gain. Under this mindset, making profits is perfectly acceptable in all industries save healthcare—money earned helping customers with their health and wellness issues is instead akin to profiteering or piracy.

The term "patient" comes with its own in-built problems. Most obviously, the term is antiquated as it suggests a passive recipient of care, an image wholly at odds with today's activated, empowered population of online information seekers and social network devotees. I don't know about you, but when my friends get sick, everyone on their Facebook feed knows about it, and many chime in with what they believe to be helpful information and even diagnoses. You can just imagine the search engines in action, scouring sites like WebMD to see what their symptoms reveal, and reaching out to others who have had the same condition. The word "patient" denies the true identity of today's healthcare brand seekers. Everyone reading this has at some point come down with some kind of illness, whether acute or chronic. What do *you* expect from a healthcare brand? What we all do: to resume a state of normalcy (i.e., an "unsick" state) as much, as quickly, and as discreetly as possible given a particular disease or condition.

Webster's defines the word "resume" as follows: **resume (ri-zoom') v. (Latin: to take up again) 1. To begin or take up again following an interruption. 2. To continue after interruption.**

The concept of resuming normal life offers a better way to understand and connect with the health and wellness customer. Whether you just get a cold and want to get rid of your nuisance illness and resume your activities, or whether you have just been diagnosed with emphysema and are seeking to resume whatever part of your identity possible, all parties want to "take up and continue" their lives, or as much of their lives as they can. Therefore, a more enlightened view of the end-user for healthcare brands is not the Consumer model, but rather the Resumer model: a consumer who has become ill and seeks to restore essential aspects of self that illness has compromised. The illustration of this model might look something like this:

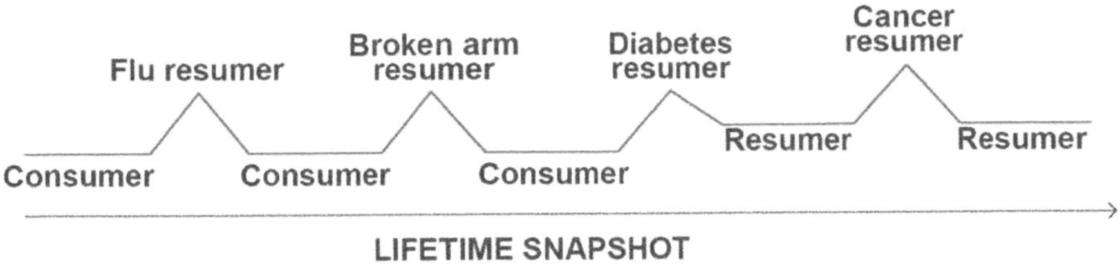

> ILLNESSES—EACH IN THEIR OWN WAY—COMPROMISE THE SELF, DISTRACTING IT FROM ITS ASPIRATION, AND IN TURN, FUNDAMENTALLY ALTERING THE WAY A SICK PERSON BEHAVES AND BUYS BRANDS, ESPECIALLY HEALTHCARE BRANDS.

And different illnesses create different types of resumer behavior. The simple but illuminating perceptual map below showcases how people with illnesses fall on just two measures: acceptance of the condition and a willingness to take some kind of remedial action. Sometimes being a resumer means popping a pill to continue one's lifestyle (as with high cholesterol). And sometimes being a resumer means denying that you are even sick in the first place (people with gout often just muddle through until the symptoms subside).

We've all been sick. And if we're honest with ourselves, we know the Mr. Hyde side of us is distinctly and unpleasantly different from our Dr. Jekyll. This is not just a subjective feeling but also a scientifically documented concept. In their landmark paper, *Health behavior, illness behavior, and sick-role behavior* (*Archives of Environmental Health* 12: 531-541; 1996), Yale School of Public Health Professors S.V. Kasl and S. Cobb discuss the primary tenets of Health Psychology: "Health and illness are important life issues that critically influence goal selection and behavior in our daily activities. As such, general models of behavioral self-regulation must be able to account for health-related behavior." In other words, health and illness significantly affect the way we make choices (goal selection), and the way that people react to their own unhealthy circumstances (behavioral self-regulation) must be taken into account when offering helpful remedies.

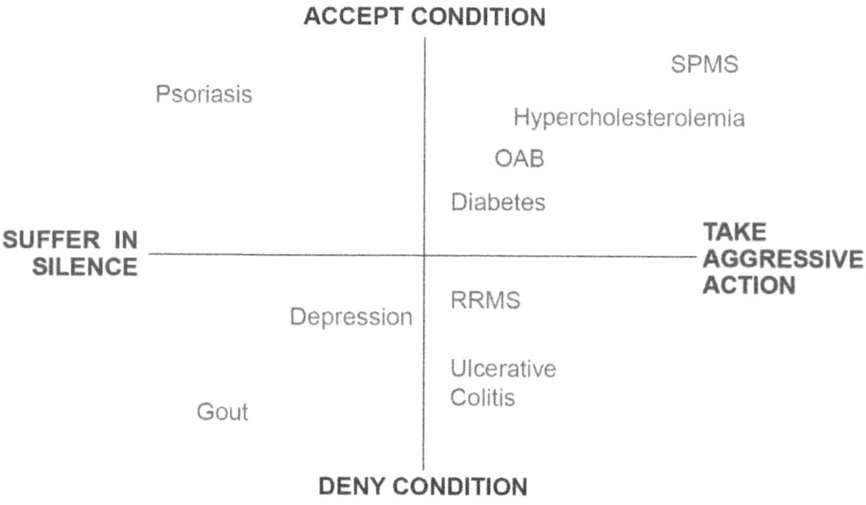

OAB = Overactive Bladder; **SPMS** = Secondary-Progressive MS; **RRMS** = Relapsing/Remitting MS.)

Additionally, *The Encyclopedia of Public Health* outlines two key aspects of how healthy behavior is compromised and redefined by malady. The most common is identified as Sick-Role Behavior.

Sick-Role Behavior involves any activity undertaken by those who consider themselves to be ill for the purpose of getting well. It generally involves a whole range of dependent behaviors and leads to some degree of forgiveness from one's usual responsibilities.

- They accept the established medical system of patient and healer
- They consider themselves exempt from carrying out normal social roles
- They are not "at fault" for their plight

My doctor told me to rest and take my medicine with meals.
I'm skipping the company meeting because I don't want to make anyone else sick.

Illness Behavior, by contrast, involves any activity undertaken by those who perceive themselves to be ill for the purpose of using their illness to define their state of being. Think normal people who flirt with having a gluten allergy to express their unique sensitivity and elicit attentiveness from others. Unlike Sick-Role behavior, it works outside the doctor/patient model and involves more independent behaviors.

- Explore self-help strategies
- Experiment with remedies on one's own
- Dismiss the symptoms altogether

With Sick-Role Behavior, a resumer's new normal is to return to as much of one's previous activities as quickly and as discreetly as possible. With Illness Behavior, as illusrated on the next page, a resumer's new normal is to seek lifestyle modifications to one's previous normal—to move away from one's life habits before the illness existed—in pursuit of a newly satisfying self-identification.

As you can see, "resumer" is not a monolithic term. It has nuanced behaviors that are affected by type of illness, age, gender and culture. For example, psoriasis is a disease of the young (15-35 years old, with most first experiencing symptoms in their 20s). The new normal sought by a psoriasis resumer might include being able to go to the beach and not feel embarrassed by the evident lesions on his/her body. Pushing into gender differences a bit (more on this below), while men with psoriasis will articulate such a desire, women with the condition will go to greater lengths to resume their normal appearance due to the burden put upon women by our culture's obsession with female body image. It's one of the reasons that women are often featured as part of the healthcare brand's visual assets even though the disease does not discriminate between women and men.

Such a new normal wish would be beyond the wildest dreams of late-stage MS resumers. Going to the beach would not even make their top 10 list, because of how these diseases specifically rob the self in very different ways, and at a different age.

"What is important for the early-stage patient is the maintenance of hope," Kasl and Cobb insightfully assert."What is important for the late-stage patient is the maintenance of purpose."

For an MS resumer in the late stage of the disease, one desire of a new normal might be the ability to operate a motor vehicle at least one day a week. For MS resumers without access to public transportation, their condition often means complete public immobility and isolation on the order of house arrest. Simply going to the grocery store will likely be in their top five of what would constitute an acceptable new normal.

For the Alzheimer resumer, there's not as much that can be done at present compared to other diseases. (The good news is that it is one of the most active areas of research in both the public and private sectors.) When one thinks of what the new normal might be for an Alzheimer resumer, the ability to remember names and faces is what comes to mind. And why not? That's the tragedy that gets played out in Hollywood dramas about people with the disease. And that's how some of the healthcare brands present the yearnings in their brand identities. However, this is not the top desire for people with Alzheimer's when you ask them to paint a picture of their acceptable new normal. The number one desire is not to be a burden to those around them. The reason I bring up Alzheimer's disease specifically is that it illustrates a unique nuance in the resumer dynamic. As Alzheimer's disease progresses, it completely erases the identity of the victim. In doing so, it creates two sets of resumers: the patient and the family who cares for him/her. (Family members and friends who play the role of seeing to a patient's healthcare needs are referred to as "caregivers.") This is why the movies and the healthcare brands focus on memory loss. Having their names remembered is one of the top desires of an Alzheimer caregiver in pursuing their acceptable new normal. Such aspects of resumer behaviors are critical to a brand's success.

Even product packaging can influence resumer behavior. It wasn't until the 1990s that prescription arthritis anti-inflammatory brands finally recognized that all the efforts they built into their brand identities were being undone by the little green or brown prescription bottles being dispensed by the pharmacist. The plastic bottles were painful and/or impossible to open by people with rheumatoid arthritis (RA). The packaging—so much a part of a consumer brand experience—was out of the marketer's control. And this one aspect of the brand experience fought mightily against a key concept of the new normal for RA patients: being independent of others for self-maintenance.

"As people come to recognize the permanence of their condition and experience its ongoing disruptions," say Kasl and Cobb, "[they] may be able to regulate a more positive self-image in the face of chronic disease if they reformulate their future self-conceptions to be compatible with the limitations of the disease."

Gender also influences resumer behavior. The differences between how men and women express and address illness are so well characterized that they have achieved the tenured status of stereotypes. Getting men to even admit that they have a medical problem is a major challenge for healthcare brands. Getting them to do something about it requires even greater resources. There are no definitive surveys on the topic, but there are general trends confirmed by several different evaluations. When either a man or a woman accepts that they are ill, they visit their doctor about the same percent of the time. That's about where the parity ends. Because of their physical differences, women become accustomed to seeing doctors on a regular basis for their gynecological health. This habitual routine leads women to consider more frequent wellness visits (i.e., they go to the doctor to monitor their health even when they do not feel sick).

Men, on the other hand, see illness as weakness. The very thought makes men feel vulnerable and dependent, even psychically impotent. They will shrug off symptoms and deny warnings, often putting off a doctor visit until the problem has gotten so bad it may make their desired new normal impossible to achieve. Outside of school- or work-mandated annual physicals, about one in seven men report never going to a doctor otherwise, compared with about one in 17 for women. (My father, who was a primary care practitioner for more than 40 years, died at the age of 86 from colon cancer, a disease that ran in our family. Colon polyps can usually be resolved by surgery if caught in time through routine colonoscopy. He never got one. When people ask what my father died of, I don't say "colon cancer"; I say "stubbornness.")

Since women are more proactive about their health, and since they are also, by default, the primary caregiver in the family (more on this later), healthcare marketers often leverage women's advocacy as a means of getting their men to develop relationships with healthcare brands. For instance, back in the 1990s, the advent of nicotine replacement therapy created an easier way for people to quit smoking cigarettes than just going cold turkey. Our agency team launched Parke-Davis's (and now Pfizer's) Nicotrol brand, a nicotine patch. Anyone who has ever smoked knows that nicotine is a powerfully addictive substance, so while replacement therapy wasn't actually a direct route to becoming unhooked, it did offer a carcinogen-free drug delivery of nicotine while waiting for one's willpower to kick in. (The joke at the time went like this: "I used to be addicted to smoking cigarettes; now, I'm addicted to nicotine patches.")

In addition to becoming physically addictive, smoking had other physical and social values that people were unwilling to give up. Pleasure was chief among them. Once learned, the habit of smoking feels good physically. It is also a means of self-control—something one can do for oneself at will whenever a problem comes to mind and one needs a moment to oneself. Even as the non-smoking movement gained momentum, it ironically reinforced the sense of self that smokers had about being mavericks, and not following the herd (Marlboro anyone?). All of these factors made getting men to quit smoking extremely difficult. Getting them to visit their doctor and create a relationship with a healthcare brand that would help them quit was a challenge on a much higher plane. How does a healthcare brand create a new normal when the idea of smoking doesn't seem like a chemical addiction, but rather a lifestyle choice?

A typical healthcare rationale didn't work. Male cigarette smokers back then did not quit out of concerns for the risk of cancer or cardiovascular disease. And neither did women. We had to find self-values that would appeal to each gender's sense of what a desired new normal would look like and then impart them to the Nicotrol brand. We started with the most primitive ideas of how men and women function in the culture. The hunter and the gatherer. The protector and the nurturer. Men concern themselves with matters of performance; women with matters of appearance. (Ever compare how the sexes talk about each other? "Hey, I met a girl." "Yeah? What does she look like?" This versus "Hey, I met a guy." "Yeah? What does he do?").

Our discovery research led us to the insight that it was the male/female relationship we could leverage in getting both genders to quit smoking with Nicotrol. They would do this for each other. As non-smokers, men could perform better and longer at being a great boyfriend, husband, and father. And women could maintain their healthy appearance and be better caretakers of their relationships. Instead of conducting a steady stream of promotion to smokers as other patches did, we pulsed activity in coordination with "couple" moments. Quitting smoking could be a couple's Christmas present or New Year's resolution together. It could be a Valentine's Day mutual commitment.

Working with medical directors from blue chip corporations such as General Motors and their insurance companies, we synchronized our Nicotrol brand offers with significant couple events like marriages and the birth of children. With women leading the activity of getting themselves and their men to commit to each other in life's joys, Nicotrol went from being an effective nicotine replacement therapy to a brand that helps cement relationships.

This same strategy can be seen again working its magic in the healthcare category of Erectile Dysfunction (ED), where Lilly's Cialis (tadalafil) woos couples romantically while Pfizer's Viagra (sildenafil) tries to get men to discover their inner horndog. Cialis is impromptu dancing in the living room and hot-tubbing together. Viagra is building campfires on the beach and repairing classic muscle cars.

Cialis and Viagra roughly split the $4 billion ED market. While Viagra has enjoyed its position as the one that started it all (the advantage of being first is a great one), Cialis has done a remarkable job of keeping pace by harnessing the values of both genders in their brand identity. Still, the dueling new normals of holding on to one's masculinity (potency) or holding onto one's relationships (protector/nurturer) are very fine examples of how to maximize resumer mindsets in pursuit of indelible healthcare identities.

Unlike with most consumer brands, where the prospect of gaining something is part of the brand promise, healthcare brands need to accommodate the resumer mindset by dealing with what is lost or potentially lost. (In the ED example above, potency and intimacy, respectively, are being threatened with loss.) This is well illustrated in the research I've done with cancer (oncology) resumers. Oncology therapies vary significantly based on tumor type, stage of the disease, and patient characteristics (e.g., family history, genotype of the cancer, etc.). Since many cancers have no cure, and since there are many different ways to attack the problem, what's called a "standard of care"—an accepted best practice on how to manage a disease—is constantly being re-evaluated and tweaked as new information and new brands influence the dynamic. However, there is one constant in the resumer mindset for which cancer treatment brands must account: a loss-framed promise is often more effective than a gain-framed promise.

RESUMERS BUY RISK REDUCTION MORE THAN THEY BUY REWARD.

Imagine a group of "naïve" or previously untreated cancer resumers. In addition to their chemotherapy regimen, they are offered a choice of radiation or not. In the risk vs. reward scenario, one can present them with a survival promise (how many years people in general live following radiation), or with an avoidance-of-mortality promise (how many years people lose from their lives without radiation). The data is identical, but the resumer is asked to contemplate years saved vs. years lost. Unlike a typical consumer mindset, where the prospect of gaining something might compel a purchase, the prospect of gaining years of life actually results in a decrease in the selection of additional radiation therapy. Those resumers presented with what they would lose if they didn't opt for radiation chose radiation more often. (Again, a resumer is trying to reduce that part of the self that is being lost.) While the entire matter is, literally, a morbid topic, it highlights the hidden identity that must be considered by brands that wish to reflect a resumer's concept of the new normal.

Another distinction between consumers and resumers can be found in the concept of "choice." Consumer brands relish the notion of freedom of choice, especially in the United States, where freedom is a core value of the American brand. It's a pretty thought. When you browse supermarket aisles, department stores, or electronics shops, you are presented with dozens and dozens of options, each with their own set of differences, some significant to performance and some merely esthetic. Which bonbon to choose? What a great time to be alive!

Not so for most healthcare resumers. What appears to be a great range of different OTC choices on the drugstore shelves are really just minor variations of each other. (The next time you are shopping for an OTC cough/cold remedy, compare the ingredients. You'll find the same three to four medicines in every one.) Even in many regulated prescription therapy categories, choices are much more limited than in the consumer goods world. (In industry speak, highly similar drugs are called "me-too" brands.)

Take the treatment of high blood pressure (hypertension). Generally speaking, the condition refers to a buildup of pressure in the circulatory system. Think of it as a garden hose set up: there's a tap, the capacity of the hose itself, and the end of the hose where the water comes out. Turn it on, and everything works fine. Now simulate hypertension: stop the water from coming out with your thumb at the end of the hose. Pressure builds to an unnatural and potentially dangerous level, threatening to burst the hose (vascular disease), ruin the tap (heart attack), or bruise your thumb (kidney disease).

There are basically three ways to treat hypertension medically. You can use diuretics to let out the water (i.e., ease up on your thumb). You can use one of several different types of agents (blockers and enzyme-converting inhibitors) to down-regulate the source (i.e., turn the tap lower). Or you can use a combination of these. They each have their own "therapeutic index" (the ratio between the drug's effectiveness and its side effects).

I choose hypertension as an example because it is a condition that has witnessed an established maturity from a drug therapy perspective. That is, there is an accepted standard of care. In other words, this is a condition that—while dangerous—has an accepted number of proven choices. For the healthcare resumer, this is a more welcome scenario than it would be for a buyer of consumer goods. When healthcare customers browse the web for details about a condition or a therapeutic solution, they learn everything from facts to opinions to myths. Vaccines cause autism (false). Hand sanitizer diminishes your immune system, making you more vulnerable to disease (arguable). Ulcers are caused by an infection in the stomach lining (true). Hepatitis C has no cure (false). And so on. They want information, and boy do they get it. So much stuff, and such confusing stuff, that they call into question their own ability to separate the wheat from the chaff. (This is admittedly truer for healthcare product brands than for healthcare service brands.)

As the 1980s Devo song points out:

Freedom of choice
is what you got.
Freedom from choice
is what you want.

Anyone with access to the Internet can learn anything they *want* in seconds about a healthcare brand. Information is everywhere. But for resumers, information is only a secondary goal. When faced with a tsunami of facts, half-truths and myths, what people *need* is an emotional refuge from choice: reassurance. Don't get me wrong. Individual choice is still a factor when building a healthcare brand. However, many resumers cannot often act without the validation that comes from being in the majority. "Just give me what everyone else is having, so I don't have to become a doctor to understand all my options."

Nowhere is this more the case than in healthcare branding, where the inherent risks to one's well-being posed by illness—and treated by therapeutic brands—compel people to play it safe and choose what the majority is getting. There's safety in numbers. Tylenol (acetaminophen) boasts that it is the number-one choice of hospitals for pain relief—this despite clinical studies that show that Tylenol is inferior to other over-the-counter medications for relieving pain. But Tylenol is considered safer than many other options, both clinically and psychically. There is comfort in the herd. My point is, we can't confuse the resumer's identity when regarding healthcare brands with the celebratory identity of surfing on iTunes, selecting smartphone cases, and finding just the right sneaker that lets you be you (like everyone else). Freedom *from* choice favors the popular healthcare brand. The brand value of reassurance suggests a simple, guided tour of the hell that is TMI (too much information) in a resumer's world. People who bought X diabetes medicine also bought Y glucose monitor, reassured by the ease and popularity of their choice.

Let's return to the topic of conditions or diseases that require the participation of a caregiver. As we saw with Alzheimer's disease, the caregiver's own desire for a new normal often trumps that of the person who has the disease. This is abnormal behavior in the consumer goods world, where people will go the extra distance to find and purchase something for a loved one. The motivating factors in such a consumer model are, again, a celebration of the self: "I'm going to show my brother/mother/friend what a generous and thoughtful person I am." But for a caregiver dealing with Alzheimer's, it is more about a protection of self: "I'm going to help my brother/mother/friend remember who I am, though not if my decision can make their condition worse."

Caregivers follow the same risk vs. reward motivations as do doctors when advocating healthcare brands for others. While contemporary trends are shifting a little from mothers to fathers in the family dynamic, it is still typically the woman's role to be the primary caregiver for the family. Whitehall-Robins, the division of Wyeth (before it was acquired by—here they come again—Pfizer), very astutely branded their flagship cough brand, Robitussin, with the woman-as-primary-caregiver in mind. Robitussin, and its sister product, Robitussin DM, contain guaifenesin and dextromethorphan respectively, two drugs approved in the 1950s. The first is a mucolytic (breaks up mucus and phlegm) and the second a cough suppressant. Again, if you examine the ingredients in dozens of OTC cough medications, one or both of these drugs is/are in virtually all of them.

So how did Whitehall-Robins create a unique and relevant brand identity? By following the branding best practice found in this book: take a value esteemed by customers and transfer it to the brand. When it comes to keeping the family healthy, mothers have the same self values as doctors: first, do no harm; and second, go with your most reliable remedy. Illness in children is no case to get fancy and take chances. The brilliant result was branding Robitussin as "Recommended by Dr. Mom." (Why they ultimately abandoned this identity is one of healthcare branding's great mysteries to me.)

When Mom is at home, everybody else is in *her* office, and she identifies as the doctor. Now if Mom gets sick, she may take a swig of knockout Nyquil, or pop a Mucinex (the exact same ingredient as Robitussin, but branded as a "powerhouse" force against evil mucus). However, as Dr. Mom, going with a brand proven over a half century to be effective and gentle reinforces her self-image as a responsible caregiver. She wants her own cough to go away fast and treats it aggressively. But for her "patients," her pride in not causing additional harm trumps her desire to treat aggressively. This is normal behavior in a caregiver mindset.

Perhaps the best example of this mindset can be seen in the hysterical (as in crazy, not funny) movement not to vaccinate young children. Every government health authority and practicing physician that I know or have met considers vaccination to be one of the greatest accomplishments of modern medicine. Due to vaccination, the world avoids the following (a very small sample):

- A 1,900% increase in polio
- 2.7 million measles deaths per year
- A whooping cough (pertussis) epidemic that could cause pneumonia and lead to brain damage, seizures, and mental retardation
- A rubella epidemic, resulting in heart defects, cataracts, mental retardation and deafness
- A 600% increase in lifelong Hepatitis B infection, resulting in a 25% death rate from liver disease.

I could go on, but it wouldn't matter to about 10% of the parents in the United States who do not vaccinate their children for various reasons:

- Religious objections (leave it in God's hands, like the Amish).
- Old diseases, like diphtheria and polio, don't exist anymore, so why vaccinate?
- Since most children are already vaccinated, it's no big deal if a few kids aren't. (Fact: at least 95% of the population needs to be vaccinated for the human "herd" immunity to the disease to be in force. The US is currently at about 90%.)
- Chicken pox is a mild disease, so my child doesn't need the vaccine. (Fact: even with vaccines, chickenpox causes more deaths than any other vaccine-preventable childhood disease—one child a week currently in the U.S.)
- Good nutrition and natural remedies offer enough protection against disease, so vaccines aren't necessary (as if it were a nutritional issue!).
- Why bother? The vaccine immunity wears out over time. (Similarly, why eat? You'll just be hungry later.)
- It's too much of a hassle to go to the doctor and remember the appointments.

I'll resist the further temptation to refute any of this nonsense because it detracts from my central point here about how a caregiver identity affects buying decisions in healthcare. Besides, healthcare transactions are not much different from consumer goods purchases when it comes to the stupidity of many people. Foolishness is too unpredictable to model by even the most expert marketers. My point is best made by the two reasons that many educated parents give about why they don't vaccinate their children:

- Vaccines can cause serious problems (autism, SIDs) or even cause the very illnesses they are trying to prevent.
- Giving a child multiple vaccinations for different diseases at the same time increases the risk of harmful side effects and overloads the immune system.

The origin of these incorrect claims can be traced to a very reputable publication, the British medical journal *The Lancet*. In 1998, Dr. Andrew Wakefield, a surgeon and medical researcher at the time (he has since had his license revoked by the British General Medical Council), published a study of 12 children, each of whom received a single vaccination to prevent three diseases: measles, mumps and rubella (MMR). He found that three of his research subjects became autistic and therefore attributed the autism to the vaccines. These are the facts:

- No other researchers have ever been able to duplicate his findings.
- Standard research trials on vaccines are done with tens of thousands of subjects (not 12).
- Dr. Wakefield excluded other medical criteria that could account for the autism.
- Dr. Wakefield was found to have some type of vested financial interest in the outcome.

The Lancet subsequently withdrew the article from its archives, but Wakefield's findings still made international headlines accompanied by predictable paranoia and conspiracy theories about government and industry covering up the truth.

Despite all evidence to the contrary, a good number of people in the anti-vaccine movement still firmly believe Dr. Wakefield's study to be valid, in good part thanks to Jennie McCarthy. A television personality and 1993 *Playboy* Playmate of the Year, McCarthy famously drew attention to Dr. Wakefield's claims, using her fame as a pulpit, and her own experience as a mother with an autistic child, and putting a spotlight on the matter that just won't be shut off. Which brings me to my point: why would a caregiver defy all logic in favor of a subjective choice to avoid a healthcare purchase for those in his/her care? As with the Robitussin example, the reason is that fear and guilt about potentially causing harm trumps the facts, even though the odds are all but guaranteed in the caregiver's favor.

A research exercise done in 1994 by Dr. David A. Asch, Professor at the Perelman School of Medicine, offers one of the most cogent portraits of caregiver values on the subject of vaccination. He posed the following scenario to a group of parents:

- There is a flu epidemic that can be fatal to children three years of age and under.
- There is a vaccine that is guaranteed to prevent any child against the flu.
- Out of every 10,000 children who DO get the vaccine, five will die.
- Out of every 10,000 children who DO NOT get the vaccine, 10 will die.

Even though *not* getting the vaccine puts one's child at twice the risk of death, many parents said that the guilt over their actions outweighed letting the chips fall where they may from their inactions. In other words, they would rather put their child at a greater risk of death than take the chance on feeling responsible for their death as a result of something *they* did. (As I write this, 14 states in America are currently witnessing a measles outbreak. The most publicized cases are in California, where Disneyland has been converted into a petri dish by vaccine deniers like Jenny McCarthy. Welcome to the Magic Kingdom.)

Stipulating once again that vaccination should be a no-brainer, it is plain but sad to see why some caregivers opt out of the choice to act. And aside from any moral or intellectual judgments, the key takeaway is that the presence of illness in life alters identity: the way that people relate to brands, especially healthcare brands. In the case above, the only thing being denied by the anti-vaccine movement is the selfishness of elevating one's own vulnerability over that of a child's. Additionally, the consumer branding model, and the accepted practice of conceptualizing customers as either sick or sick-to-be, are inadequate to develop effectively the kind of brand identities needed for healthcare products, services, and companies. Consumers buy clothes and fragrances and living room furniture. Consumers buy brands to celebrate the self. Resumers buy a return to normalcy as much as possible, and as such, buy back parts of themselves and their abilities when they buy healthcare brands. Caregivers act in preservation of themselves as well as those for whom they're caring, choosing to do nothing when doing something has even the slightest possibility of harming their sick charges.

Let no healthcare brand ever again confuse or confound their customers' identities lest they risk great peril to their brand's equity and stature in the marketplace.

5

Neglecting Physicians' Unique Identities

Another common cause of identity crisis in healthcare marketing is the use of misguided or misinformed assumptions about physicians and how they approach their tasks of healing. Healthcare professionals (HCPs) are not the "end-user" in the process of care. That role falls to the patients. However, while doctors do not use medicines and devices to treat themselves, their recommendation to their patients of one brand over another is clearly related to the doctors' own identities. A myth persists even today that HCPs are emotionally detached from the brands they prescribe for their patients, relying solely on data and research to formulate their decisions. However, experience—and data!—show that physician brand loyalty often depends upon how the brands reinforce the doctor's sense of self and personal style of medical practice.

My father provides a perfect example. He ran his general medical practice out of the same house in which he and my mother lived. Whenever I visited them, I would always accept a tour to see what was new in his office and treatment rooms. Part of it was a good-natured interest in his life, and part of it was a reconnaissance mission to see which healthcare brands my father was using in his practice from one year to the next. As part of my fact-gathering, I would always look inside his sample closet (where trial sizes of medications were kept), scan the waiting room for brand name placement items, and collect the stack of promotional materials left behind by sales representatives from the various pharma, biotech, and device companies. He was all too happy to comply with my requests to save them for me because, as he said, they meant nothing to him. As far as he was concerned, he based all of his prescribing decisions on data and sound medical judgment and not on the colorful, branded brochures that outlined the drug's virtues, data, and fair-balance side effects. This was the late 1980s, long before the advent of digital media or Rx brands being promoted on TV. Print promotion was king in those days, and the marketing brochures piled up quickly in the time between my visits to my father's office.

During one of my visits, I asked him if he was using any of the newer ACE inhibitors, a class of drugs used to treat hypertension. He replied that he had been using two of them: Zestril and Prinivil.

"I like them both," he said, as we stood beside his stout wooden desk. "They're both good, but based on what I've seen, Zestril is much stronger and gets the job done better."

I pulled out a bright red folder from the pile with the Zestril logo emblazoned across it. "You mean this one?" I asked.

"Yes," he said. He pointed to the theme line. "See. It says '24-hour Power.' Prinivil doesn't have that. It's gentler."

He fished out the Prinivil brochure, which had color photographs of people enjoying the great outdoors, summiting mountains or snorkeling in pristine waters. The headline read "A new way of living." He was very proud to discuss the differences he experienced with each brand, and I listened earnestly.

What my father didn't know was that I was on the team that delivered the Zestril brand experience and developed many of the Zestril brochures that he said meant nothing to him—but whose message he had clearly internalized. Another thing he didn't know was that Zestril and Prinivil are the exact same drug, lisinopril, sold under two different brand names in the exact same dosage strength (much as Advil and Nuprin were both ibuprofen in the same strength). But for my father, Zestril was the brand of choice, and his reasoning was based on the impressions he had retained as if by osmosis from a marketing brochure given to him by a company salesperson.

I mention this anecdote not to project the idea of my father as an uninformed prescriber, but rather to show him as the human being that he and all doctors are. He was a gifted diagnostician, an expert on human anatomy, and a caring, thoughtful mentor to his patients. However, when it came to branded healthcare products, he was influenced in much the same way as anyone else in any other field of endeavor. Like all other doctors, he would never admit to being swayed by branding. To him and other physicians, such an admission seems to threaten their sense of intelligence, as if they could be "fooled" by marketers.

Let me be very clear here. Healthcare brands don't fool doctors. Brands aspire to be a flattering reflection of doctors' values. No self-respecting doctor would ever select an inferior brand over a better one. Most of the time, the choice is between two or three equally good brands. If a brand doesn't live up to its own treatment promises, then no physician would ever risk his/her reputation by prescribing it.

Salespeople also influence the uptake of the brand experience for physicians. While doctors often cite respected medical journals as their source of information about new or existing drug therapies or devices, it is often the drug/device sales representative who, figuratively, *becomes* the brand experience and gets inextricably associated with one brand vs. another. Speaking with one sales representative for a device company just the other day, I asked her to create a pie chart of what influences the doctor's choice of similar devices in the category. Here is what she drew:

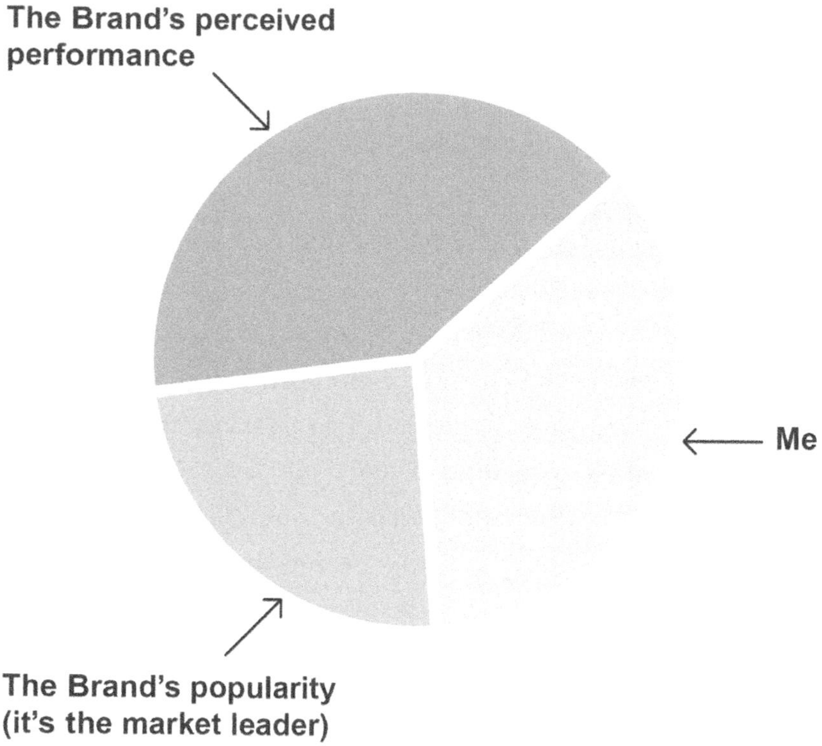

Basically, more than a third of the brand's equity was being delivered not by the actual brand, but rather by the value of the personal relationship that the sales representative added to the doctor's esteem for the brand. It's no wonder that pharmaceutical, biotech and device companies highly value their sales teams. They can make or break the brand experience, regardless of how effective the other aspects of marketing and promotion are.

Perhaps doctors need to feel completely in control of their thoughts and actions, and resist the idea that there are subconscious factors in play when selecting brands for their patients. Maybe, out of tacit respect or fear of this emperor-has-no-clothes denial, this is why so many healthcare brands insist on creating brand identities that are about the product or service's functional attributes, and not the more engaging ideas of practical and emotional benefits that dare not speak their names. As I said, doctors are only being human. Ask them (as I and many others have done) which TV shows are their favorites, and many will insist either that they don't watch TV, or if they do, it's *60 Minutes* and cable news. Very serious stuff. However, if you ask them, say, what they think about Candice Glover winning *American Idol* this season, some of them might correct you by pointing out that she won last season; Caleb Johnson was the winner this season. As with any living creature wary to put its vulnerability on the line, one must approach doctors in an entirely different way to account for their need to be perceived as wholly objective to anything but the facts about a brand.

My father's reaction to the Zestril/Prinivil branding was not an isolated case. A majority of the medical community felt the exact same way. Merck had developed the lisinopril molecule. Its sister Merck brand, Vasotec (enalapril), was not only on the market, but was also the sales leader. Merck's marketing strategy was to avoid cannibalizing Vasotec sales while at the same time maximizing the investment in lisinopril by licensing it out to Stuart Pharmaceuticals (now AstraZeneca) to market as its own separate brand. Merck's thinking at the time went like this: Merck was Goliath to Stuart's David. Stuart had very little experience in the cardiovascular category and would probably get beaten soundly in a head-to-head competition with Merck's own marketing machine. Stuart would lose out and still pay Merck a fee for their lisinopril marketing rights. The branding that Merck put forth for Prinivil was very typical of other ACE inhibitors at the time: a focus on an improved quality of life (likewise, Vasotec's branding showed a farmer happily leading one of his horses out of a barn). Stuart needed to differentiate Zestril from other brands in the category or it didn't stand much of a chance against the competition. That's where our agency team came in.

The only clinical data available for lisinopril at the time was a comparison against placebo. Not very impressive. However, the trial for lisinopril happened to use a breakthrough technology at the time: ambulatory blood pressure monitoring. Trial subjects wore a monitor all day and night. It recorded their blood pressure automatically every hour for 24 hours. No other antihypertensive agent had been studied in this way, including Vasotec.

Rather than shrink away from the unimpressive data that showed lisinopril was only effective enough to beat a placebo in blood pressure control, our branding team capitalized instead on a key emotional insight about physicians. High blood pressure is an extremely serious matter. Physicians want to be very certain that whatever medicine they prescribe to treat it would exert its full effect over the course of an entire day without waning. And lisinopril was the only molecule that had proof of that enduring effect. (Who knew if all the others did as well?)

Physicians take great pride in being ever watchful and vigilant of the lives in their care, and the Zestril brand could reflect these values by reassuring doctors that—like them—it wouldn't quit on their patients before the day was out. 'Twenty-four hour power' wasn't just a property of the drug. It was a battle cry to physicians to be more powerful than the condition that threatened their patients. The logo featured two innovations to project the tone of the promise: (1) it was rendered at a 40° angle, and (2) it contained a yellow exclamation point. Taken together, the logo and theme line suggested robust success. By the end of the first 12 month of sales, Zestril had 70% of the lisinopril market to Prinivil's 30%. And they were the exact same molecule and dosage. What compelled physicians to prefer Zestril more than two-to-one over Prinivil? Its brand identity. The Zestril brand went on to become the best-selling ACE inhibitor of all time.

It is essential for us to acknowledge that doctors are doctors only while they are on the job. That is, they have private lives beyond the job—personalities, preferences, hobbies, and so on. When they step into their professional roles, it is difficult (if not impossible) to shut out the very things that define their private selves. With notable exceptions, doctors relate to healthcare brands less because of the features of the brand, and more because of how the values of the brand create a flattering reflection of the practitioner they strive to be—a reflection born out of a personal, subjective aspiration. It's not that the features of the brand are not relevant. Far from it. It's that the features have value only in relation to how they enhance the prescriber's self-image.

Further, doctors' personal aspirations are very different depending on the medical specialty they have chosen. While it is true that people who become doctors all go to college and medical school, the differences in who they turn out to be is where the true insights lay. I'll skip over the vast landscape of differentiation that concerns age, gender, and geography, and go straight to my central point: medical students don't just become doctors; they become specialists in different fields of medicine that reflect their own unique disposition, and, in turn, their own relationship to the healthcare brands they employ to define their personal and professional reputations.

I don't have space in this book to explore every single medical specialty and deconstruct the personalities that they attract, so I will select certain specialties to demonstrate my thesis that healthcare brands must accommodate how doctors' personal motivations and ambitions influence the different choices they make when prescribing or advocating a healthcare brand. Additionally, it bears pointing out that most people—the doctors themselves especially—think that because physicians receive so much post-graduate education and because they are experts in their chosen fields, they must be experts in many other things as well. They're not. As mentioned in previous chapters, doctors are taught very little in medical school about weight management, nutrition, exercise and other subjects germane to the practice of good health. While they do learn the basics about drug treatments and the use of devices, after about five years out of school, everything doctors learn about new drugs and devices usually comes from healthcare manufacturers—the makers of the drugs and devices—via online presentations, print promotion and, yes, the sales representatives. (This is especially true for device companies because the sales representatives are usually the ones teaching the surgeon, hands on, how to use the latest laser or instructing the psychiatrist on the intricacies of properly administering transcranial magnetic stimulation. The central idea here bears repeating:

> AFTER ABOUT FIVE YEARS OUT OF MEDICAL SCHOOL, EVERYTHING DOCTORS LEARN ABOUT NEW DRUGS AND DEVICES USUALLY COMES FROM HEALTHCARE MANUFACTURERS.

There are, of course, some specialists who have a significant command of drug chemistry and drug trials for brands, but they are still human and want the brands they prescribe to reflect their own values as doctors. For example, oncologists are very fluent in the molecules and regimens they use to attack cancer and reduce or eliminate its viability. And psychiatrists are especially astute about the nuances of drug and brain chemistry. Not only do these two medical specialties attract the kind of people who have a fascination for such minute detail—as well as a healthy obsession with parsing clinical trial data—but they also play chess with two of the greatest medical foes facing humanity: cancer and mental illness. For all the good the science does—and it does a world of good—these two frontiers remain, for the most part, mysteries that resist cures. The origins of the respective pathologies continue to evade the best researchers in these fields. The correct path of treatment in each individual case is a journey in and of itself. The people who join these two fraternities of medical specialists share a fascination with the dark unknown and liken themselves to pioneers of the *terra incognita*. It might be easy to dismiss the idea that such sophisticated and intellectual medical specialists are immune to a brand's identity, but they are as human as any and are as willing to hope as the rest of us.

> MEDICAL STUDENTS DON'T BECOME DOCTORS; THEY BECOME SPECIALISTS IN DIFFERENT FIELDS OF MEDICINE THAT REFLECT THEIR OWN RELATIONSHIP TO THE HEALTHCARE BRANDS THEY EMPLOY TO DEFINE THEIR PERSONAL AND PROFESSIONAL REPUTATIONS.

One of the most successful rebranding initiatives in the field of oncology succeeded precisely because the brand identity acknowledged and honored the predisposition of oncologists. The brand is Gemzar (gemcitabine). It is a cytotoxic agent (i.e., it kills cancer cells) indicated for a variety of tumors. However, its cytotoxicity is weaker than that of other drugs used in chemotherapy, and it has a much more benign side effect and safety profile. It eventually earned the reputation among oncologists as "gentle Gem."

When one markets a brand that is expected to face down cancer (like the doctor who prescribes it), "gentle" is not the nickname you want doctors to associate with your drug. The manufacturer, Eli Lilly

& Company, used the occasion of a new indication in breast cancer to engage my team in rethinking Gemzar's brand identity. Instead of trying to win the hearts and minds of oncologists with Gemzar's own fine merits, our branding team took a different approach by appealing to the unique way that oncologists attack cancer. Doctors who treat cancer don't just use a single drug in most cases, but rather a "cocktail" of several different drugs. The elements that make up the cocktail, therefore, take collective credit for whatever good and bad they do. Gemzar was a good drug partner because it added another degree of effectiveness against tumors without contributing to the significant side effects associated with other agents in the "cocktail" of chemotherapy (oncologists use combinations of drugs and agents to attack cancer). Using the insights outlined above about the types of people who enter the field of oncology, we re-positioned the Gemzar brand as, literally, the lead dog of a team that gets one through an arduous journey (in this case, the Iditarod dogsled race, inspired by the real story of transporting life-saving medicine to ice-bound cities such as Nome).

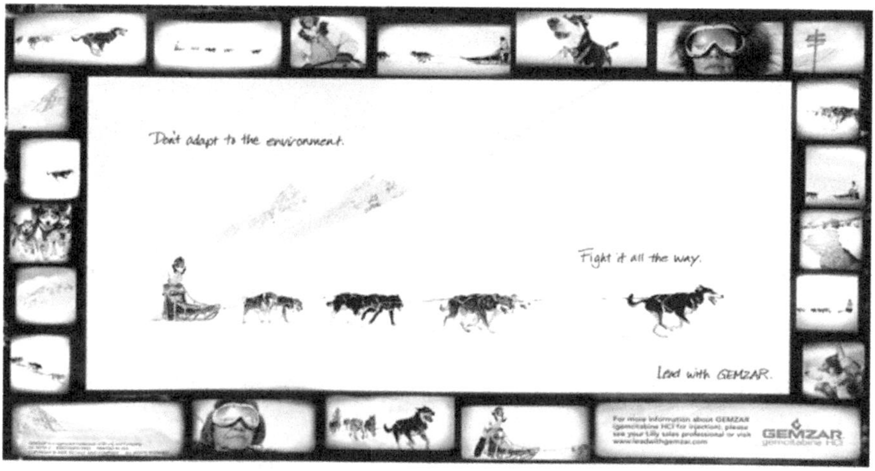

Our team happened to actually find a professional "musher" who had breast cancer, and photographed her in various scenarios to establish an image library for consistency of visual presentation across global campaigns. "Don't adapt to the environment," the headline states imperatively. "Fight it all the way. Lead with Gemzar." The copy and visuals are designed to appeal not only to the patients oncologists are seeing every day—women with a fighting spirit, determined to beat breast cancer—but to the oncologist's own identity as well. They see themselves as empowering their patients to endure a harsh journey that, in the end, will hopefully be their best chance at survival.

In addition to having a self-image as being keenly smart, some physician specialists embody a level of self-confidence that not only borders on egotism, but also really thrives on it. I think most of us would agree that we don't mind this trait if our fates depend on another person. In fact, I, for one, expect it. For example, I want my surgeon to feel that he or she is borderline divine as I drift off, helpless, under the effects of anesthesia. Nowhere is this better dramatized than in the 1993 film *Malice*, when a surgeon, played by Alec Baldwin, replies to a deposition inquiry in a typically incisive Aaron Sorkin monologue:

> "I have an MD from Harvard. I am board certified in cardiothoracic medicine and trauma surgery. I have been awarded citations from seven different medical boards in New England . . . So I ask you: when someone goes into that chapel and falls on their knees and they pray to God that their wife doesn't miscarry, or that their daughter doesn't bleed to death, or that their mother doesn't suffer acute neural trauma from post-operative shock, who do you think they are praying to? You ask me if I have a God complex? Let me tell you something: I am God."

This scene is arguably over-the-top, but I recall it here as an insight to healthcare branders: locate the traits that make your customers see a reflection of themselves in your brand, even if those traits seem extreme.

A case in point is Ethicon, Johnson & Johnson's premier surgical supply company and a leading producer of many items that surgeons use to perform their jobs effectively. Most notable among them are the specialized needles and thread used to stitch up wounds. Ethicon also sells a different type of wound-closing technology called Dermabond (2-Octyl Cyanoacrylate). Dermabond is a topical skin adhesive, a technology first developed during the Vietnam War to close battlefield wounds quickly and effectively (think medical-grade Krazy Glue). On paper, Dermabond has a lot going for it. It closes wounds in 30 seconds with the same strength as a hand-sewn thread suture. Unlike thread sutures, it creates a waterproof and anti-microbial barrier. You can take a shower after the administration of Dermabond, and it won't compromise the wound closure. There's also less scarring with Dermabond. Surgeons found these advantages very interesting and even exciting, especially ER surgeons who race against time and a packed waiting room to treat everyone quickly and well. Yet despite its many attractive features, the brand wasn't selling well.

My team was brought in to help solve a mystery: why did Dermabond have 98% awareness and 96% esteem among surgeons and yet have only a 2% share of the closure market? By the time we arrived, the company had tried many different remedies. They produced a new campaign, re-organized information in their selling materials, interviewed surgeons and surgical nurses about the brand, even switched advertising agencies—everything except asking the surgeons about *themselves*.

What we know is that surgeons are a unique breed of medical doctor. First, their primary means of delivering patient care is not by using medicine at all, but rather by cutting, repairing, replacing and stitching with their own two hands. Second, while most doctors fancy themselves as managing life-and-death matters, surgeons are by far the closest to these matters in their daily lives. They face significant jeopardy by opening up their patients and themselves to risks of infections, complications, and the grim prospect of the ailing subject expiring on the table or in the recovery room after. (Their malpractice insurance runs into the tens of thousands of dollars, which means they must earn twice that before taxes just to open the doors of their practice.) Third, they do not work alone. They command a team of diverse disciplines—nurses, anesthesiologists, other doctors—and take responsibility for them all. They don't do this just once a day, but often several times a day (understandably, this is so onerous that they don't operate every day). Fourth, because of the nature of their business, they must operate outside the confines of their offices in hospitals or surgical centers. This means that other professions enter into the equation. The surgical department head, the hospital inventory manager, the ethics committees, and the hospital pharmacy personnel are all exerting influence on the daily execution of surgeons' jobs. All of the above dynamics were well known to Ethicon. But they had overlooked one major factor: what kind of people go into a line of work like this?

In the world of consumer goods, profiling the customer's deeper reasons for engaging with brands is commonplace. It is rarely so in healthcare, and there is regularly a lack of insight into the doctors who use and prescribe healthcare brands. One possible explanation for this is that since doctors deny the emotional drivers behind their brand choices, marketers in turn accommodate this pretense by respectfully never probing. My clients often fear that an interrogation about personal values will antagonize the doctors, the executives in their own company, or both. Clients eventually accept my counsel only if they have exhausted every other avenue and/or after I prove to them that I have done similar exercises before with good results and no negative consequences.

It all comes down to avoiding the error of imagining healthcare providers as having identities of emotionless automatons, and in the case of Dermabond, we needed insight into the kind of surgeons who might use the brand and why. This is where the art of healthcare branding comes in.

Our fundamental observations included the facts that surgeons have strong personalities and that there are many different types of surgeons. In addition, as distinct as surgeons are from their other medical school counterparts, they are equally dissimilar from each other. Cardiovascular (CV) surgeons are the professionals who might first come to mind when thinking about surgery. Heart transplants, coronary artery bypass grafts (CABG or "cabbage," as it is commonly referred to) and other complex procedures were developed by pioneering CV surgeons in the last 50 years. But it is only in the last 30 that they have come to be seen as miraculously routine, life-saving events. And as such, their patients, colleagues, and the general public revere the surgeons who perform these operations.

This is quite different from, say, orthopedic surgeons who revitalize knees, hips, and shoulders. Unlike cardiovascular surgery, orthopedic procedures are fairly bloodless and can be viewed as a form of carpentry on the body. In contrast, Ob/Gyn surgeons primarily go into their field not for the pathologies they resolve, but rather to bring new life into the world. Plastic surgeons have a public image skewed toward cosmetic procedures despite the fact that many perform much-needed reconstructive surgeries on birth defects and deformations from traumatic accidents. The people who go into each one of these surgical specialties have very different personalities that must be accounted for if one wishes to create a healthcare brand that is a true reflection of these doctors' diverse and nuanced self-images.

For example, patient care—the desire to work and interact with patients—is a primary motivator for an Ob/Gyn physician, but not for a CV surgeon. I'm not saying that CV surgeons do not care about their patients. They do. But consider the nature of the interactions: CV surgeons might meet you for one or two brief visits before the surgery; they do their work when you are unconscious; they stop by afterward to see how you are doing. What draws them to their chosen field? It is the big stage. They are not just performers but also leaders. They lead a team to face down premature death from CV disease and defy it.

Ob/Gyn physicians have very different motivators. They like the balance of patient care and surgery. They love babies and keeping women's reproductive systems healthy for the eventual joys of delivering the children of patients who have been going to them for years.

On the other hand, orthopedic surgeons rarely deal in life-and-death matters. And that's the way they like it. They occupy somewhat of a middle ground between an Ob/Gyn and CV surgeon. Like CV surgeons, their procedures are restorative, and they take great pride in "fixing" the body. And like Ob/Gyn surgeons, their patients keep coming back to them, so they, too, maintain relationships that may be as brief as their CV counterparts, but as long-standing as their Ob/Gyn colleagues. There are two each of shoulder, hip, and knee. It's only a matter of time before these break down and require ongoing visits to the orthopedist.

When we examined the research Ethicon had done to date on Dermabond with surgeons, not only were the questions they'd asked all about the product, but also each surgical specialty had been interviewed separately. ER surgeons praised Dermabond for certain reasons; Plastic Surgeons, Ob/Gyn surgeons, and CV surgeons liked it for their own, different reasons. With these findings in hand, Ethicon had developed individual selling materials for each surgical specialty, which was clearly responsible for Dermabond's brand awareness amongst surgeons in general.

This actually seems like a reasonable strategy on first glance. But just imagine if, say, Buick conducted branding research in the same way that Ethicon did. That is, they would talk to plumbers and lawyers and housewives and construction workers and bankers separately about what they liked about cars and then develop separate branding plans for each type of person based on their answers about Buick. Buick is the safe choice. Buick is the frugal choice. Buick is the classy choice. And so on. The result would be the same as what happened with Dermabond: lots of brand awareness in the community, but no single, strong brand identity with which to self-identify. As different customer segments become aware of the brand standing for other customers' values, they all tend to distance themselves from the brand because its diffuse and uncommitted identity ceases to be special to them.

Ethicon had made the common mistake of trying to transfer as many values as possible to their brand, and the result was an identity crisis for Dermabond. After completing my review of their branding strategy thus far, I recommended we scrap the multi-surgeon marketing approach and instead develop a central identity for Dermabond that reflected a single core value to all types of surgeon.

> BRANDING IS NOT ABOUT TRANSFERRING AS MANY VALUES AS POSSIBLE TO ONE'S BRAND. INSTEAD, IT IS ABOUT DISTILLING ONE OR TWO CENTRAL VALUES THAT UNITE A COMMUNITY AROUND A BRAND.

I will explore branding research methodology in Chapter 7. For now, here is what my team and I did in the case of Dermabond once Ethicon agreed to let us go forward. We simulated the community that Dermabond sought to woo. We assembled groups of 12 surgeons, each comprising pairs of six surgical specialties (Noah's Ark-style). We conducted the groups in various geographies to see if there were any regional biases (not much, it turned out).

For the first half of the research, we set Dermabond aside and, instead, led the group in a discussion about why they became doctors, why they became surgeons, and why they became a specific type of surgeon. Here are some of the insights that came out of the dialogue (this is heavily paraphrased):

Q: What's the difference between a doctor and a surgeon?
A: A surgeon is a doctor who actually resolves things.

Q: What's the greatest pleasure you get from your job each day?
A: Fixing things.

Q: What's your greatest concern during the course of doing your job?
A: That I won't be able to fix the problem.

Q: And your patients will suffer or even die?
A: Yes, that and the effect it would have on my team.

Q: Your team? How so?
A: They'll lose confidence in me.

Let's think about these excerpts from a much longer conversation. Surgeons feel superior to non-surgeons and have as evidence the immediate repair of a serious problem that they can "fix" quickly. The focus of their day is not centrally about the patient, but rather the task of applying their restorative skills—reaching inside a human body and "fixing" it—so that they secure their reputation and the respect and admiration of their team.

Once we had a good idea of what makes surgeons tick, we dropped Dermabond into this mix. But instead of asking the surgeons straightforward questions about the brand (to which we already knew the answers), we asked them to come together as a community and work with each other in a series of exploratory exercises. We separated the original groups of 12 surgeons into two groups of six, assuring that each group had one of each of the surgical sub-specialties in it. The exercises we took them through were based on behavioral psychology practices designed to make wary research subjects comfortable giving their opinions without fear of judgment or failure.

One such exercise is an oldie but goodie: a projective technique. We asked the surgeons to imagine surgical closure technologies as modes of transportation. One group was given thread sutures and the other Dermabond. The results were startling.

The first group declared that sutures would be "a steam locomotive" because:

- It is part of a long heritage and time-honored tradition
- It is driven by an engine that pulled all the weight of the other cars
- It would take a monumental crisis to derail it
- It is ideal for moving a great volume of people

Clearly, the surgeons collectively saw a reflection of themselves in sutures. What the research subjects were telling us is that they are proud they are members of a legendary guild of surgeons. They are uncomplicated, prefer to follow the same routine for their volume of patients, do not take risks, and feel that they are the "engine" that pulls the weight of the team.

The other group declared that Dermabond was a "Vespa" because:

- It is more of a toy than a serious way to get around
- It would be easy to tip it over on the road
- It has no power

Yikes. Clearly the surgeons felt that Dermabond trivialized their good work, presented a risk to their procedures, and lacked the gravitas worthy of their sense of power on the team and in the hospital. Put simply, they felt the brand made them look silly, despite the fact that they admired many of Dermabond's functional qualities. Fortunately, they also saw some of their values reflected in the Vespa:

- It is environmentally responsible, not using much gas
- It is easy to get around in tight spaces
- It is fast and can zip through traffic

In other words, the surgeons were telling us that they liked to be seen as good public citizens, respectful of the environment. Further, there were some occasions when they need some maneuverability in tight spaces, or a burst of speed.

We knew that by factoring in how the brand could reflect the self-values of our target customers (all types of surgeons), Dermabond could become more about them than itself, which would remove the perceptual impediments to engage with the brand and use it more often. In other words, even though Dermabond was proven clinically and on the battlefield to be able to close large wounds quickly and effectively, this idea was perceived to be risky and primitive—not qualities surgeons saw when they looked in the mirror. So, based on these and other findings from our new rounds of research, we updated the logo to look more formidable (powerful) and advised changing the packaging from what the surgeons described as "like a crayon" to something worthy of sitting on a tray next to the scalpels and clamps. We re-launched Dermabond's identity as a progressive wound-closure technology that was perfect for small incisions (tight spaces), which we collectively agreed would be two centimeters or less, and/or on an area of the body with creases.

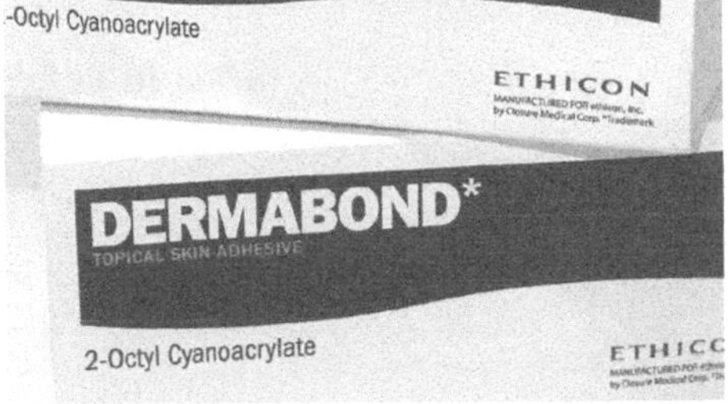

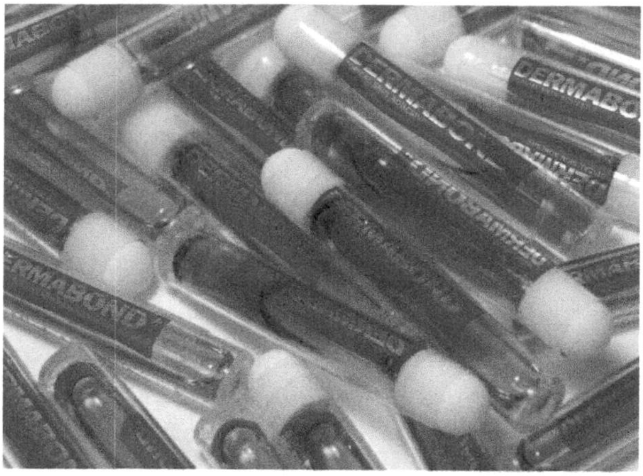
DERMABOND

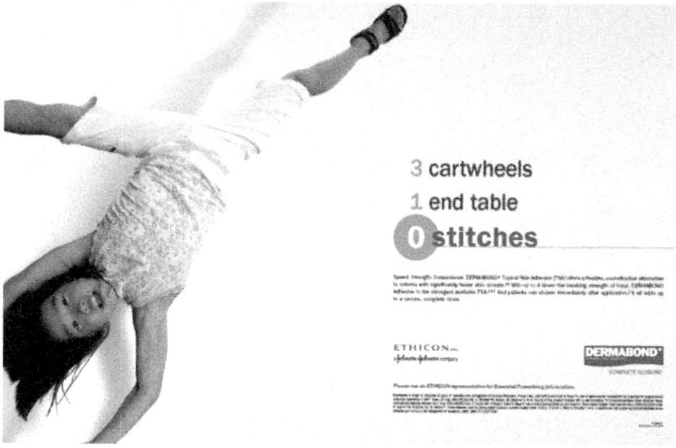
3 cartwheels
1 end table
0 stitches
ETHICON
DERMABOND

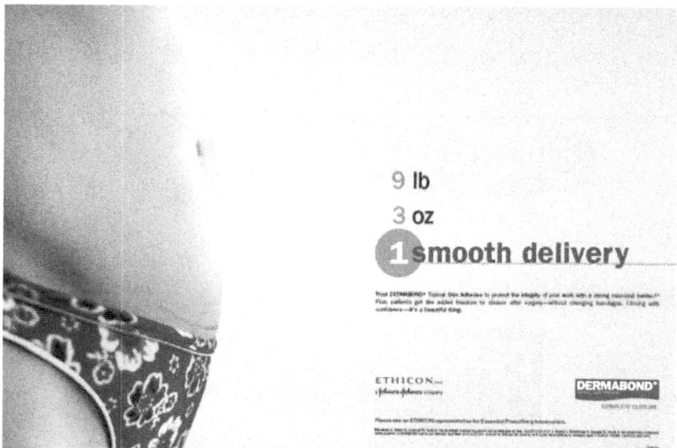
9 lb
3 oz
1 smooth delivery
ETHICON
DERMABOND

The new tag line of Complete Closure, while alluding to putting the finishing touches on surgery, also evoked the idea of what closure means to surgeons: the problem fixed and a job well done. With our new brand identity in place, Dermabond sales soared. The ER surgeons made it their go-to option for small cuts around the forehead and eyes. The CV surgeons would never use it for the open-heart incisions of CABG, but they would for harvesting the small graft of the saphenous vein in the thigh. The orthopedic surgeon thought it would be perfect for the tiny incisions used to debride the cartilage meniscus in the knee. In fact, as it turns out, the fastest-growing segment of surgeries are procedures that use minimally invasive incisions, such as laparoscopies, and Dermabond is a perfect solution for closing these small incisions.

Our success with creating momentum behind Dermabond was only possible because Ethicon agreed to let us ask doctors about themselves rather than their brand. In the case of Dermabond, we were dealing with surgeons, perhaps the most super-human of all specialists. And guess what? Once we got inside their heads, they were just as human as any of us.

In the larger picture, be assured that there's no risk in picking doctors' brains to find out what makes them tick. In fact, it's key to building a successful healthcare brand identity, no matter which discipline of the medical profession is a key to success. Remember: there are healthcare professionals who treat and healthcare professionals who influence treatment. For example, the surgeon relies on the pathologist to reveal if the biopsy is malignant or benign. The Intensive Care Unit (ICU) nurse manages the day-to-day support for patients. Pediatric nurses are often the ones giving babies their vaccines, as many pediatricians do not want their small patients to grow up associating them with a painful experience.

The personalities of these allied colleagues must also be considered when crafting a brand identity. For example, when marketing a brand to radiologists, it is not the patient from whom respect and esteem is sought, but rather the physicians who rely on the radiologists for diagnosis. Going back to my father as an example, at Christmas time, when my father, the general practitioner, received presents from some of his patients, he also received generous gift baskets and top-shelf spirits from his radiology colleagues as a thank you for all the referrals. Doctors go into radiology because they value the medical lifestyle, but they don't particularly want to deal with patients. Reading an X-ray or a CAT scan is a very different proposition than handholding a patient through a cancer diagnosis and treatment. Still, radiologists are typically very sociable by nature and fulfill their need for camaraderie by partnering with other doctors in getting the job done. Ultimately, their physician colleagues must put great trust in their judgment to correctly assess what they see on the various scans and X-rays. Is it a tumor? Has it spread to other parts of the body? Has the rotator cuff in the shoulder torn? If so, by how much? If one referring physician calls their reputation into question, it could have a ripple effect and ruin their practice. Radiologists are the eyes of other doctors, an extension of their senses, so a brand identity reflecting radiologists' values must also take into account the radiologists' relationships to the doctors with whom they are allied.

For example, when I was developing an identity for a brand of contrast media—a type of "dye" that radiologists inject at the scan site to highlight pathology—I super-imposed the radiologist's own talents onto the brand. The tag line read, "The image you seek in every vial," as if the secret to what lay beneath the surface was already contained in the brand. But more so, it was the radiologist's own self-image that resonated in response to the branding in research. Radiologists could see the burnishing of their own image every time they used the brand to enhance the scans. 'The (self) image you seek in every vial' is their colleagues' admiration, smiling and giving thanks.

As I hope is clear by now, we don't create healthcare brands for doctors. We create hints for the puzzles of people who become Neurologists, or secret passwords that magically open locked doors for the people who become Oncologists, or enduring relationships for those who choose General Practice, or magic tricks for the sleight-of-hand artists who become Plastic Surgeons. Most doctors feel too foolish or vulnerable to admit that emotions are behind many of their healthcare brand preferences. Likewise, most healthcare product and service providers defer to this delusion rather than risk ruffling feathers of their would-be customers.

It is our job to honor this psychographic dynamic, work within its framework, and make a brand's identity seem primarily about its functional aspects while winking at the other, just as real, influential factors at work. If we wish to create brands for people who have graduated medical school or are an allied health professional, then we must remember to ask ourselves: what's the private life of the man/woman who goes out each working day and heals in his/her own way? Whose values exactly am I trying to understand? The answers will not only surprise you—they'll endear you and your brand to healthcare practitioners for a good long while.

In the next chapter, I'll deal with another key problem of how to align customer values with healthcare concepts: the identity crises caused by misconceptions around branding medical conditions and disorders.

6

Identifying the Enemy: How Branding Health Conditions Can Help Us Defeat Them

When done properly, health condition branding—the discipline of creating brand identities for conditions, syndromes, and diseases—can enlighten an entire society about the best course of action to take when an illness causes segments of the general populace to suffer. Also, such branding initiatives can transform the way an entire society perceives how illness compromises many of the people we know and even ourselves. When done badly, condition branding ends up helping no one and can even contribute to harming the diagnosis, dialogue, and treatment approaches in a disease category. In this chapter, we'll look at the best practices in health condition branding and also some of the identity crises academic physicians, advocacy groups, and marketers generate by improperly branding health conditions, despite their good intentions.

Condition branding—a new term I coined (the existing one was called "nosology") in a 2003 article for the industry publication *Medical Marketing & Media*—involves acknowledging or discovering pathologies behind human ills and behaviors and instilling them with an identity:

a universally accepted name and/or acronym. Conditions like multiple sclerosis, bi-polar disorder, overactive bladder, AIDS, carpal tunnel syndrome, to name just a few, were once mythical, misunderstood sets of symptoms that puzzled and oppressed society. However, through condition branding we have come to acknowledge and understand them as legitimate illnesses worth studying and treating by professionals and having covered under insurance policies. We have neutralized the confusing power they had over us by giving them brand identities. Even in cases such as Alzheimer's disease or multiple sclerosis, where no significant solution or cure exists, branding these pathologies encourages a collective recognition of the need to fund, research, treat, reimburse, and invest in further medical solutions.

Physicians and patients want better ways to identify and discuss health conditions, and proper branding can provide a framework and language to facilitate this discussion. In addition, insurance companies want greater clarity on conditions that affect health costs in the long run, and condition branding helps here, too. So before I get into some of the common identity crises that are created in health condition branding, let's look back and learn how and why such a practice arose and why it is essential to do it the right way.

Years ago, when the winter season rolled around, I looked forward to it in all but one respect: my uncle's withering pessimism about the whole holiday tradition. For him, celebration and good cheer were out of the question. "Why should we be compelled to feel happy on a given set of days when the world would be essentially the same afterward?" he would grumble to anyone within earshot. Humbug. Then, in the 1980s, an influential doctor identified the condition that gave shape to my uncle's annual acrimony: Seasonal Affective Disorder (SAD), a type of depression that makes people feel sad and tired during seasonal changes, especially winter, because there is less light during the daytime (and light—we now know—affects mood).

This identification of a formerly unnamed mental illness transformed my uncle in my eyes from an unpleasant curmudgeon to a sympathetic victim through the coining of a simple, elegant identity. Additionally, there was a known treatment for SAD to allow him and the others who suffered in the company of his depressed self to better celebrate the joys of the season and be happier human beings.

Norman E. Rosenthal, M.D., and his associates at the National Institute of Mental Health (NIMH) framed the concept of SAD in 1984. Dr. Rosenthal was investigating the cause of his own depression as daylight dwindled in the winter. He developed and conducted a placebo-controlled clinical trial and published it in a well-respected medical journal, *Archives of General Psychiatry.* His trial showed that dark moods caused by the diminished winter sun could be effectively resolved by exposure to light therapy: a low-cost, low-tech solution to a health problem that potentially affects everyone living in a place with short winter days. Today, there are many antidepressants on the market available to treat SAD as well.

Despite the positive results of his experiment, many authorities initially questioned the existence of SAD and voiced skepticism of Dr. Rosenthal's findings. These skeptics, it turns out, never personally experienced SAD, so they reflexively dismissed it. Fortunately, medical authorities other than Dr. Rosenthal felt the seasonal mood changes in their own lives and observed them in their patients as well. The science of SAD grew over the years until it became a formally recognized subset of major depressive disorder in the fourth edition of the *Diagnostic and Statistical Manual of Mental Disorders*, or DSM-4 (1987), the ever-evolving desk reference used by psychiatrists and therapists to cast light a little further into the darkness of how our minds work. In DSM-5 (2013), SAD is no longer listed as a separate mood disorder, but as an exacerbation of an existing depressive disorder. And as the years unfold, perhaps we'll come to understand it in even different ways.

Condition branding, as the name implies, is not a random act or discovery, but rather the purposeful, concerted effort on the collective part of marketers, academic physicians, and doctor and patient organizations to identify and lend support and validity to health and wellness concepts. The great majority of the time, the government has no hand in the matter. Instead, condition brands generally arise out of a grassroots movement to gain greater recognition of a condition, an educational initiative on the part of healthcare groups and pharmaceutical manufacturers, or both.

Unlike with product and service branding, where identities become known almost exclusively through paid promotion, successful condition branding can come to fruition only through cooperative efforts involving pharmaceutical companies, authorities at leading academic schools of medicine (referred to in the trade as 'thought leaders'), the entire medical community that treats patients, support societies, advocacy groups, and consumers. Further, the effort must be coordinated with multiple communication agencies in the fields of branding, advertising, education, and public relations for the condition brand to be successfully established. Once a condition brand has reached a critical mass of recognition, it becomes self-sustaining and "owned" by society as a whole rather than by a manufacturer or special interest group. When a single party tries to create a condition brand unilaterally on its own, the usual result is a complete failure. One entity rarely speaks for every constituency (more on this later in the chapter).

Why must all parties unify around a condition brand concept? Because each constituent in the collective has a different agenda for creating a condition brand identity; and as with all identities, the goal is to find a core idea in which everyone can see a flattering reflection of these disparate agendas. Academic medical thought leaders—those in public health and/or who publish in medical journals and conduct clinical trials—want a condition brand that honors the scientific rigor of their chosen profession. Advocacy groups want a condition brand that's considerate and relevant to their constituents. Practicing doctors and their patients are looking for a "password" that opens up a fruitful dialogue and facilitates diagnosis and treatment. And pharmaceutical companies are seeking a condition brand identity that points to their own product brands as potential remedies.

Condition branding is an essential aspect of healthcare best practices, but may not be right for every situation. If you are a marketer trying to decide if condition branding offers an effective means to bring clarity to a solvable healthcare problem, ask yourself the following questions.

Is condition branding right for your product brand and its customers?

1. **Does your product or service help resolve a scientifically proven pathology or a set of symptoms that is considered credible and relevant to the medical community yet is not yet branded?** If your brand can raise awareness of, and advocacy for, a new perspective on either an existing condition that is poorly branded or a physical or mental circumstance that has yet to be well articulated, then all constituencies would embrace a condition branding initiative. The healthcare community at large and the general public will rally around an effort that reduces human suffering and healthcare costs and helps clinicians better care for their patients.
2. **Does your product or service help resolve a disease in a new way—via a new pathway, at a new site of action, addressing an underlying cause versus relieving symptoms—that would benefit from rebranding the disease to highlight the difference?** The perceived value of solving a problem increases remarkably when the problem is more finely understood. Further, the value of fostering such an understanding—thereby expanding physician/patient dialogue and comfort—can be made to accrue to your

product brand as part of a comprehensive condition branding initiative. If your brand works in a new way, then the problem it solves may be branded to elevate the distinct and significant impact your product makes.

3. **Are there stigmas/social concerns associated with the condition your product treats that would hinder a physician/patient dialogue?** By re-branding a condition that engenders embarrassment, a product can help foster a new, more reputable way to think about the condition that (a) legitimizes the subject as worthy of scientific research, funding, and reimbursement; (b) encourages consumers to come forward and present as a newly identified patient segment; and (c) acts as a password between physician and patient that initiates an open, productive dialogue.
4. **Does your product or service have significant benefits for a condition that has little or no awareness?** A product brand can help identify a new market segment by calling attention to, and aligning itself with, a freshly branded condition. In some cases, the product brand does not even have to be the only one of its kind on the market to gain a preferred link to the condition. Product brands can create a branded condition using nomenclature that builds on the product's unique properties. In other instances, recognized symptoms and/or diagnoses can be linked into a universally accepted "syndrome" that can be associated with a product.
5. **Are there competitive efforts to devalue or marginalize your product as beneficial only for a condition that is not perceived as an important health risk?** Condition branding may also be used to counter negative perceptions generated by competitors that are attempting to narrow your product's scope of influence. By changing the nomenclature to reflect a broader

value or rebranding condition names that are more relevant to customers, your product brand can reframe the debate in favor of its unique benefits.

Once the decision has been made to brand or rebrand a health or medical condition identity, a best-practice model derived from past successes is the most efficient and prudent route to pursue. Here's how a proper condition branding effort should proceed (it's a lot like rallying votes for a bill in the US Senate):

- A primary interested party (e.g., a patient advocacy group, physician medical society, or healthcare manufacturer with a remedy in hand or in development) takes a leadership position and creates a mission to brand or rebrand a healthcare condition that is overlooked, misunderstood, or poorly branded in the first place.
- The primary party networks with other constituencies mentioned above that are essential to creating the critical mass needed for grassroots acceptance.
- As part of the networking process, the primary party surveys each constituency to understand the outcome it seeks as part of the branding/rebranding initiative.
- A one- or two-day summit is convened with an agenda designed to align the various desired outcomes of the constituencies around a central brand identity strategy (i.e., the criteria that a condition brand name must satisfy in this particular situation). Not surprisingly, a condition branding strategy conforms to the same model as a product or service branding strategy: you collectively develop a Brand Threat (opposite of a Brand Promise) and a Brand Personality using Step 2 in the Goldilocks Process, found in Chapter 8.

- Based on the consensus strategy, the collective group brainstorms and generates condition brand name candidates, and prioritizes a list of viable condition brand names.
- The brand name candidates are tested with patients and clinicians for their appeal and also to gain feedback on the pros and cons of how the names deliver on the consensus strategy.
- The summit group (or steering committee) convenes once more to review the research feedback and select a condition brand name.
- The various constituencies then depart and begin to implement the agreed-upon condition brand identity in their various media channels: member newsletters, promotion, public relations, articles and papers in well-regarded medical journals, and so on. The general public learns of this rebranded or newly branded condition identity from a variety of sources, and if the identity resonates, it takes root in our lexicon. (The Obama administration tried to get the general public to call its healthcare legislation by its official name, The Affordable Care Act. The public preferred to call it "Obamacare," which helps or hurts the concept depending on your view of President Obama. Take note as this chapter proceeds on how to avoid losing control of health condition branding.)

One shining example of condition branding that succeeded is Overactive Bladder, or OAB. OAB is a best-practice example of re-branding "incontinence." All constituencies backed the concept because all constituencies were consulted when the brand name was created. Academic healthcare thought leaders respected the sobriety of losing the "bed wetting" image of incontinence in favor of a more anatomical concept. Advocacy groups were pleased that the newly branded Overactive Bladder took the stigma out of the condition for its members and blamed the problem not on a loss of personal control, but rather a faulty muscle in the bladder. (Hey, it happens to us all after a while.) Doctors and patients liked the discreet, simple "password" OAB, which immediately set in motion an entirely new protocol for an unembarrassed and frank discussion. And Wyeth (now part of Pfizer)—the pharmaceutical manufacturer who helped sponsor the rebranding at the time—was satisfied that the concept reinforced the mechanism of action of their brand Detrol (tolterodine) to resolve the problem. Detrol works by increasing the "activity" of the detrusor muscle (a sphincter in the bladder) thereby enabling it to control the spasms that cause OAB. OAB was a lock that made Detrol a turnkey solution for all parties.

It's important to note once again that condition branding is not an act in and of itself to advance the agenda of any one party. Condition branding is an approach to resolving a specific problem in diagnosing and addressing a particular disease, disorder, or syndrome. Assuming the cooperation of all necessary parties, there are three principal strategies for condition branding:

- Developing a new condition brand to build recognition for an unmet need
- Redefining an existing condition brand to reduce a stigma
- Subcategorizing an existing condition brand to recognize illness subsets

Let's take them one at a time.

Developing a new condition brand to build recognition for an unmet need.

In 1981, Glaxo (now GlaxoSmithKline, GSK) successfully launched the prescription medication Zantac (ranitidine hydrochloride) as a treatment for ulcers. The second indication Glaxo pursued with Zantac was commonly called "heartburn" at the time. In the heartburn paradigm, overeating or eating spicy foods occasionally requires self-treatment with an OTC remedy such as Tums or Alka-Seltzer. Why would anyone go to a doctor and get a prescription for something so trivial? With further scientific investigation, Glaxo discovered that spicy foods do not cause chronic heartburn. Rather, chronic heartburn was due to an exacerbation of an underlying condition in which the esophageal sphincter (the closure leading from the esophagus to the stomach) becomes weakened and fails to close completely. This anatomical weakness enables stomach acid to wash up into the esophagus, causing inflammation, pain, potential long-term tissue damage, or even esophageal cancer. Unlike Tums or Alka-Seltzer, Zantac is an H2-receptor antagonist. It does not neutralize acid, but rather slows down the production of acid in the stomach, a much more sophisticated and effective means of resolving acid back-washing into the esophagus on a chronic basis.

I was part of the joint marketing/agency team advising GSK at the time. We followed the best-practice protocols I've outlined above, reviewed past condition branding protocols in search of lessons learned, and set the following strategic and branding goals:

1. The condition brand must scientifically address the seriousness of the illness to alert those with "chronic heartburn" that their condition could be much more dangerous than they had assumed.
2. The condition brand must be complex enough to legitimize it as a form of pathology worthy of treatment by a doctor, but simple enough to act as a "password" in discussions with patients.
3. The condition must appeal to academic and clinical practitioners as a *bona fide* disease backed up by physiological data.
4. The Brand Threat was: Condition X is a serious, chronic threat to the well being of the upper GI tract, leading to increased morbidity and mortality.
5. The Brand Personality was: Aggressive, Insidious, and Complex.

Using the appropriate processes of building a consensus among the medical community and other constituencies, we were able to successfully launch a new condition brand identity known as gastro-esophageal reflux disease, or GERD. This was not just a re-naming of heartburn for financial gain. Identifying the condition and branding it as GERD completely altered the conversation and mandated an entirely new approach of diagnosis and treatment agreed upon by doctors, insurance companies, the general public, and the associations that support them all.

HEARTBURN	GERD
No big deal	Serious and potentially dangerous
Occurs once in a while	Occurs chronically
Caused by eating spicy foods	Caused by acid reflux due to a weakness in the esophageal sphincter
Self-treat with OTC remedies	Medical professional diagnoses and treats with an Rx

This is a far cry from the "plop-plop, fizz-fizz" perception of heartburn expressed in 1970s Alka-Seltzer commercials. Of course, Alka-Seltzer has its place for acute heartburn, but if you've ever suffered from GERD, then you know it's a much more serious condition than occasional over-indulgence on pizza or Buffalo wings.

Glaxo launched a well-coordinated initiative by creating the Glaxo Institute for Digestive Health (GIDH), which served as a platform for education and awareness. The GIDH sponsored research awards in the area of gastrointestinal (GI) health, discussed GERD in the context of other, more serious GI diseases, involved powerful third-party advocates such as the American College of Gastroenterology, and fielded a public relations effort called Heartburn Across America.

Not only did Glaxo double the percentage of physicians who perceived them as leaders in GI health, but it also realized an annual sales increase for Zantac to more than $2 billion at peak, 65% of which was accounted for by GERD. By 1988, Zantac was the world's largest selling prescription brand. If you visit the GSK campus in Research Triangle Park in North Carolina, one of the main buildings is shaped like the chemical structure of Zantac, so great was its influence on GI medicine and GSK's reputation for innovation. In the years since Zantac transferred to OTC status, many other, more sophisticated and effective prescription brands have been released, evolving the paradigm Zantac created by rebranding a condition because of a hidden unmet need.

GERD has been decried by cynics as one of the most over-aggressive means by which a pharmaceutical company helps generate sales for its brands. As shown above, Glaxo did not work alone on this initiative, but rather in concert with all interested constituencies. Further, one major storyline always goes unmentioned when cynics cite the financial profitability of condition branding for companies such as Glaxo: ALL THE GOOD THAT CAME OF IT for improving people's lives.

- According to the National Institutes of Health (NIH), the annual prevalence of GERD ranges between 20% and 30% in North America.
- Since the advent of the GERD brand identity, there have been significant annual decreases in hospitalizations (3.1 million at peak) and deaths with GERD as the primary diagnosis (1,150 at peak).
- Further, studies have shown that people with GERD have a lower reported health-related quality of life, which includes reduced enjoyment of food (80%), sleep problems (60%), and work-concentration difficulties when symptoms are present (40%).

- And the American College of Gastroenterology estimates that the symptoms of GERD result in almost $2 billion in lost productivity each year.

Glaxo and its brand Zantac set in motion a paradigm shift to reduce the significant burden of illness on society through a well-coordinated condition branding initiative, as well as with the power of Zantac to resolve GERD. So, clearly, when condition branding is done right, it enlightens and buoys our entire society. Everybody wins.

Redefining an existing condition brand identity to reduce a stigma.

Whereas Glaxo identified a new condition brand (GERD) to build recognition for an unmet need, sometimes existing health condition brands are considered medically relevant, yet they suffer from an association with social embarrassment. Often, the stigma surrounding these conditions has been worsened by a history of OTC remedies whose low-budget or lowbrow promotional efforts push patients further into hiding.

Perhaps the most prominent example today of a company redefining an existing condition to reduce social stigma is Pfizer and its effort to give a new brand identity to impotence. Impotence has long existed as a recognized medical condition, but the term was always associated with either a disability linked to physical trauma or, more commonly, with a loss of libido—both of which contribute to low self-esteem. Furthermore, the remedies developed for impotence over the years were often invasive and their implementation indiscreet. And finally, regardless of whether one considers a diminishment of sexual function with age a legitimate medical condition, the psychological ramifications certainly venture into the realm of depression, anxiety, and other mental illnesses.

Linking the condition brand with its drug Viagra (sildenafil citrate), Pfizer successfully led an initiative that rebranded impotence using the new term "erectile dysfunction" (ED). This new condition brand identity realigned a socially embarrassing condition associated with a lack of potency (i.e., male virility) with the more enlightened concept of a physical loss of function that could be simply reversed. Like GERD, the new identity of ED was captured in an acronym suitable for mass consumer promotion and functioning as an easy password between physician and patient to initiate a formerly difficult and embarrassing conversation. Furthermore, the brand personality of ED—simple, discreet and empowering—aligned beautifully with that of Viagra, an elegant and effective solution to this rebranded identity.

Subcategorizing an existing condition brand to recognize illness subsets.

No illness categories are more welcoming of condition branding than those found in the fields of psychology and psychiatry, where illness is rarely based on measurable physical symptoms and, therefore, open to multiple, confusing definitions. Watching the Diagnostic and Statistical Manual of Mental Disorders (DSM) balloon in size over the decades to its current mammoth dimensions would have us believe that the world is a more mentally unstable place today than ever. In fact, the disorder categories have just gotten more specific, and their descriptions require more room.

Without a blood test or a biopsy or any yardstick whatsoever, how is anyone able to determine scientifically where the line is that distinguishes normal human behavior from a mental illness—for example, a crank from someone with Major Depressive Disorder, an absent-minded aunt from one with Minor Neurocognitive Disorder, or a gluttonous pig from someone who suffers from Binge Eating Disorder? These are all newly identified diagnostic categories to be found in DSM-5 (2013).

The treatment of mental illness remains somewhat of a mystery, leaving the door open for considerable debate. For example, Dr. Allen Frances, chairman of the DSM-4 task force, considers DSM-5 conditions such as Disruptive Mood Dysregulation Disorder (excessive temper tantrums) and Gender Dysphoria (feeling like you were born the wrong sex, e.g., Caitlyn Jenner) to be "fad diagnoses" and "pet ideas." Admittedly, it is an inexact science. However, for the most part, branding conditions of mental health is a noble enterprise. It helps patients realize that they may be able to get attention for a formerly un-identified disorder; it removes the stigma associated with socially embarrassing behaviors due to illness; it gives doctors expanded knowledge to help more of their patients; and it shines light a little further into the darkness that is illness of the human mind. The trustees who approved the criteria in DSM-5 may not have gotten everything "right," but some consensus of what's "right" must exist for the common good. In my opinion, the trustees did the difficult work that had to be done, and we're better off for it.

The increasing number of identified emotional conditions has resulted, in good part, from subcategorizing existing conditions into their component segments to better assess treatment options (we saw this earlier in the chapter as SAD is now subcategorized as an exacerbation of an existing depressive condition). Not surprisingly, many of these newly coined conditions were brought to light through direct funding by pharmaceutical companies in research, public relations, or both because there are meager funds set aside for such activities in the public sector.

A legendary example of subcategorizing an existing condition brand to recognize an illness subset resulted from research funded by Upjohn (now Pfizer) the makers of Xanax (alprazolam) for what we now know to be Panic Disorder. In DSM-2 (1968), the description of what would become Panic Disorder in DSM-3R (1987) fell under the catchall category of anxiety neurosis. Without a well-branded condition, patients experiencing panic attacks often went to cardiologists, thinking their problem was a heart condition, only to be labeled "cardiac complainers" and hypochondriacs due to a lack of physical pathology. For those unfamiliar with the symptoms of panic attack, they can mimic a heart attack and include:

- Shortness of breath or hyperventilation
- Heart palpitations or a racing heart
- Chest pain or discomfort
- Trembling or shaking
- A choking feeling

Dr. David Sheehan, a pioneering thought leader in the field of panic, helped characterize the condition and push for a new way to diagnose and treat it. Upjohn helped fund Sheehan's early research, as well as publications and speaking tours aimed at cardiologists to help raise awareness of the heart-brain connection in the minds of Panic Disorder patients. Xanax was the only benzodiazepine (an anxiety medication) to be studied that showed clear evidence of effectiveness against Panic Disorder. Through an unrestricted grant by Upjohn to the National Institute of Mental Health, a three-day condition branding summit resulted in a published consensus on the diagnostic criteria of Panic Disorder and how best to treat it.

Xanax was the first to receive an exclusive indication, thereby establishing its leadership in anxiety disorders. Since the release of DSM-3R in 1987, which first recognized Panic Disorder as a distinct condition, its reported incidence has grown 1,000-fold, and newer antidepressants have been studied in response to expanding ideas about this condition.

Another example of subcategorizing an existing condition brand is the recognition of pre-menstrual dysphoric disorder (PMDD) in DSM-4 as a severe form of pre-menstrual syndrome (PMS), and its subsequent successful treatment with Sarafem (fluoxetine hydrochloride) from Lilly. As many industry insiders know, Sarafem is identical in formula and dose to the anti-depressant Prozac, so the branding strategy that helped build awareness for both the new condition and the drug were fascinatingly integrated.

I was part of the team that helped raise awareness for this branded condition, as well as the pharmaceutical solution proffered by Lilly. A Lilly-sponsored prelaunch initiative built awareness for the newly recognized condition, recasting diagnosis to conform to the DSM-4 criteria. While the PMDD brand effectively captured the concept of a decrease in wellness associated with hormonal transition, the remedy (Prozac) evoked conflicting notions of a mental disorder for female patients. (Women in research recalled unpleasant echoes of "It's all in your head.") By changing the brand identity of the PMDD remedy from Prozac to Sarafem—packaged in a lavender-colored pill and promoted with images of sunflowers and smart women—we helped Lilly create a brand that better aligned with the personality of the condition brand and reflected the values of the doctors and patients for a hand-in-glove fit.

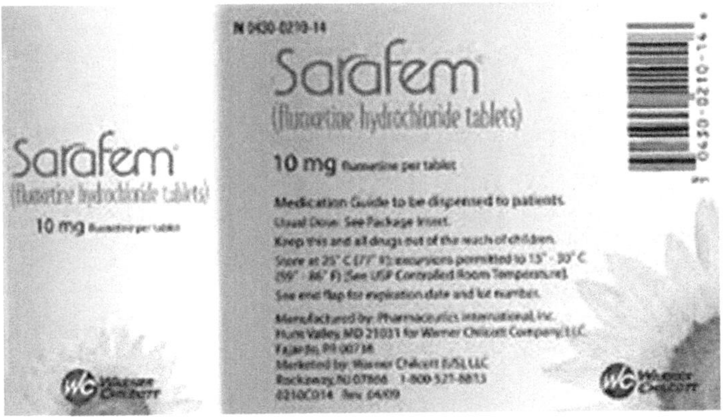

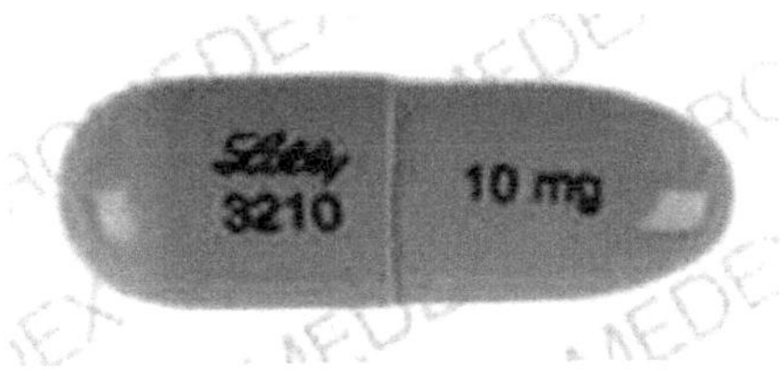

The flip side of the coin: when identity crises are created in condition branding.

Not all efforts at condition branding are justified or result in the degree of societal success as those examples outlined above. Most times, failure is due to incompetence. And in rare instances, failure is due to disingenuous intentions. The legacy of the snake oil salesman still haunts what has become a very noble enterprise today. Take, for example, the reprehensible dealings in the early days of Listerine. In the 1920s, Warner-Lambert was looking for an opportunity to expand the market for its Listerine brand. Although the antiseptic solution was being marketed for everything from dandruff to wound irrigation, sales were flat. Warner-Lambert found its answer by creating awareness—and anxiety—around a newly coined, sinister medical identity brand: halitosis. Whereas the harmless concept of bad breath never caused much of a public stir, halitosis—through scare-tactic branding—became feared and demonized for a range of social casualties from lack of career advancement to divorce.

As the antidote for this "newfound" condition, Listerine had a sales increase from $100,000 to $4 million over the next six years and helped make halitosis a household word.

This would not only be disreputable and inexcusable behavior on the part of regulated healthcare constituencies today, it would also be illegal thanks to the 1962 Kefauver-Harris amendment to the Food, Drug, and Cosmetic Act and other such legislation. Healthcare manufacturers absolutely want to make as much money as possible on their brands. What company doesn't? But today's laws prevent this blatant exploitation of consumer fears. And even if it didn't, there are enough checks and balances in today's healthcare system to prevent phony illnesses from surviving the 24-hour news cycle.

"Sorry, Watkins
—but we're cutting down"
THAT'S the explanation they gave him, but they were letting him go for another reason entirely . . . one that Watkins didn't even suspect. Without realizing it, he had offended a number of the firm's best customers and they had complained to the boss. It was sort of tragic . . . to have this happen just when he thought he was getting some place. A good man, Watkins—and an ambitious one—but just a little bit careless.*
You can't get away with it
Maybe a few super-employees get away with *halitosis (bad breath), but lesser ones shouldn't even try. This offensive condition, of which anyone may be guilty, is the fault unpardonable in business, and social life. Business firms should insist that their employees use Listerine Antiseptic every day, to take precautions against offending.
While some bad breath is due to systemic conditions, most cases, say some authorities, are due to the fermentation of tiny food particles that may take place even in normal mouths.
Listerine used as a mouth rinse and gargle quickly halts this fermentation and then overcomes the odors it causes. The breath becomes sweeter, more wholesome, less likely to be obnoxious.
Make your breath more agreeable
If you are trying to get ahead in business, don't risk offending. If you want people to like you, get in the habit of using Listerine Antiseptic systematically every morning and night, and between times before business and social engagements.
This wholly delightful precaution against a condition that anyone may have at some time or other without realizing it may pay you rich dividends in popularity.
Lambert Pharmacal Co., St. Louis, Mo.

There are three categories of bad condition branding in healthcare:

- When one constituency unilaterally brands the condition based on where or with whom the condition was first observed, thereby obscuring symptoms or the proper remedies.
- When the branded condition is so off-putting that doctors and patients find it impractical and fail to engage.
- When the branded condition is so vague that it lacks a defined set of symptoms and therefore is useless as a guiding concept.

Again, let's take them one at a time.

Branding the condition based on where or with whom the condition was first observed.

My next-door neighbor has an awful joke that's never funny, but nonetheless useful when I discuss condition branding. For decades, Lou Gehrig, the Hall of Fame New York Yankee, once held the record for most consecutive major league baseball games played (2,130 over 17 seasons), earning him the nickname, "The Iron Horse." That is, he was never injured or sick enough to miss a game. Ironically and tragically, he died at the young age of 37 of amyotrophic lateral sclerosis (ALS). According to the ALS Association, the disease is:

> A progressive neurodegenerative disease that affects nerve cells in the brain and the spinal cord. A-myo-trophic comes from the Greek language. "A" means no. "Myo" refers to muscle, and "Trophic" means nourishment—"No muscle nourishment." When a muscle has no nourishment, it "atrophies" or wastes away. "Lateral" identifies the areas in a person's spinal cord where portions of the nerve cells that signal and control the muscles are located. As this area degenerates it leads to scarring or hardening ("sclerosis") in the region.

It was a very thorough and scientific naming strategy but a horrible effort at creating a condition brand identity because it fails to illuminate the problem or its symptoms for a lay audience not quite caught up on their command of classic root languages. Hence ALS became known popularly as Lou Gehrig's Disease, since the Yankee first baseman was the most famous person to die from it. Here's where my neighbor's joke comes in. In 1995, the Baltimore Orioles' Cal Ripken, Jr., another Hall of Famer who had a similar nickname (The Iron Man), broke Gehrig's record for most consecutive games. My neighbor's punch line: "Now I guess we'll have to call it Cal Ripken's Disease." Dumb humor, yes; but his inadvertent point is well taken. Even after millions of dollars were raised for ALS in 2013 with the viral Bucket Challenge that witnessed the famous and unknown alike dousing themselves with water in the name of raising research money and awareness for ALS, the great majority of citizens still can neither articulate the full disease name nor list out the symptoms. The disease brand is stuck in 1941 along with the name of its most famous victim.

We've come a long way since ALS was first coined in the 1920s, but still there remains a strong penchant for knee-jerk branding among today's first responders to new or puzzling medical conditions. Lyme Disease gets its name because those healthcare professionals on the front lines first discovered it in Lyme, Connecticut. And Legionnaire's Disease—a form of pneumonia—was coined because of an outbreak of infections at an American Legion convention in Philadelphia in 1976. Even the newly discovered pathogen was called *Legionella* in tribute to one of the most unscientific acts of branding in medical history. While the intentions of public health officials and others are noble, the public relations nightmares of, say, the tourism bureau of America's western state parks (Rocky Mountain Spotted Fever, anyone?), or the need to endure constant jokes for anyone named Alzheimer, is impractical and unfair. The Centers for Disease Control (CDC) dodged a major catastrophe in bypassing their brand name candidates 4H (hemophiliacs, homosexuals, heroin users, Haitians) and GRID (gay-related immune deficiency) before landing on Auto-Immune Deficiency Syndrome (AIDS) (although the maker of AYDS, an OTC weight loss lozenge, threw a fit).

The World Health Organization (WHO) issued a set of guidelines in 2015 that—while not enforceable—certainly points in the right direction of good condition branding practices. The two most germane to our discussion here are:

1. Eschew references to people, places, and specific occupations.
2. Avoid names that might instill panic: "fatal," "epidemic," "catastrophic."

Hopefully this will help ensure that the world will never again have condition brand identities such as Stockholm Syndrome (those poor Swedes, forever associated with Svengali-like captors) or Epstein-Barr Virus, a form of herpes, though what ordinary citizen would know that other than the descendants of the disease's eponymous discoverers, Anthony Epstein and Yvonne Barr?

When the branded condition is so off-putting that doctors and patients find it impractical and fail to engage.

One of the most egregious and tragic branding mishaps in this category—and one with which I and others have worked diligently to try to change without cooperation from manufacturers or women's support groups—is Vulvovaginal Atrophy (VVA). Yes, that's what it's actually called by the medical community, which clearly never looked beyond their medical dictionaries before launching this vile identity into the world. The clinical definition is as follows: thinning, drying, and inflammation of the vaginal walls due to women producing less estrogen primarily as a result of menopause. This is an important condition to brand, but the resulting effort is completely tone deaf. Research with women aged 45 and older shows that the condition brand, Vulvovaginal Atrophy, evokes horror, laughter, outrage, embarrassment, and denial among women who have it. We cringe at the thought just as we cringe in the torture scene from *Casino Royal*, where Le Chiffre repeatedly swats the genitals of James Bond with a thick rope. Think of the constructive and humane "Erectile Dysfunction (ED)" on the male side of the branding equation to articulate the breakdown of genital function brought about by aging, and one can see why the idea of a woman's vagina "atrophying"—or "wasting away and shriveling up"—as she approaches and undergoes menopause would surely qualify as a violation of the Geneva Convention. As a result, women never bring it up with their doctors. And doctors are reluctant to bring it up with their patients because the clinicians fear they'll get a negative reaction from their patients. So no one talks about it. The term actually works *against* the sound practices for condition branding articulated above.

Working with the condition brand they've been given, several pharmaceutical companies with various remedies at the ready urge women through TV and magazine promotions to speak with their doctors about VVA. Acknowledging the gender bias that many medical conditions for women have not received the same attention and medical solutions as they have for men, there are still other factors at work with this poorly branded condition. First, for the same reason doctors do not treat weight, they do not treat age: VVA is not pathological; it's normal. Menopause is a natural part of aging, so the tendency is to let it take its natural course.

Second, since doctors do treat pain, that is where pharmaceutical companies involved with VVA are spending the bulk of the money in their efforts to stir up a dialogue around the condition and potential medical responses.

You do not have to look far these days to see the smiling women, alone in a color photo, telling sufferers and doctors alike that sex shouldn't be painful. Aside from the devotees of *Fifty Shades of Grey*, who could disagree? Well, the problem is twofold: (1) VVA doesn't cause painful sex. It causes a cluster of symptoms that are very unpleasant and, sometimes, results in sex that is painful; and (2) believe it or not, painful sex isn't the number-one complaint of women with VVA (it's itching). So the idea is simple and clear, but not clearly relevant.

Like any condition that is poorly branded, VVA will never gain the power it seeks to resolve misunderstandings and promote positive dialogues unless better language is coined and adopted using the proper protocols for successfully branding a healthcare condition cited above. It begins with the active participation of women, healthcare marketers, healthcare professionals, and the advocacy groups supporting them. Remember: all constituencies must be brought to the table in a concerted workshop or series of workshops to brainstorm ideas that answer the following questions:

1. Does the branded condition offer all constituencies a way to advance their agendas in a concerted way?
2. Does the branded condition offer both doctors and patients a means of having a productive dialogue on diagnosis and treatment?
3. Does the branded condition offer some direction or hope for a potential resolution, either now or in the immediate future?

Some efforts have been made with VVA, but the constituencies that were invited to the table were far from a quorum. The North American Menopause Society (NAMS) and The International Society for the Study of Women's Sexual Health (ISSWSH), two advocacy groups promoting women's health, took a shot at rebranding VVA in May 2013. They failed to invite other important constituencies to participate (I volunteered to no avail), so their odds of success were hobbled from the start. In the absence of any marketing partners in branding and public relations, or any actual peri-menopausal, menopausal, or post-menopausal women who could offer a perspective on the viability of the resulting condition brand name, the two advocacy groups came up with GSM: genitourinary syndrome of menopause. Does this seem helpful or less off-putting than VVA? Hardly. NAMS and ISSWSH had the right idea, but—like the guys in white coats who named VVA—they went about it in the wrong way: they never invited the communications experts, medical opinion leaders, or the very women who suffer from the condition to help with the rebranding.

Separately from the women's advocacy groups, the marketers of Osphena, a relatively new brand indicated for "dyspareunia," or . . . wait for it . . . painful sex, have also tried their hand at rebranding the condition, but they, too, go it alone. They take a laudable approach of co-opting existing nomenclature with a promotional message that directs our attention to "the other ED (estrogen deficiency)."

While their instincts are correct in identifying a "deficiency" that can simply be supplemented or replaced, their analogy falls short. ED or erectile dysfunction is a branded condition that is simple and has one specific symptom: the penis cannot achieve rigidity, ergo Erectile Dysfunction. Not so VVA/GSM, the symptoms of which include dryness, inflammation, soreness, itching, urinary incontinence, and urinary urgency among others. "Estrogen deficiency" is a valiant try, but reduces the issue to its lowest common denominator, thereby making it inadequate. Additionally, since VVA/GSM is a cluster of symptoms, the better definition should involve the term "syndrome" found in the GSM brand. Estrogen Deficiency Syndrome—or EDS—might seem like only a slight variation, but when it comes to condition branding, success is all in the specifics. EDS, as I have advocated with at least one manufacturer, meets all three criteria listed above. It adequately addresses the agendas of all parties; it provides a welcome starting point for a productive dialogue; and it points to a clear resolution, namely, when there is a deficiency of estrogen, replenish it. (Of note: Osphena is not a form of estrogen, so they wouldn't be keen on EDS.) No need to evoke images of a vagina imploding or conjure the unpleasant and mainly irrelevant ideas about not satisfying "your man" in bed. Estrogen Deficiency Syndrome—or something more workable for all—would be a welcome topic of conversation in medical journals and women's consumer magazines. Vulvovaginal Atrophy and GSM harken back to the 1920s techniques that spawned ALS: scientifically accurate, but opaque to a lay audience and completely demotivating to those who wish to self-identify and engage in discussion.

Another example of condition branding that epically fails is the condition known as "Female Sexual Dysfunction." The Mayo Clinic website defines the term as follows: "Persistent, recurrent problems with sexual response, desire, orgasm or pain—that distress you or strain your relationship with your partner."

It meets one of the criteria I cited at the beginning of this chapter of a situation where bad condition branding is at work: the branded condition is so vague that it lacks specific meaning and therefore has no meaning at all. By the accepted "clinical" definition, nearly every woman could qualify as having Female Sexual Dysfunction at some point in her life. In this case, the brand name begs an open-ended question: What is sexual dysfunction? Not having an orgasm? Not having an enduring orgasm? Not having as many orgasms as one did when younger? Not having a high quality of orgasms? A lack of desire to have sex? These are not just questions aimed at highlighting confusion over the branding of this condition, but also the types of questions posed by drug companies during clinical trials to see if their brands can resolve one or more of these complaints. If you don't feel this is scientifically rigorous, then you're right. This is the kind of mistaken condition branding that critics cite when calling the practice into question, and I couldn't agree more in this instance.

Female Sexual Dysfunction is one of the conditions that cynics cite most often when making their spurious argument that most condition branding is a hoax intended to scare doctors into over-prescribing and patients into over-treating. (Hopefully by now I have offered enough examples and evidence to show that proper condition branding is a concerted effort that improves healthy discussions and health outcomes and is put forth by many diverse constituencies rather than one rogue entity on a misguided mission.) And while I denounce the concept of Female Sexual Dysfunction, I don't believe it's a hoax, but rather a condition brand name that fails every constituency miserably. Let me be clear: some women have real psychological and physical barriers to enjoying sexual intercourse and/or sexual intimacy. It is a legitimate area for research and therapeutic discovery. However, a condition brand that is open to having so many meanings ends up having no specific meaning at all and leaves women dissatisfied and unfulfilled (pun intended) in pursuit of relief that is safe, discreet, and effective. A doctor/patient scene from one of my favorite contemporary fiction writers, Lorrie Moore, sums up the dilemma aptly in her usual cogent, black-humor style:

"He removed the mole and put it floating in a pathologist's vial . . . he said, 'Precancer'—like a secret or a zodiac sign. 'Precancer?' she had repeated quietly, for she was a quiet woman. 'Isn't that . . . like life?' (Like Life, Knopf, 1990, page 132.)

I have the same concerns about Generalized Anxiety Disorder, which the DSM-5 defines as "an anxiety disorder characterized by excessive, uncontrollable and often irrational worry (i.e., apprehensive expectation about events or activities)." "Irrational worry?" Are they serious? For every parent out there with daughters apoplectic about what to wear to the prom, many of us who have friends who will never, ever dip their toe in an ocean for fear of being attacked by a great white shark, and maybe even you, reader, who exerts a vise-like grip on the stranger seated next to you as your airplane experiences some turbulence, is it Generalized Anxiety Disorder or is it, as Lorrie Moore's character says, like *life*?

Early in this chapter, I acknowledge and continue to acknowledge that drawing the line between pathological medical conditions and normal human emotions is a difficult but essential job (remember my uncle with SAD?). However, this third type of bad condition branding, where the brand name is so vague that it becomes meaningless and impotent to do its job, only points to the task ahead for those contemplating DSM-6 and the broad constituencies who must work in concert to effectively cage the monsters that threaten our emotional well-being inside the chamber of an effective condition brand identity so that they no longer have power over us. Condition branding is an essential aspect of healthcare best practices. The ideal solutions in peoples' minds are predicated on precisely defining the problems besetting us. Do it right and the world will be forever enlightened; make the common mistakes and the world will be unmoved at best, or plunged further into confusion and despair at worst.

With the major issues and challenges around healthcare branding now articulated, let's get to the finish line by discussing the simple, proven three-step process (The Goldilocks Process) for how to create healthcare brand identities and avoid the mistakes and failures perpetrated by those who refuse to recognize the established rituals that make healthcare branding unique and successful apart from any other type of marketing activity.

7

The Goldilocks Process Part 1: Discovery: Avoiding Identity Crises In Branding Research

In the previous chapters, I've explored how the concepts of health and wellness exert a unique influence on the identities of key players in the transaction model (healthcare professionals, patients, and care-givers) and how those key players make brand choices. Let's now examine what I call The Goldilocks Process for developing effective healthcare brand identities.

As the name might indicate, The Goldilocks Process is not too long, not too short, but just right. How do I know? Because over the course of my 30-year career as a leader of agencies, creative departments of agencies, and branding companies, I have seen dozens and dozens of processes, and I have learned the difference between what is essential and what is just a duplication or triplication of effort and a waste of time and money. The Goldilocks Process for creating a healthcare brand identity involves three steps: Discovery, Strategic Convergence, and Brand Experience Design. Others might argue that a fourth step would be Brand Equity Measurement, but this is just another form of

Discovery. So think of these three steps not so much as a linear process, but rather a circular one:

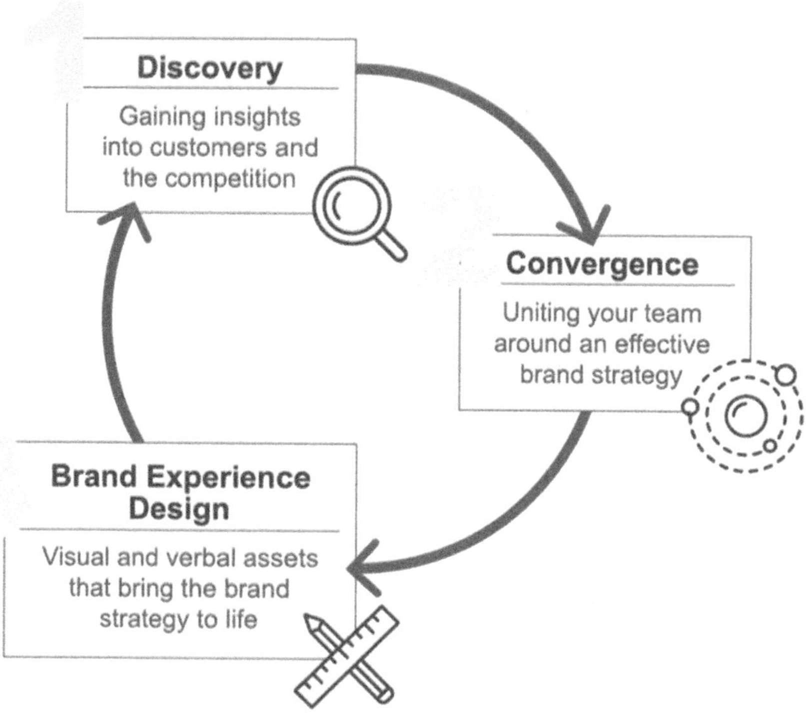

> ANY HEALTHCARE BRAND IDENTITY PROCESS LONGER THAN THREE STEPS IS INEFFICIENT, AND ANY SUCH PROCESS SHORTER THAN THREE STEPS IS INCOMPLETE.

This chapter will delve deeply into the process of Discovery: Gaining insights into customers and the competition. The other two steps will be covered in Chapters 8 and 9, respectively.

Throughout this book, I've revealed the identity crises fostered by healthcare marketers and their agencies brought on by using misguided approaches to building healthcare brands. The root of the deep confusion about the role that healthcare brands play in our society usually originates with the methodologies for comprehending what goes on in customers' minds. You would think we could all agree on paper that there is a difference between information and knowledge and between data and wisdom. Yet I am constantly surprised by what passes for knowledge and wisdom in the field of healthcare branding.

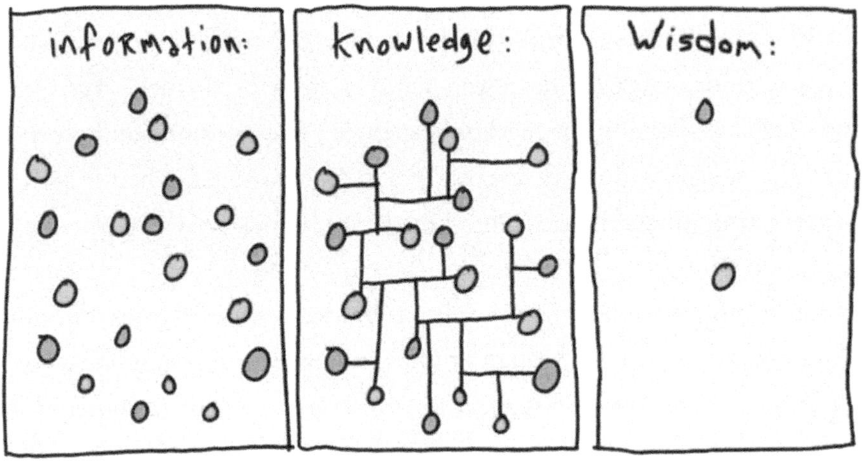

When clients or agencies call my team in to work on a brand identity project, our proposal always includes Discovery: connecting directly with customers to understand how the client's brand can best fit into their identities. Almost without exception, we're told that Discovery research has already been undertaken, so our expertise won't be needed in that regard. We then obediently examine their Discovery research and almost always find they've spent a lot of money asking their customers all the wrong questions about branding. Studies commissioned from market research vendors—some of them very robust and extensive—typically offer pages and pages of written analysis and dazzling graphs that answer the following questions: What do you think about our brand? When might you use it? With whom might you use it? How often would you use it? Where does it fit into your hierarchy of choices? These may all be good questions to gather information and data, but they rarely yield knowledge and wisdom about your customers.

Instead of Who, What, Where, When and How questions, the Discovery research I know to be most effective seeks to understand Why: why would customers see a flattering reflection of themselves in your brand? When one discovers the answer to this question, true wisdom and valuable insights into customers and competition will begin to fall in line right behind it.

Many healthcare companies have some form of insight-mining capability in house, from a single market researcher to an entire department of analysts and databases. Usually, the methodologies they use are sound and proven, reflecting a legacy of good research practices. However, when it comes to generating unique insights into healthcare brands for the purposes of developing or studying brand identity, these methodologies fail. The reason? Research models for health and wellness brands—especially prescription drugs and devices—have been built to capture sales and promotional data about the category and surface data about the behaviors of customers, but not the underlying customer psychology—how customer identities think and behave regarding health, wellness, and healthcare brands.

> BRAND IDENTITY RESEARCH IS NOT ABOUT WHAT COMPANIES ARE SELLING, BUT RATHER ABOUT WHY CUSTOMERS ARE BUYING.

In the early 1990s, when pharmaceutical advances in pain and inflammation were taking shape for the first time in more than a decade, we were working on the identity of a blockbuster Cox-II inhibitor, Vioxx (rofecoxib). The company, Merck, had hired a major consulting firm to conduct research and develop strategy. It cost the client around $2 million, and the effort took 18 months. When they were done, they presented their findings, among which was a patient segmentation study. Such a study attempts to create profiles—or segments—of customers that highlight the differences among them in such measures as degree of illness, age, attitudes toward life, and so on. The Vioxx research featured 28 different segments—28 distinctly different pools of customers that the consultant argued would need to be targeted in specific ways. The brand director turned to me and said, "What the hell am I supposed to do with this?"

Indeed, the information proved voluminous but non-actionable. Although it is easy to fault the vendor for delivering this shock-and-awe offensive on the brand's behalf, some of the blame lies with clients, who—out of fear of leaving no stone unturned—upend every object in the landscape in search of answers. (As you might imagine, there is a lot of money riding on these answers and therefore a lot of upper-management scrutiny, hence the tendency toward an all-encompassing approach, often called CYA: cover your ass.)

Sophisticated, expensive studies sometimes have their place, but when it comes to proper brand identity Discovery, we're better off sticking to the basics of these three essential principles:

1. The goal in brand identity research is not to ask every question, but rather to ask the right questions;
2. The information derived has to be actionable. That is, the insights have to point specifically to a finite series of branding strategies one could pursue; and
3. Unlike messaging research or other inquiries where one wishes to understand all possible varieties of responses, brand identity research operates at a macro level, seeking to distill similarities, not explore differences.

Let me explain this last point in greater depth. Brands create a "community" of belief—a set of values shared by those who esteem the brand. And a brand identity must act as a beacon, signaling to that community a central idea of what's it's like to reside there. Yankee Stadium hosts up to 49,642 people for each of its 81 regular season home games. If you wish to conduct a research study to see what food and beverages should be available for purchase to please most of them, you would want to account for the different tastes, preferences, and economic standings of people in the cheap seats and the upper decks, as well as those behind home plate. In this case, you might take a sample of, say, 10–20%, and survey 5,000–10,000 ticket holders. However, if you seek to understand what they all prize about the Yankees brand, you need talk to only about 100 and you'd get a great idea what the brand means in everyone's minds. Why? These stadium attendees lead individual lives, with a great diversity of family, friends, vacations, jobs and other activities. But when they go to the ballpark or pop on a Yankees cap, they are all part of one community: Yankees fans. And what it means to be a Yankees fan is pride—a feeling that you are a part of a legendary heritage of winning. That's what the Yankees brand identity is about. Must you interview all 49,642 to find this out? Experience shouts from the bleachers, "No!" (Note: Should you hate the New York Yankees on principle, please substitute your favorite sports franchise. The sample sizes will still be the same.)

Whereas the shock-and-awe Vioxx vendor paralyzed the client with information and data, our goal was to distill and refine our Discovery research into knowledge and wisdom about Vioxx customers and present the client with an actionable plan. So, instead of finding the differences among 28 segments of patients, we sought to identify what one or two values they might all have in common. From the start, we knew that the pain category is habitually stuck between two polarities of values: effectiveness and safety—either treating pain regardless of side effects, or treating pain less ably, but sparing the patient from further injury (e.g., gastrointestinal bleeding, addiction). Everyone reading this has experienced pain and inflammation, whether it's a common headache or something much worse such as excruciating back pain or arthritis. While Vioxx could be used for the former, it found its greatest utility and promise in those with chronic pain and inflammation because it was a new kind of anti-inflammatory that was effective, non-addictive, and shown to be gentler on the gastrointestinal tract than other agents commonly in use, such as our old friend Advil. Pfizer's Celebrex (celicoxib) is another such agent.

Experience shows that both healthcare professionals and patients alike perceive that a brand cannot be both powerful and safe at the same time. That is, human nature perceives a powerful drug as being less safe than a less powerful drug. Likewise, a drug with minimal addictive properties and side effects is automatically perceived as less powerful. In our research, we sought to avoid the polarity of the brand being either safe or effective. In order to accomplish this, we had to ask different kinds of questions to get Vioxx out of this "either/or" paradigm.

Pain, by its very nature, is a category that resists objective measurement, unlike, say, hypertension, which can be verified by anyone using a blood pressure monitor (sphygmomanometer). Clinical trials set up standard historical models for measuring patients' responses to pain, but the models are based on subjective self-reporting. One such model involves subjects who are getting their wisdom teeth pulled, with individuals rating their own pain levels using the famous Wong-Baker FACES® Pain Rating Scale: Circle your level of pain based on the chart below:

Wong-Baker FACES® Pain Rating Scale

0	2	4	6	8	10
No Hurt	Hurts Little Bit	Hurts Little More	Hurts Even More	Hurts Whole Lot	Hurts Worst

©1983 Wong-Baker FACES Foundation. www.WongBakerFACES.org
Used with permission. Originally published in *Whaley & Wong's Nursing Care of Infants and Children*. ©Elsevier Inc.

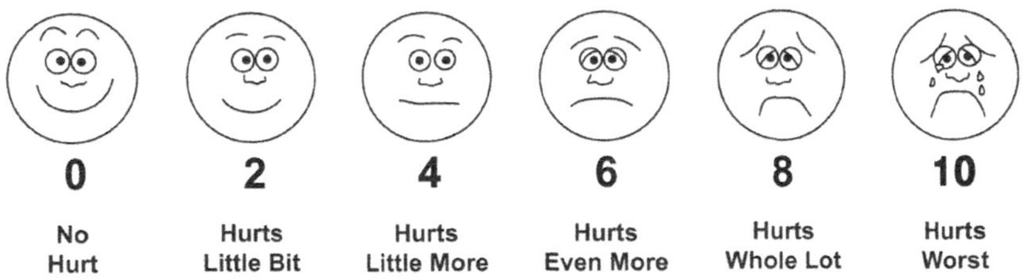

While saying that "pain is all in your head" is a cruel and untrue claim, the mental perceptions of pain actually vary immensely from one person to another. Simply put, some people have higher pain tolerance than others. Not surprisingly, placebo response rates in clinical trials are in the ≥34% range—a much higher rate than patient self-measures for other conditions.

So where does our Vioxx research fit into all of this? We sought to use the emotional perceptions of pain as our research guide rather than the more functional polarities of clinical efficacy and safety. After all, how do physicians know if the pain medication is working or not? Answer: they don't hear complaints from their patients. Silence and tranquility equal relief.

Unlike the existing pain research the client had commissioned, our insight-mining techniques put patients through a series of exercises not about their pain, but rather about their concept of relief. One such exercise used collaging techniques: patients used popular magazines and cut out images of what relief looked like to them. As it turns out, the concept of relief has three key, universal aspects across global geographies and sources of patient pain:

- Relief from the physical feelings of pain;
- Relief from the psychological worry that the medicine will cause further pain or injury (e.g., ulcers, addiction); and
- Relief that is not fleeting, but rather a constant state of being

Our insights led to the central strategy of Enduring Relief—a concept that reflected what all 28 patient segments sought in common. Our study took six weeks and cost more than 80% less than the previous 18-month-long shock-and-awe strategy study. More importantly, it provided a simple, actionable answer to what the brand's identity should be about for doctors, patients, caregivers, allied care professionals, insurance companies, and pharmacists. An early test concept for the brand took the idea of building a "community of belief" quite literally and suggested that Enduring Relief was an actual place that people could go in their minds with Vioxx. It looked something like this:

Ultimately, the Vioxx brand team selected one of our other concepts, a more global celebration entitled "A new world of relief."

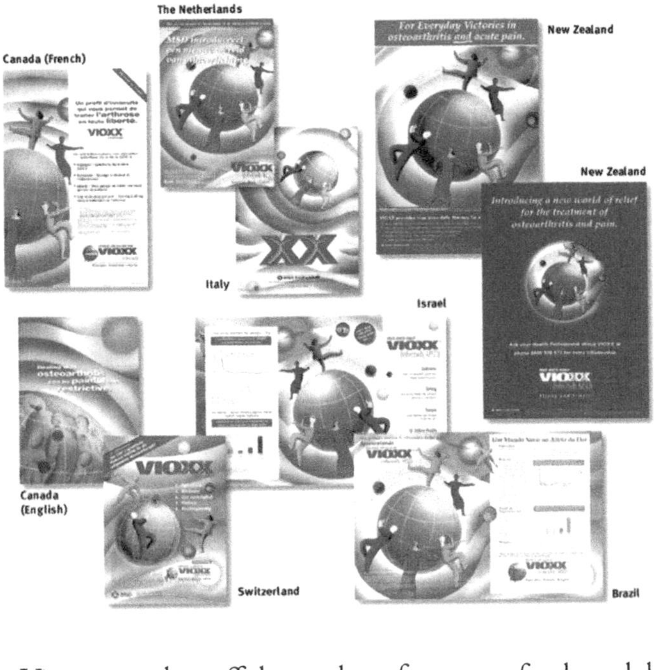

Sadly, Vioxx was taken off the market a few years after launch because its use in the general population became associated with cardiac events. Still, it serves as a good example of how asking the right questions in brand identity research yields fresh thinking about why customers buy healthcare brands.

One of the hidden problems in most brand identity research is that it's conducted in a one-dimensional plane. Most of the questions are simple and straightforward and, most egregiously, are about the product not the customer. To fully understand the three-dimensional associations that customers have with brands, let's examine a model called Belief Dynamics. There are three components to Belief Dynamics:

1. It Beliefs
2. Me Beliefs
3. Them Beliefs

It Beliefs are usually the singular focus of most brand identity research. It Beliefs are all about how customers respond to questions about your brand—the "it" in question. What do you think about it? What makes it special? How might it change your life for the better? These beliefs yield important data and information. However, it is the other two components—Me Beliefs and Them Beliefs—which yield more robust knowledge and wisdom, yet are rarely examined.

- Me Beliefs: how a customer feels about him/herself when engaging with your brand; and
- Them Beliefs: how a customer feels about how others see him/her when engaging with your brand.

[THE BARRIERS TO BRAND ENGAGEMENT WITH CUSTOMERS ARE RARELY FOUND IN "IT BELIEFS," THE RELATIONSHIP BETWEEN THE CUSTOMER AND THE BRAND ALONE.]

Brands are a reflection of our values, and healthcare professionals and patients are keenly aware of—and vulnerable to—the attention and judgment they draw to themselves when embracing healthcare brands.

In Chapter 5, when discussing the liquid tissue adhesive Dermabond, we saw that while surgeons had several It Beliefs about the brand that were positive—environmentally responsible, good in tight spaces, fast—it was their Me Beliefs and Them Beliefs that prevented them from esteeming the Dermabond brand. "I can't see myself associating with a brand that lacks power," (I'm a powerful figure, a Me Belief). "If my surgical team sees that I made an unconventional choice and something goes wrong, they'll lose trust in me," (I have a reputation to maintain, a Them Belief).

Once again, healthcare marketers perpetrate a brand identity crisis by misunderstanding Belief Dynamics. Many years ago, as the car brand Porsche began experiencing a migration of sales to Audi and BMW, Belief Dynamics revealed why. The research team interviewed likely Porsche buyers and found these most common characteristics: 45-65 years of age, high income levels, leadership position in companies, kids grown and moved out, in a long-term relationship, and looking to reflect their status. When these customers were asked what they valued about the Porsche brand, the most common It Belief was "German engineering and craftsmanship." However, this "truth" broke down with follow-up questions such as: what other German-engineered products do you currently own? Most couldn't name one. That's because asking about It Beliefs alone does not always reveal authentic responses about how people's identities engage with brands.

Then the researchers asked the potential customers to do an exercise that would reveal Me and Them Beliefs. They gave the research subjects a picture of a man similar to them sitting in a Porsche and asked them to fill in the thought bubble over his head as if it were them in the car. Not surprisingly, the men filled in responses like: I'm successful, cool, rich, and still sexy. Hmm. So the Porsche seems to deeply resonate with their aspirational self-values, their Me Beliefs. So far, so good.

Next, they gave the research subjects another picture—this one of two younger women who might happen to be in another car next to them at a red light. They asked the men to fill in the thought bubble over the women's heads about what the men suspected the women felt about them. The responses were remarkably different: He's having a mid-life crisis. He's over-compensating for his dull life. He looks silly in that car. With the revelation of these Them Beliefs, this group of likely Porsche buyers seems to crumple under the weight of what others think about them and their brand choice.

It wasn't the car that was the problem for these potential customers (It and Me Beliefs); it was their fear of what the car brand was in other people's minds (Them Beliefs). That is, the Porsche brand was so associated with the cliché of trying to buy back one's youth and coolness in others' minds that it had potential Porsche buyers turning to less stigmatized brand choices like Audi and BMW.

A thought-bubble exercise or collaging techniques may appear on the surface to be silly, playful, and therefore illegitimate as a means of conducting serious research about serious medicine. Also, there are many charlatans out there who don't know how properly to conduct and interpret such exercises, and they give the practice a bad name (more on this shortly). Actually these methodologies (and others like them) are derived from the field of behavioral psychology. They were originally conceived as a means of getting at the underlying issues of a person who is too guarded, too inarticulate, or too unenlightened about themselves to provide reliable feedback. It is part of what's called *discovery learning*, which espouses that people are most revealing when they are led to discover aspects about the world and themselves on their own. (I call proper brand identity research Discovery, and *discovery learning* is a part of Discovery.)

Another way to view the technique of using behavioral psychology exercises to reveal insights is to see them as object lessons: things people learn about themselves when viewing the self as an object in a journey or task, rather than as a subject. It yields more objective information from the research participant, rather than less valid, subjective assertions and beliefs. For example, while working with 40-to-55-year-old women in conjunction with hormone replacement therapy for menopause symptoms, we used an object lesson to delve deeply into matters that were fraught with stigma, embarrassment, fear, and anger. In this case, we conducted an auction of ideas and feelings. we gave each of the women an imaginary sum of $1,000. We then revealed a dozen or so values that they could bid on: sexiness, wisdom, peace of mind, courage, and so on. The idea was to think of what they were going through as they experienced the various stages and symptoms of menopause and then purchase the value(s) they most cherished. Sexiness went for $100 and had just two bids. Courage upped the sale to $375 and drew six bids. Peace of mind saw a frenzy of activity, with one woman actually standing and bidding her entire $1,000. What does this tell us about these customers that could impact the development or refinement of a brand identity? That among many desires, the loss of sexiness is not that big a deal for either Me Beliefs or Them Beliefs. Many women can live without it and still feel good about themselves. The medium-level bidding for courage indicated that menopause was so daunting a challenge that they nearly quadrupled what they were willing to pay for it over sexiness. When we asked the winning bidder why she bought peace of mind and now had no money to purchase anything else, she replied, "If I knew that I would be alright getting through this, then I couldn't care less if I were sexy or brave or wise or any of the other feelings." You cannot get such profound wisdom by merely asking It Belief questions. I have found exercises and object lessons such as this one indispensable in brand identity research.

Belief Dynamics even works with existing brand identities. When trying to assess the equity of an existing brand in the treatment of liver cancer, we were initially faced with oncologists giving their usual replies about efficacy and safety and compatibility with other therapies and so on. When I switched to an analogy exercise, look what happened. The exercise was seemingly simple, as follows.

Fill in the blank:
The brand is to liver cancer as ____________ is to ____________.

Here are some of the responses we received:

The brand is to liver cancer as a

- Fireplace is to fire
- Seat belt is to auto safety
- Earthquake insurance is to California

What did this exercise reveal to our participants and me? That the brand was more essential to their treatment approaches than they had originally assumed. It is essential to have a fireplace if starting a fire in one's home. Buckling up is essential to safety while driving. Further, taking the responses together, the brand stood for a basic fail-safe in their treatment protocol. That is, without this brand, a huge piece of the puzzle would be missing in their practices. The exercise not only confirmed a key aspect of the brand's identity, but it also elevated the brand in their minds beyond what it was before the exercise. (Another version of this technique is to have the subjects imagine what would be lost in the world if the brand never existed.)

As I mentioned earlier, the reputation of these types of exercises has been maligned by people who either dabble in them or just assume that any exercise whatsoever is just as valid as anything else. This is not just a mistaken notion, but also ignorance or fraud or both. We were brought in to create and develop a brand identity in a life-and-death therapeutic category. The healthcare advertising agency that would eventually create the promotional concepts for the brand insisted on attending the research. I insisted on it, too. More people participating in research and strategy will ultimately benefit the brand because such an inclusive practice insures group ownership of the brand identity and helps eliminate competing ideas that often result from bitterness at not being invited to the party. Also, as in the case I'm discussing now, agency inclusion dispels resentment that someone like myself is not needed because the agency "knows how to do research exercises, too."

Even so, it didn't go as well this time as I had hoped. Instead of honoring our respective expertise and putting the client and brand above politics and ego, the agency essentially badgered the client into letting it design half of the Discovery exercises out of "fairness." I reluctantly agreed under the condition that we would each moderate and interpret the results of our own respective exercises.

There were to be four exercises in total, two apiece for my group and the agency. For my first, I had a group of 12 doctors separate into two groups of six participants, and role-play: they would personify the brand and—as if the brand were an actual person—write letters to customers in the voice and personality they imagined for the brand. Each sub-group of six would take one of two audiences: patients or other doctors in their specialty.

Since the drug brand in question was going to be used in conjunction with another type of therapy, my second exercise was a projective one: imagine the two brands (ours and the one with which it was to be used) as a famous duo. Who would they be and why? The doctors could choose any famous duo from, for example, the entertainment industry (e.g., Abbott and Costello), sports (e.g., quarterback and receiver), politics (e.g., running mates), and so on.

In contrast, for their first exercise, the advertising agency gave each doctor a pad of small sticky notes and asked them to jot down things they admired most about what they had read about the brand (the agency had provided a backgrounder, which the doctors got in advance of the research exercises). The agency's moderator then organized the sticky notes by topic and led a discussion about them.

For their second exercise, the agency had printed up about 30 cards, each with the logo of a famous consumer goods brand on it: Budweiser, Apple, Nike, Whole Foods, John Deere, etc. They then asked the doctors, as a group, to select a total of five branded cards that they felt best represented the qualities of our brand under study.

By this point in the book, I'm hoping that readers will have already figured out why the agency's exercises failed at the task of identifying values that could resonate with doctors about the brand. If so, please indulge my analysis. The agency's first exercise generated typical It Beliefs. It did deliver information on the features of the brand that intrigued the doctors. However, as we have seen about It Beliefs, they revealed nothing about why the doctors could see a flattering reflection of themselves in the brand identity. Even more useless, the sticky note exercise basically was an exercise in how well the doctors could play back messages they were given before the exercise. We'd like you to read about our tall, handsome, intelligent brand. Now tell us, what do you like about it? Well, of course, that it's tall, intelligent, and handsome.

I must admit that I have never seen anything as inane as the agency's second exercise, but I was curious to see what, if anything, it would reveal. The five brand cards that the doctors chose were: Apple, Nike, Macy's, Burger King, and Toyota. When the moderator probed on each of these, here's a sampling of the answers he got:

Q: Why did you choose Apple?
A: I like Apple, and I think I'll like this brand. It seems well engineered.

Q: You also chose Nike, and Apple and Nike are two of the world's top brands. Does this mean that you believe our brand to be the best of its kind?
A: Well, we also chose Macy's and Burger King. And those are good, but not as good as Apple and Nike.

Q: So what are you saying then?
A: That the brand seems like it could be a big deal, but depending on how well it works out in the real world, maybe it will just be second rate.

Q: Why did you choose Toyota?

A: You said we needed five, so we added this in. It's a decent car, not too flashy or expensive. I would have chosen Honda, but that wasn't represented on any of the cards.

Oh, boy. Unlike the collage exercise I mentioned earlier, the agency's exercises restricted the doctors' choices to what they were given. Further, by forcing the doctors to choose five surrogate brands (why five?), we'll never know if—given their druthers—they might have selected only one or two, thereby better distilling the information into something approaching an insight. But the real tragedy is that this exercise might have yielded actual knowledge had the moderator asked the right questions: How many of you own and use Apple products? What value do these Apple products have for you in your everyday life? The doctors might have said: I feel Apple keeps me on the forefront of what's best in technology (innovative); I'd be lost without my iPhone—my life is in there (essential); or iTunes lets me organize my music any way I wish so easily (intuitive, the brand "gets" me). These values—innovative, essential, and intuitive—are the kinds of values that can be acted upon in developing a brand identity, as we'll explore further in the next two chapters.

I'm not here to bash this agency's efforts—they earnestly felt they knew what they were doing and wanted to contribute to our group efforts. But their amateur execution and pitiable results remind me of a video gaming friend of mine who bragged about his prowess on *Guitar Hero* and asked me if I knew how to play it. I replied no, but that I had been playing a real guitar for more than 40 years. My point is that learning about behavioral methodologies, studying the exercises, knowing which are the right ones to discover the values one seeks, and doing this 100% of the time in the course of one's job are not matters one can fake one's way through (at the client's expense, no less). Dabbling is not real expertise, just as playing *Guitar Hero* is not playing a real guitar.

On the flip side, here are a couple of insights (out of many more) that my role-playing/letter-writing exercise yielded:

- The tone of voice in the letter that "the brand" wrote to doctors was straightforward, urgent, and passionate, while the letter to patients was straightforward, nurturing, and reassuring.
- In both letters, the groups admitted to imagining the brand to be a man's voice talking to a woman.

What knowledge was gained? The straightforward tone was common to both audiences, so that is one value that should be explored in rendering the brand identity. Using a masculine voice was interpreted by the doctors as believing that the brand was authoritative, strong, and confident—other values that were actionable in crafting a brand identity.

For my dynamic duo projective exercise, I also separated the 12 doctors into two groups of six. One group broke the rules by selecting a combination that wasn't human: peanut butter and jelly. (That's OK. Open-ended exercises don't create a bias for pre-selected options from which to choose.) They saw our brand and the one with which it would be used together as being equal partners in a satisfying outcome. The other brand was seen as jelly because it was easier to spread (i.e., easier to use), sweet (i.e., patients loved it), and came in different flavors (i.e., dosing forms). Our brand was the peanut butter because it provided a salty alternative to the sweet jelly (i.e., a complementary action to attack the illness) and added a much different texture and binding action to create a 1+1=3 effect.

The other group selected Fred Astaire and Ginger Rogers, with our brand being Fred. They, too, saw the two brands as equal partners in the dance they created together. They, too, admired the two different approaches, in this case, one masculine and one feminine. And while

Avoiding a Brand Identity Crisis in Customer Research

1. **Never demand a pathological diagnosis**

   Healthcare professionals are trained to find something wrong. Where we see a pretty face, they'll see a potentially cancerous mole. Indeed, if they cannot find something wrong, chances are they feel they have failed in some way. They ask, "What's the problem?" not "Is there a problem?" So avoid this natural bias by staying away from questions about your brand that ask them to be critical in a negative way. No brand identity has ever been built on what people don't like about it. Instead, try "What do you like best about these ideas?" This will yield actionable information.

2. **Don't award honorary marketing degrees**

   Do not ask doctors how they would market your brand. Questions like "How would you order the information about our brand?" and "What would you need to know in order to recommend this brand to your colleagues?" The answers? "It doesn't really matter," and "More data," respectively. They are being smug because you've made them uncomfortable. When you go into a restaurant, the chef doesn't come out and ask what kind of cuisine he should be preparing for you. That's his job. If you are a brand director or a branding researcher, don't ask doctors to be marketers. That's your job. Instead, try "Why do you feel that the idea you've selected might also be appealing to your colleagues?" This reveals how peer-to-peer selling might take place.

3. **Don't assume the audience is inside your bubble**

As marketers, your entire day's work is concentrated on your brand. Even your performance review, your bonus, your raise, and your promotion may depend upon your brand's success. Conversely, healthcare professionals and patients alike think about your brand, or the prospect of your brand, for no more than a fraction of their day, if at all. Don't force them into your world and expect anything but pat responses. Instead, get them to invite your brand to join their world. Talk about them, their practices/daily lives, and their joys and concerns. And only then do you let the brand enter that context, where it will be met with the same thoughtfulness and respect that you accorded your research subjects.

4. **Don't presume that because it's being said, it's being owned**

Competitive brand identity assessments fail most often when they are taken at face value, or literally. Communicating a certain set of values in visual and verbal assets doesn't mean that the brand experience *delivers* on these values. For example, in evaluating different brands of skin moisturizers with dermatologists, one brand claimed over and over again that they were the brand with "rejuvenating science." This doesn't mean that customers believe it (or even know what it means). Brands must make a commitment to walk the walk, or customers and the competition will brand them accordingly. Instead ask, "What value did you (the dermatologists) assign to the brand in question?" You have a better chance of getting the insight you wanted, "That's the expensive one." Perception—not a promotional claim—is reality.

5. Don't think in isolation

When branding regulated healthcare entities, such as prescription drugs and hospital products, clients often rely on a staple of market research: the one-on-one interview. Here's the problem: these healthcare brand identities are not consumed on a one-on-one basis. Rather, there are many parties involved—patients, generalists, specialists, nurses, caregivers, etc.—a community that must unify around the brand in order for it to achieve esteem and market share. If a group buys into a brand as a community, then simulate the community in research. Instead of one-on-ones, put together groups of diverse disciplines in the same room and see how they interact when discussing your brand. Any weak link in the chain undermines the brand with the entire community.

they did not see the 1+1=3 effect, they did note that Fred Astaire had danced with a number of partners, but that the magic he made with Ginger was of paragon quality. These examples revealed a number of values for serious consideration: synergistic, elegant, and satisfying.

Let's turn to the topic of research formats, another key area of Discovery where getting it wrong can lead to a brand identity crisis. Many of the common research venues can aid in understanding why customers might see a flattering reflection of themselves in your brand. I've conducted online surveys and one-on-one interviews, as well as done dyads and triads to form mini-groups. However while these venues can be very helpful in flushing out general themes around which to build brands, I wish to highlight two proprietary research formats: Brand Insight Groups and Group Revolutions.

As discussed earlier, brands build a community of belief, so the best formats for gaining customer insights about brand identities simulate the very communities in which the brands will be esteemed. One of the best ways I've developed to do this is through what I call Brand Insight Groups, or BIGs for short. BIGs may look like typical focus groups because they involve eight-to-12 people sitting around a conference table, but that's where the similarity ends. One major difference is that I choose BIG participants based on how they might interact with others where the brand is concerned. For example, hospital brands must reflect the identities of many different professionals: doctors, nurses, hospital pharmacists, department heads, procurement, and so on. Clients will often speak to these diverse disciplines individually, because that's how most focus groups are done for research about messaging, or sales, or other topics where the goal is to uncover important nuances among the different target groups.

Our goal as branding experts is different. We want to distill the values that bind together all parties in the treatment community. By inviting, say, two of each of these different professionals into a single group (Noah's Ark-style), we can simulate the environment where the brand will actually perform and where its unifying values will be discovered by the group as a whole.

In this way, BIGs help us zero in on one or two big unifying values, not the smattering of little ones generated by standard focus groups. BIGs also involve many of the interactive exercises about which I've been writing. For instance, rather than creating a moderator-versus-group dynamic, I divide BIG participants into small groups by either splitting the number in half or by creating dyads and triads. The participants then ideate over a given exercise, presenting their results to the other small groups. This simulates the way they would talk about a brand among themselves, but in a guided exercise that lets us peer into the branding insights behind their interactions.

Another proprietary research methodology I recommend is called a Group Revolution. One hidden and often misunderstood transaction in healthcare branding is the "point of sale"—the dialogue between doctor and patient that results in a prescription, or not. We cannot be present for such a transactional conversation, yet without any insights about this conversational dynamic, we are flying blind when developing a brand identity that might work to unite both parties in a mutually satisfactory transaction. In looking for insights about this transaction, a typical researcher interviews doctors and patients separately, mistakenly believing that in this way they can capture the true doctor-patient dynamic. As we've seen with interview subjects during a brand identity exercise, participants cannot be trusted to volunteer their true feelings. Instead, they give answers that reflect an idealized self.

To help capture a better picture of how doctors and patients converse, and more importantly, the role of the brand in acting as a unifying agent in that conversation, we use a different format that simulates the interaction as it might happen in a doctor's examination room. The proprietary exercise we specifically developed for this purpose we call a Group Revolution. We bring six doctors into a research setting, one-way mirror and all. We talk about the disease or medical condition that our brand treats, get an understanding of how often it comes up in their practice, and then probe about how the conversation proceeds. Here are some of the topics we discuss:

- Who brings up the subject?
- How long does the conversation take?
- Do you use any visual materials in explaining things to your patients? If so, what?
- Do you present brand choices or lead with a specific brand? Why?
- What are the common obstacles to a satisfying conversation?

We then bring the doctors back into the observation room, where they can watch the next group from their hidden position behind the two-way mirror. The next group we bring in are patients (but not the doctors' actual patients) that have the condition our brand treats, which we've been discussing with the doctors. We ask the patients the exact same questions we asked the doctors.

Finally, we bring both groups together around the conference table, pointing out areas of discord and agreement. Additionally, we identify conversational cues that would make the dialogue easier and more satisfying for both parties. These cues can be transferred to the brand so that the brand can serve as a *password* that unlocks conversational doors. I call this a Group Revolution because of the "revolving" parties in and out of the room during the course of the study. This process also happens to be revolutionary, which accounts for why it has become the research technique most "stolen" by other agencies from my intellectual property.

Below is an outcome map from one such Group Revolution. It was conducted for a new implanted blood insulin pump—a device located under the skin, like a pacemaker, that automatically pumps insulin into the body at prescribed intervals, thereby insuring proper compliance. As you might imagine, the idea of having an implanted device both challenged and complemented patients' identities depending on their personalities. The participants were type-II diabetics (i.e., patients who produce insulin naturally but still have high blood sugar) as well as the types of doctors who treat them.

We discovered that there wasn't one doctor-patient conversation in the room, but rather four different types, depending on the disposition of the patient (a.k.a. the patient's Counseling Profile): Seeker, Deliberator, Natural, and Battler. Each of these profiles viewed the doctor as playing a different role in the conversation. For example, Deliberators wanted the doctor to be a mentor to them, while Battlers saw the doctor as a parental figure, admonishing them. Bringing the doctor and patient groups together in the final session allowed us to better understand what types of dialogues work best with the four Counseling Profiles we identified. Results from this Group Revolution research led us to build in brand values that stimulated more productive doctor-patient conversations: compassion, patience and confidence.

PATIENT PROFILE	RELATIONSHIP TO PHYSICIAN	COUNSELING PROFILE
Seeker Adventurous, medium complier wants to avoid limitations to active lifestyle; technophile.	**Trusting and obedient**: sees doctor as authority figure. **Behavior**: Asks doctor, "What's new/what's right?"	Dialogue should be about the brand and its advantages. Time should be spent understanding how the device works to remove obstacles and make therapy "mindless."
Deliberator Cautious, wants all the info before making any decision, wants to research and speak with others in same situation; medium complier.	**Tentative and wary**: sees doctor as mentor. **Behavior**: Asks doctor to outline the pros and cons of different approaches.	Dialogue should be about learning more. Time should be spent understanding best sources to access and a repeat appointment for consideration of therapy.
Natural Sees pump as foreign object that's "in me"; responsible, good complier, likes habit and routine, wants to control own situation.	**Self-realized**: sees doctor as advisor. **Behavior**: Tells doctor about what's important to them. They set the pace of follow up.	Dialogue should be about the best natural process of insulin regulation. Time should be spent understanding how a choice for the pump is an act of personal control as well as proper insulin regulation.
Battler Poor acceptance of responsibility, takes medicine only as a last resort, vain, puts lifestyle and appearance over internal health; poor complier.	**Rebellious and immature**: sees doctor as parent. **Behavior**: Tell doctor about upcoming plans (e.g. marriage/new child). Ask how options will affect them.	Dialogue should be about preserving pleasing aspects of life. Time should be spent understanding how choices impact other life activities and/or may put a burden on friends and family.

In addition to Discovery work that reveals key insights about customer values and how they can be transferred to a brand to create a flattering self-reflection, research is also needed to understand the comparative set of brands and the composition of their identities. I will defer a discussion on this until Chapter 9, where I review best practices for expressing values in design, so that the connection between the research and the resulting visual assets (logo, color, typography, iconography) is clearer.

For now, suffice it to say that in order to avoid an identity crisis, Discovery is best conducted in formats that simulate the role the brand plays/will play in real-world environments. Our goal is not to generate a volume of information, but rather to distill the distinct values important to all parties in the community so that they can be incorporated into the brand. Typical questions about how audiences see the brand (It Beliefs) are worthwhile, but Me and Them Beliefs are the keys to gaining a deeper sense of how a brand can create a flattering reflection of audience values. Asking the right questions (vs. asking every single question under the sun) is the proven way to gain actionable insights—ideas that can be purposefully used in crafting a unique and effective brand identity strategy, the subject of my next chapter.

8

The Goldilocks Process Part 2: Convergence: Avoiding Branding Strategy's Multiple Personality Disorder

It will come as no surprise that if healthcare marketers and their agencies do not understand how to mine customer insights properly, they end up with little actionable information as input for their branding strategy methodologies. However, even given good insights, the great majority of strategic methods employed by healthcare marketers today have hidden flaws that can produce a brand identity crisis.

Go to any agency or any branding company, and they tout their own process for branding strategy. Brand essence. Spike attributes. Brand character. Brand voice. Brand impact. Brand magnetism. Positioning. Brand aspiration. Brand truth. Brand ladder. The Unique Selling Proposition (USP). Brand pyramid. Brand values. In the best cases, the terms given to components of one agency's brand identity strategy are really just a re-naming of the same things in others' strategic models. In the worst cases, some agencies use a handful of the above terms in the same strategic model.

Here's a graphic from the first advertisement my inVentiv Health business unit, Y Brand, used to lampoon this whole mess:

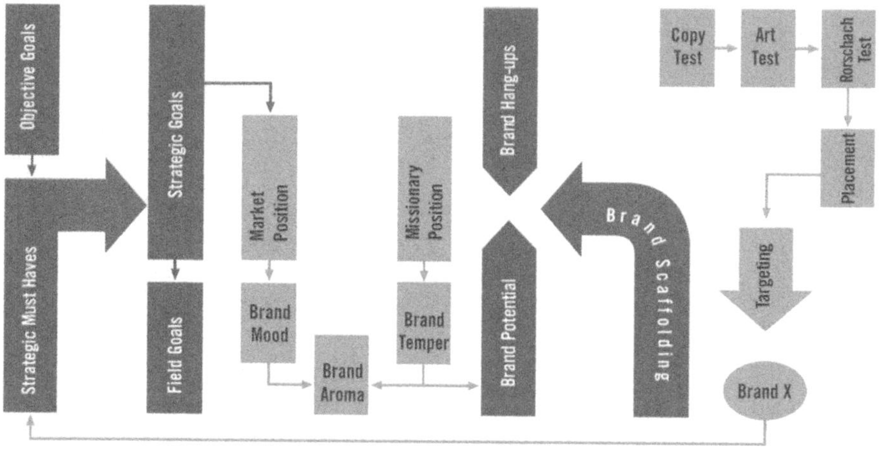

It's a fun piece, but there's a truth behind its humor: too many brand strategy maps resemble the convoluted schematic of how to electrically wire a house. Zoom your eyes out from the page and you can see "Huh?" spelled out. Brand identity crises often occur because the branding strategy processes themselves suffer from multiple personality disorder: they have no idea what they want to be. Yet there's a simple remedy for this disorder that I've been using for decades. Let me illustrate with an analogy about a similar process: the preparation of food to be used in a meal.

Many years ago, I decided to learn how to cook. I took an introductory course called "Knife Skills" at the International Culinary Center (formerly the French Culinary Institute) in New York City. Knife Skills was pretty much what it sounds like. I learned to cut everything from fruits and vegetables to fresh spices to meat to poultry to fish. The course was two hours long. How could one learn every possible way to slice, dice, julienne, fillet, and debone in such a short time? Because there was one way—the best way—to do each of these tasks.

The best way had been defined and refined over the centuries and throughout the world. If you walk into a professional kitchen in

Tokyo, you will see them dice an onion using the same exact technique as their counterparts would in Rome, Barcelona, Chicago, and Prague. You might imagine that over the many decades, innovative souls—inflated with self-confidence—tried a variety of other ways to dice the onion with the suspicion that they, alone, would reveal what thousands and thousands of other chefs had failed to notice. Nope. In the end, there still remains one way to dice an onion quickly, uniformly and without tears. (It involves a series of equal cuts crosswise, lengthwise, and widthwise to produce a perfect, uniform dice and minimize exposure to the onion's acidic gas. Google it, and you'll see.)

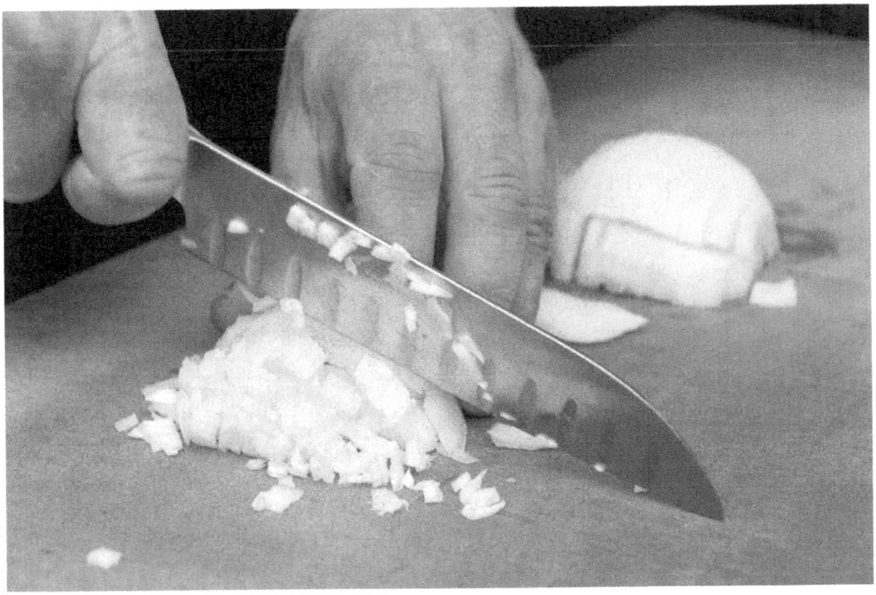

Cooking (promotional tactics) is a creative act. Go crazy. Prepping food to be cooked (branding strategy) is a disciplined, uniform practice that should never be forced to get re-invented. Yet the overwhelming majority of marketers reject such fundamentals, prepping their brands with the inefficiency and confusion that stem from trying to "get creative" with an established foundational practice.

I have led, worked at, and worked with a dozen different agencies over the course of my career. Half of them would change their brand strategy models every couple of years. That's because advertising people excel at constantly inventing new ways to showcase brands in promotion. And they apply this itchy creativity to brand identity strategy because they fear that their clients or their colleagues—or especially themselves—are growing bored with their existing methods. It's like a fashionable man or woman trying on different hairstyles to refresh the way they feel about themselves. The surface may change, but the person remains essentially the same. This is change for change's sake. It may look pretty, but it's a waste of time, not to mention a waste of the client's money if an agency chooses to make them the subject of their little experiments. Branding has evolved into a foundational discipline over the last 50 years. And like the bedrock principles of my Knife Skills class, the elements of a brand identity strategy have been reduced to their simplest, most effective form. Try as they might, agencies and branding companies cannot improve upon this best-practice model.

A BRAND IDENTITY STRATEGY HAS ONLY TWO ELEMENTS:

- BRAND PROMISE: THE COMMITMENT A BRAND MAKES TO CUSTOMERS
- BRAND PERSONALITY: THE TONE AND ATTITUDE WITH WHICH THE PROMISE GETS EXPRESSED OR DELIVERED

These two elements work in concert to establish the cornerstone strategy for the development of imagery and behavior for a brand, summed up in the term "Brand Experience." Let's hypothesize a brand of anxiety medication and see how a proper branding strategy achieves its goals simply and effectively.

- Brand Promise for Brand X: Anxiety relief for your toughest challenges
- Brand Personality for Brand X: Confident, Elegant, and Reassuring

A creative director at an agency asks three writers to each come up with one tag line to patients for Brand X using the above branding strategy. A few hours later, they turn in their results:

1. Brand X: Show anxiety who's boss!
2. Brand X: Live every day on your terms
3. Brand X: Lets you do the best you can

Rather than rely on the "I like it/I don't like it" commentary on full display for a variety of Creative Directors who think such comments are, indeed, "direction," a Creative Director who understands branding strategy would use it to provide an understanding and guidance to his/her staff. It might go something like this:

1. Number one delivers on the Brand Promise (Anxiety relief for your toughest challenges) by implying that no challenge can stand up to a person on Brand X. The Brand Personality (tone) is certainly Confident (even over-confident), but is it Reassuring and Elegant? Direction to the creative team: Needs more work.
2. Number two delivers on the Brand Promise because it asks the customer to imagine a world where no matter what the challenges, they are going to be in control. The Personality of the line is Confident without being cocky; is Reassuring because it promises self-control; and is Elegantly stated as a gentle encouragement to the customer. Nice job.
3. Number three fails on all counts. It doesn't deliver on the Brand Promise because a customer with anxiety is already doing the best

he/she can . . . and not succeeding. The Personality of the line is flat and lacks Confidence, Reassurance, and Elegance. Maybe you should switch to account services.

Try this test for a variety of branding assets other than a tag line, and you will see how simply and easily it works to provide guidance. For example, the client wants to do a consumer TV spot with a voice-over and asks: should the voice over be a man's or a woman's? The voice must be Confident, Reassuring and Elegant, so either gender could provide those tonal qualities. However, with the Brand Promise being "Anxiety relief for your toughest challenges," I would recommend auditioning male voices because of the traditional belief that a deep, bass-y tone might best evoke "toughness." That's not just me talking; that's what the strategy is saying.

The worst Creative Directors I've encountered work backwards from their own egos to the strategy. If they come up with a line or an idea that they feel is "really cool" but off strategy, they'll just re-write the strategy to make the line or idea "on brand." So much for all the time and money the client has invested in it. Why not just throw the dart and draw the target around it? The answer of course is: putting one's ego over the needs of the brand is a sure path to fracturing the careful establishment of a brand's identity. Imagine if every creative person attempted this retrofitting of strategy to creative ideas? Find a brand with an identity crisis, and I'll wager some narcissistic Creative Directors or Brand Managers are responsible.

A BRAND PROMISE ISN'T JUST A STATEMENT. IT'S A TRANSFER OF ENTHUSIASM FOR THE POSSIBILITIES OF WHAT A BRAND CAN BE IN THE MINDS OF CUSTOMERS.

While there is no magical formula for devising a proper branding strategy, there is a proven process for building unity and enthusiasm among a brand team for a Brand Promise and Brand Personality. And if done properly, it doesn't take weeks or months, but rather a single day to get this task accomplished. Not every moderator can promise such a result. There are many, many branding workshops that do not result in an ownable, effective unanimous strategy by day's end. That's not the fault of the concept of a brand strategy workshop, but rather a failure on the part of the moderators who lack the skills to build consensus each step of the way.

Learning which exercises to employ and how to use them could be another book in and of itself. Moderating any workshop, let alone a branding workshop, is a learned skill and requires some basic personal characteristics, the essentials of which are:

- Confidence to speak comfortably in front of a group of strangers;
- Authority of voice and body language so people will follow your leadership without perceiving you as overbearing;
- Bravery to speak "truth to power" (i.e. to challenge powerful executives without upsetting or embarrassing them);
- A fluency with dialogue, especially how to create and sustain discussions; and
- The organizational skills to keep a group on topic and on time.

I have listed at least a half dozen exercises that we use in our workshops, which we gleaned from having worked with two behavioral psychologists. Like many common but non-formalized processes and trades, moderating an effective branding workshop cannot be learned solely from a book. My advice to brand planners is to have a working familiarity with the concept of Behavioral Psychology and to have good mentors. If you have the requisite skills listed above, then you should be able to master the task by watching other, more qualified moderators perform; work your way up by moderating one or two of the exercises in that moderator's workshop; and then go solo with a group no larger than six-to-eight people at first. On-the-job training is essential for moderation excellence.

Taking this discussion to the next level, let's spell out the five best practices for a successful brand strategy workshop:

1. **All hands on deck.** Any stakeholder that will be reviewing and/or producing ideas or materials on the part of the brand must be represented in the workshop by members of that discipline, including but not limited to marketing, agency, sales, clinical, and upper management. Everyone must feel ownership of the day's output or else those who didn't feel included will always question the strategy's validity.
2. **Divide and Conquer.** Split the entire group into smaller groups of 4–7 people, and make certain that no single discipline dominates the small group (i.e., the small groups should have an even mix of marketing, sales, agency, etc. No cliques!). Everyone will get to participate, and no dominant voice can over-influence beyond the confines of their small group—this makes building consensus for a large group easier. That is, getting 21 people to agree on a brand strategy is much easier if you first build consensus among three tables of seven people each. That's just three potential ideas competing instead of 21.
3. **Conduct only exercises that yield practical results.** Exercises may look like games, but they are designed to achieve very specific objectives. The goal of a brand strategy workshop is to distill insights and ideas as you progress so that building a consensus by day's end is achievable. Exercises that expand the number of ideas at each step prevent distillation (i.e., no sticky-note exercises, please). Each exercise should generate a few good ideas for consideration, not

dozens of ideas that make consensus impossible. If you are unsure about whether your exercises will prove actionable, then rehearse with your colleagues and get them to challenge your thinking so you can adjust or discard the exercise.

4. **Show progress as you go**. After each exercise, capture both Brand Promise ideas and Brand Personality traits for consideration so that the workshop attendees see that what might appear to be fun, kiddie projects (looking at you, collage work) actually yield actionable ideas.
5. **Take the subjectivity out of the final decision**. Once again, strategy is an objective discipline (remember the anxiety drug example we discussed above?), not an "I like it/I don't like it" coin toss. If you've followed practices 1–4 in this section, you will have several brand promises from which to choose. Moderate the large group, and have them evaluate each brand promise candidate objectively through my SCORE criteria as follows.

Sustainable: Does the brand have the institutional will and resources to keep driving this promise forward? (Every brand team wants to be Nike, but very few have the funds or institutional will to sustain such an unwavering marketing commitment.)

Credible: Is this brand promise believable in the minds of the customers? (Greatest in the world? Really? People should know when they are expressing a desire for commercial success instead of selecting a Brand Promise that's credible.)

Ownable: Is this a promise that the brand can co-opt to the exclusion of others? (Any brand can try to stake a claim on a Brand Promise, but can you truly "own" it to the exclusion of others in customers' minds?)

Relevant: Is this highly meaningful to all audiences? (Having the most cup-holders in a brand of automobile isn't the real reason why people are buying it.)

Exciting: Is this promise motivational to both internal and external audiences? (A Brand Promise isn't just a statement. It's a transfer of enthusiasm for the possibilities of what a brand can be in the minds of customers.)

Some of the workshop ideas will be based on a Functional Benefit (or Attribute), such as efficacy or a proprietary mechanism of action (MOA); some on a Practical Benefit such as "makes therapy easier to administer," or "saves time and money;" and some on an Emotional Benefit such as "makes me feel I can outsmart the disease," or "elevates my treatment standards." As you can see, the ideas must be simply stated and cogently phrased, but remember: the workshop is not the place to wordsmith by committee. Treat these ideas as "concepts," and let a writer sharpen the phrasing post-consensus. Don't waste time arguing over whether the word "smart" should be "savvy" or "intelligent." You get the idea.

Following the SCORE Criteria exercise, the group will be faced with an objective view of just how strong their ideas are, and which would make a better brand promise. Here is a blinded example:

IDEA	SUSTAINABLE	CREDIBLE	OWNABLE	RELEVANT	EXCITING
FUNCTIONAL IDEA 1	X	XXX	XX	XX	XX
FUNCTIONAL IDEA 2	X	XX	X	XX	XX
PRACTICAL IDEA 1	XX	XXX	X	XX	XX
PRACTICAL IDEA 2	XXX	XXX	XXX	XXX	XXX
PRACTICAL IDEA 3	XX	XXX	X	XX	X
EMOTIONAL IDEA 1	X	XX	X	XX	X
EMOTIONAL IDEA 2	XX	XXX	X	XX	XX
EMOTIONAL IDEA 3	XX	XX	XXX	XX	XXX

As for Brand Personality, the workshop is likely to yield dozens of brand personality traits that the moderator has captured and discussed after each exercise. In order to build consensus, you must again conduct the exercise so that everyone can see and react to each other's decisions. Some people want to lead, other people want to follow, and still others may want to exert their influence in ways that favor their particular agenda. All of this should be out in the open.

The simplest way to build consensus on personality traits is to pass out five stickers to each participant to have them vote on the traits as they please: pick five, place all five stickers on one trait to offset a lack of interest shown by others, put one on one trait and four on another, or any variation in between. The goal is for the group to agree on three-to-five traits. (More than five traits make the personality so diffuse that it can often become unfocused. Less than three traits make the personality so simple that the brand lacks character. Having three-to-five ensures that at any given moment, the brand has the flexibility to deliver one or a few traits, never all. Just like you and me, a brand's personality comes out in different ways in different situations.)

After the voting, you will be pleasantly surprised to see that the group has built consensus around six-to-seven traits that garner way more votes than all the others. I say "pleasantly surprised" because you might expect there to be a dozen or more. Again, by showing progress along the way in the workshop (best practice number four above) you are tacitly simplifying the choices for this final consensus. Here's another surprise: out of the six or seven traits, two or three will be of a kind. Trustworthy, Reliable and Dependable all really mean the same thing. Innovative, Imaginative and Smart can be made to mean the same thing as long as you treat these traits not as words to be smithed, but rather as concepts. A good moderator should be able to whittle down the half dozen traits in 15 minutes or less using these best practices, plus one more.

Not all personality traits are the same. They fall into three groups:

- **Inward-looking traits**: Traits that are about the brand. A brand can claim to be Confident, Strong, and Wise because it has direct influence over these characteristics through words and deeds.

- **Outward-looking traits**: Traits that the brand cannot claim about itself unless others confirm the observations. A brand can claim to be Reassuring, Enlightening, and Helpful, but it cannot become so unless others feel Reassured, Enlightened, or Helped.
- **Forward-looking traits**: Traits that may not immediately manifest themselves in the short term, but will in the long term. Visionary, Liberating, and Empowering are grand traits that may take time to become apparent.

If your workshop attendees are having trouble getting down to three-to-five traits and the other strategies above are not working, try pointing out that the personality is poorly balanced by having too many of any one of the three trait categories. Imagine a Match.com profile, where the eager suitor claims a personality that is Confident, Smart, Worldly, Optimistic, Charming, Clever, Fun and Visionary. He or she is going to come off as a little full of themselves and turn suitors off. Pointing this out to the workshop team quickly gets the number of traits in line with a more realistic and actionable Brand Personality.

How do I—and many other experts like me—know that only two elements of a brand strategy are needed? Because with these two elements—and these two elements only—every aspect of a brand identity can be produced. Any other strategic components are gratuitous—shiny tools without a purpose. A client recently asked me where a Brand Vision fits in the mix. After establishing that a Brand Vision (in their strategic model) was an internal statement assessing how the brand will impact the treatment paradigm, I asked for an example. One was for a pain medication. It went like this: Change the definition of what is mild pain. I asked her how does the "tool" of a Brand Vision enable marketers to create materials for the brand to enhance its identity? Turns out, it doesn't have a function in brand identity development, but rather in motivating the team to realize what the ultimate goal is in being in the pain-medication business. I told her it was a lovely thought but that it seemed to get in the way of the central mission of a brand identity strategy: to create a flattering reflection of customers' self-values in the brand and not a declaration of the brand's worldly aspirations, however noble they are.

As with a knife in knife skills, a branding strategy model is only as effective as its ability to do its specific job. The knife must be sharp (so it cuts effectively) and versatile (so it can be used for a broad variety of cutting tasks). Like a knife, a brand identity strategy doesn't have to be fancy or innovative. The simpler the better. And like a knife, a brand identity strategy model is not an end, but rather a means to an end. It is a tool used by many key brand stakeholders—those who are responsible for delivering tactics or initiatives on the part of the brand: designers, writers, art directors, photographers, and marketing personnel to name just a few. Therefore, the model must be sharp (simple and to the point) and versatile (so it can be used to create any identity for any type of brand). Simplicity and versatility are the only two qualities the model needs to have because that's how people are going to use it to bring the Brand Experience to life visually, verbally, and behaviorally. Yet I am continually flustered to see agencies fuss over their models to the point where it becomes an unwieldy tool that fails to do its job.

Failure here is defined in three ways:

1. Failure to develop a strategy that is grounded in specific customer insights;
2. Failure to forge an effective and ownable strategy that will have impact on the market; and (the greatest one of all)
3. Failure to instill group ownership and enthusiasm of the strategy among the internal marketing team.

Let's take the third one first.

> THE GREATEST OBSTACLE TO A BRAND'S SUCCESS IS A LACK OF INTERNAL CONSENSUS AMONG THE CLIENT'S BRAND TEAM.

If the various constituencies of a brand team cannot agree on the brand's identity across customers and geographies, then customers never will either. Further, lack of agreement among the team inevitably leads to a multiple personality disorder that makes the brand vulnerable to be positioned in the minds of customers by the competition, which are eager to exploit the fractured identity left out in the wild to fend for itself.

When we were working on Lilly's Zyprexa (olanzapine), our team conducted a workshop that forged a consensus that was born out of customer insights and highly differentiating from the competition. At the time, Zyprexa was categorized as an anti-psychotic, indicated to treat schizophrenia and bi-polar disorder (other indications are now part of its label). As you might imagine, these are some of the toughest mental health conditions to live with and treat. They are fraught with potential for violence and suicide, and often render the patient unfit to build relationships or hold jobs. Before the advent of newer anti-psychotics such as Zyprexa, the drugs at psychiatrists' disposal were powerful and crude—basically the equivalent of a medicinal straightjacket (think *One Flew Over the Cuckoo's Nest*). People felt safer around these patients on therapy, but the patients themselves were stupefied. Drugs like Zyprexa could control the symptoms of these diseases and at the same time keep the patients highly functional.

In branding research, psychiatrists described a continuum of challenges ranging from mild symptoms that could be controlled on a daily basis with oral medication to psychotic episodes that required immediate action with an injectable form of the drug for rapid onset. Psychiatrists were extra cautious when treating these types of patients and were seeking a partnership with a therapy that could have their backs in every situation along the continuum. The brand promise developed by the collective client brand team was simply phrased: Zyprexa creates a therapeutic alliance with you for effective management. A promotional excerpt from the resulting campaign is shown below: the "Z" in the Zyprexa logo is seen as a literal support on which the psychiatrist stands as he rescues a patient from the metaphorical dangerous waters of psychosis.

While it may not sound sexy, the strategy had broad implications for how the Zyprexa brand could keep this promise with physicians in highly practical ways (e.g., a variety of dosing forms), as well as service programs (e.g., updates on the latest clinical research in the field). Further, like all good branding strategies, the promise wasn't relevant only to the treating physicians, but also to patients. To patients, an "alliance" meant a therapy that helped them find the new normal, with support programs as supplementation. Every single marketing person on the client team was thrilled at what they had created. The one problem: not a single colleague from sales was in the room.

Pharmaceutical sales forces constitute the front line of physician interaction for a prescription brand. Sales representatives must themselves forge an "alliance" with psychiatrists in order to foster the kind of relationship whereby the physicians feel truly supported and the representatives' brand offerings are genuinely esteemed for their effectiveness. Without their voices being heard on what the brand should stand for, sales management took a different route in delivering the brand experience. They felt that Zyprexa was aggressive control for aggressive conditions. In their sales calls, they focused on the havoc that psychotic disorders wreak on the lives of patients and placed Zyprexa in the role of a fierce warrior, helping psychiatrists win the battle. The tone was urgent, forthright and definitive, versus the confident, nurturing and supportive brand personality of Therapeutic Alliance. Surveys with psychiatrists post-sales calls revealed that the in-person promise for the brand was completely at odds with the promotional materials. Instead of feeling kinship in the struggle with mental disorders, the doctors felt antagonism—all due to a lack of internal consensus among the team charged with delivering a unified idea about the brand identity.

Lilly happens to be a company that is very in touch with the needs of its customers and very competent at changing course when mistakes are made. They quickly re-framed their strategy, this time involving both sales and marketing. The result was a hybrid idea that appealed to all parties and still resonated with what they were hearing in customer research. Both psychiatrists and patients did see the confrontation with psychotic disorders as a battle. But instead of Zyprexa being the warrior leading the charge, it remained their "ally," like a corner man outside the boxing ring, shouting enthusiasm, giving important guidance between rounds, and empowering them to win. On the next page is an excerpt from the resulting promotional campaign that deservedly won creative awards but, more importantly, united the collective brand team and, therefore, also united healthcare professionals and patients around a cohesive brand identity.

I FIGHT FOR MY DIGNITY
Every day I fight.
To be accepted.
To be comfortable.

Lilly

I fight
for one more day with my daughter

Lilly

As you can see, failure to instill group ownership and enthusiasm of the strategy among the internal marketing team caused a brand identity crisis. Lilly saw its error, made the correction, and united its team behind the new strategy.

Now that we've dealt with my third reason that brand strategies fail to foster a meaningful brand identity, let's look at the other two:

1. Failure to develop a strategy that is grounded in specific customer insights; and
2. Failure to forge an effective and ownable strategy that will have impact on the market.

We saw in Chapter 7 how crucial proper customer research is to develop actionable brand insights. Strategies are meaningless without customer relevance. Sounds obvious, but all too often companies conceive marketing strategies without ever doing branding research with customers to understand the values they esteem in their lives or practices.

In 1991, the FDA granted approval for a remarkable new prescription therapy, Neupogen (filgrastim). Neupogen was groundbreaking because it was proven to raise white blood cell counts—the front-line cells in the body responsible for fighting diseases. Neupogen was one of the first blockbuster bioengineered brands. That is, instead of the trial-and-error method used by scientists in building a molecule in a lab using chemical reactions, Neupogen was engineered to integrate with—and normalize—body functions using something called Applied Molecular Genetics, the biotechnology that gave rise to the company that makes Neupogen, Amgen. Put bluntly and simply, during the course of chemotherapy for a variety of cancers, the chemotoxic agents kill cancer cells, but not without also killing off the patient's ability to naturally defend against cancer, its white cell count. Patients often experience neutropenia—a dangerous drop in white cells that exposes the body to life-threatening infections because the white cells are depleted and cannot defend their territory. Oncologists face the dilemma of killing the cancer before the chemo kills their patients. If the patient is deteriorating as a result of the chemotherapy, oncologists are often forced to abandon or postpone the chemotherapy, thereby allowing the cancer to continue to thrive, or they must consider different, less aggressive anti-cancer therapies that may not be as effective. It was a Hobson's choice up until the approval of Neupogen, which reduced the incidence of neutropenia (white cell death) by 38% in clinical trials.

At the time, Amgen—a company in its infancy—was riding high, its stock price soaring well beyond those of large pharmaceutical companies. The scientists and young employees who got in on the ground floor all became millionaires in just a few years. Neupogen flew off the wholesale shelves, earning billions . . . until growth flattened off two years later in 1993. When Amgen put up the brand for review to understand what had gone wrong, I was part of the agency team that won the account, not with flashy creative ads touting the advent of Neupogen, but rather with an idea that was as yet unheard of to the scientists-turned-marketers at Amgen: a branding strategy grounded in customer insights and effectively put into practice in every aspect of the Neupogen brand experience.

Back when biotech companies were first getting started (and even with many new biotech firms today), employees were so mesmerized by the scientific advances they were creating that they often violated the most basic principle of marketing and branding: assuming It Beliefs equated with branding strategy. In their minds, the brand was the star, and everyone should marvel at the brand's merits just as they did. It was all about the science: the gorgeous graphs and tables, and the breakthrough data in avoiding white cell count suppression. The oncologists seemed grateful at first, so what made them become ungrateful?

Unlike some clients, Amgen hadn't done bad branding research. They'd done no branding research at all. Their brand strategy—selling the miracle of Neupogen—was conceived in a vacuum. Oncologists at first flocked to Neupogen like they do to any new drug that offers the promise of greater results in a life-and-death category with no true cure. But greater results was not what Neupogen was promising. Neupogen was promising the magic of Neupogen, and our subsequent Discovery research with customers revealed that Neupogen's brand promise pissed off oncologists in a big way, creating an identity crisis for the brand. Here's a summary of some of the lowlights in the oncologists' points of view:

- Neupogen doesn't do anything to the cancer; it is supportive—like anti-nausea drugs—and not therapeutic at all;
- All the sales representatives care about is selling Neupogen, not taking an interest in my patients and me;
- Every press release seems to focus on the stock price, not cancer; and
- Chemotherapy may be harsh, but it gets the job done. I trust it. Neupogen makes me feel like I'm doing a bad job and hurting my patients with chemo. Chemo is not the enemy, cancer is.

The clients seemed shocked by our Discovery research. More importantly for this chapter, they were scratching their heads, wondering how in the world we could find a strategy that would come from such admonishment. We convened our strategy workshop, inviting participants from clinical research, marketing, sales, and upper management. We put the workshop team through a series of exercises that had them play the roles of oncologist and patient. The goal was to see the value of Neupogen as it fit into their customers' lives and not just their own. We didn't even refer to the benefits of the drug until late in the day, after the workshop team had accepted the object lessons of self-learning: seeing for themselves how it feels to face down cancer and try to beat it with any means possible, however coarse.

The resulting brand promise was simple, powerful, and grounded in customer insights: Put forth your best treatment strategy. It was an imperative, encouraging both oncologists and patients to take the path they feel is best. If they wish to pursue high-dose chemo, then they can do so knowing that, with Neupogen, the course they have chosen won't be interrupted due to neutropenia. Additionally there's a potential issue with a concept called "planned dose on time": a patient must carve out the time needed for regular chemotherapy infusions from an already busy schedule; if patients are forced to diverge from such a schedule, it becomes burdensome. Neupogen will help make sure that therapy is never delayed. Neupogen became chemo's best friend: a behind-the-scenes cheerleader helping it to do its dirty-but-necessary job. And physicians fell in love with the brand all over again. The sales force was re-trained to dialogue with oncologists about their cases and regimens before ever mentioning where Neupogen fit in . . . or not. Amgen sponsored clinical trials for many of the academic physicians conducting original research, providing free drug to test if oncologists could treat even more aggressively with Neupogen in the mix.

Today, the leading biotech companies, including Amgen, are some of the most savvy and admired marketers in the world. And many of their engineered drugs are truly miracles of modern medicine with a very promising future for all of us. But the miracles could never be fully appreciated until the scientists looked up from their microscopes and saw the true purpose of a healthcare branding strategy: being a flattering reflection of their customers' self-values and not a mirror of narcissistic pride in their own achievements, however noteworthy.

Let's turn our attention now to our remaining reason for failure: a failure to forge an effective and ownable strategy that will have impact on the market. What are the root causes of why healthcare branding strategies foster multiple personality disorder for brands? Things begin to fall apart with the very processes used by healthcare marketers and their advertising agencies to create effective and unique strategies. Here are three reasons why:

- Their processes are over-complicated and unwieldy, with so many steps that marketers lose sight of the central goal;
- The outcome of the process—the elements of the branding strategy—are so multidimensional that they send mixed signals that confuse the design choices and promotional tactics that the strategy is supposed to drive; and
- Marketers and agencies reject proven best practices in pursuit of something they can put their fingerprints on out of silly, personal pride (at the expense of the brand)

Such poor executions and behaviors still remain in healthcare branding because strategists on both the client and agency sides of the equation are still using outdated and disproven models to find their answer. If you are old enough or work with people who are old enough, you might have run across an early strategic model called a "brand ladder."

As seen in the illustration, the model suggests a progression from the aspects that make up the product, service, or company (Features and Attributes) to the different Product, Customer, and Emotional benefits, the last of which resides at the top of the ladder labeled the "Highest order of benefits." Forgetting terminology for the moment, the helpful thing about the model is that it recognizes that there are different aspects of how customers can engage with a brand. The big problem that makes the model ineffective as the sole tool to build a branding strategy is this: the metaphor of the ladder implies that the optimum brand identity strategy should always reside on the top rung of the ladder. This isn't always the case.

Brand Ladder Model

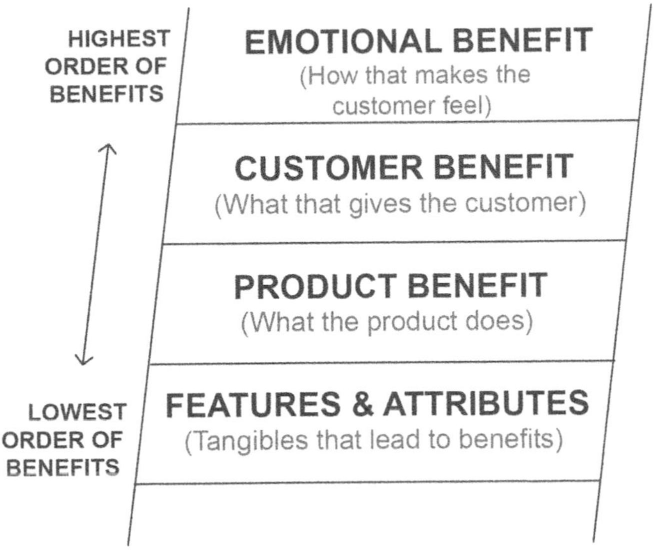

While working on brand identity for the anti-depressant Effexor (venlafaxine), one of the marketing consultants used a brand ladder to argue for an emotional benefit to drive the Effexor identity strategy. At the time, Lilly's Prozac (fluoxetine) was the market leader. Prozac's brand identity strategy was ingenious: Prozac takes depression out of the darkness for a more enlightened solution. Prozac wasn't merely a safer (no addiction potential) and easier (once-daily dosing with no need for titration) anti-depressant. It enabled family doctors to become the front line for treatment and removed the stigma of patients needing to go to a psychiatrist for their mild-to-moderate mood disorders.

Effexor was no such game changer because it wasn't part of the new class to which Prozac belonged (see Chapter 11 for more on this). Pre-launch trials with the drug showed that it was, as its name echoes, highly effective, especially in patients with moderate-to-severe depression.

Rather than use The Goldilocks Process to come up with a workshopped brand strategy, the Effexor brand team was fixated on using only a Brand Ladder to achieve the highest order of benefit, which our Discovery research showed was not credible or ownable with customers. In the end, Effexor did quite well, largely because we were able to convince the brand team that the top rung of the branding ladder isn't always the threshold to success for a brand identity strategy. In fact, the Brand Promise upon which we finally built consensus, "Greater power

Effexor Brand Ladder

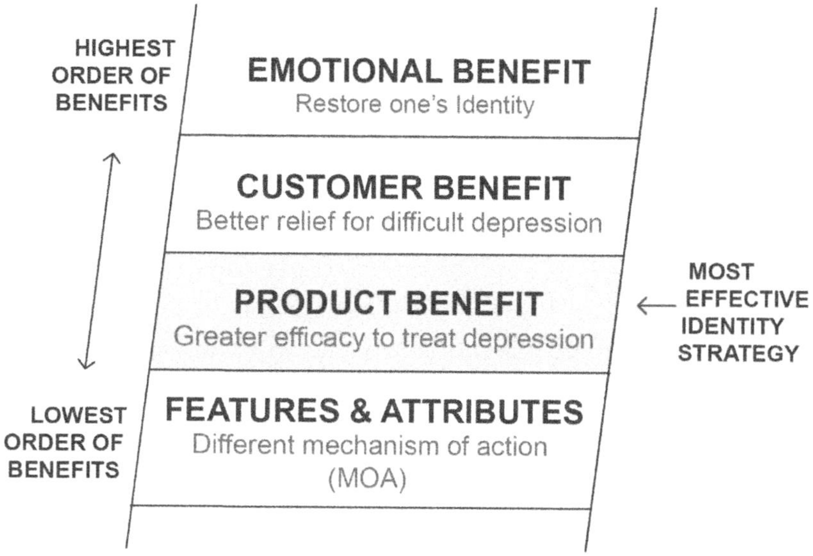

to succeed," is actually derived from the second lowest rung on the brand ladder. If you search the Internet for the Effexor logo (Pfizer denied permission for inclusion in this book) you can see how the strategy also played well off of the brand name and inspired a bold, block letter logo. Additionally, the double-colored X in the name was highlighted to convey Effexor's unique MOA: working on both the serotonin and norepinephrine pathways.

Bottom line, the brand ladder is a flawed model that—when used on its own—can easily induce a brand identity crisis. "Which rung am

I supposed to be on?" In my experience, I've seen clients waste time and money using this model without getting a clear answer to what is best for their brand. Even for something as simple as dental floss, one exercise with a client yielded this brand ladder:

Dental Floss Brand Ladder

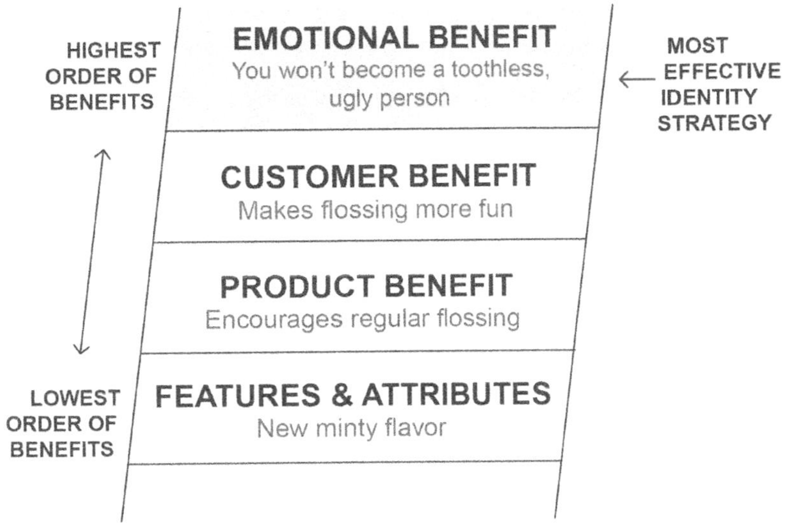

Once again, the model led a brand team astray. Discovery research showed that the dental floss's new mint flavor would simply make flossing more fun, the third rung on the ladder. It was that simple. Not every brand saves the world. No customers realistically associated the simple act of flossing with their teeth falling out and becoming a toothless ugly person. Try this out with any brand, no matter how trivial. The top rung of the ladder always results in something on the order of less fear of death or preservation of the species. You get the point.

Like the brand ladder, the brand pyramid is another widely used model that appears to be a good idea but misleads those who trust in its results. If you Google "brand pyramid," you will see about two dozen versions of it, some more complicated than others. (That should be a sign that it is a flawed model: there are too many conflicting versions.) Here are two examples:

Brand Pyramid

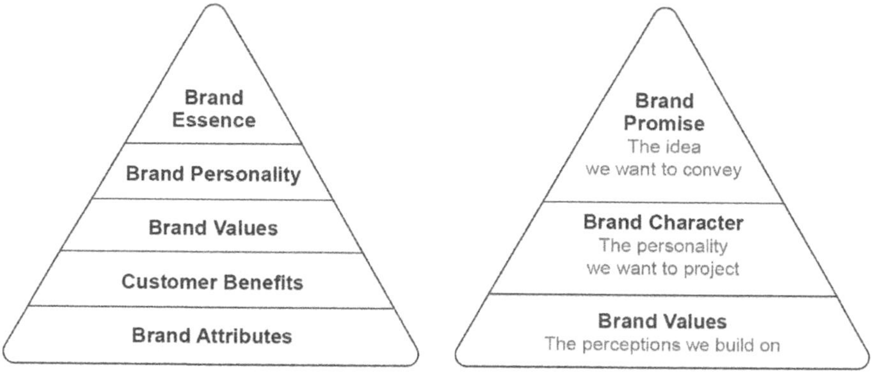

Unlike the metaphor of a brand ladder, the metaphor of a pyramid suggests that there are foundational elements supporting each layer above, with the top of the pyramid containing the one big idea that constitutes the brand identity strategy (Brand Essence and Brand Promise, respectively, in our two examples.)

The pyramid on the left suffers from having too many confusing levels. As in the brand ladder, Brand Attributes lead into Customer Benefits. Then we have the curiosity of Brand Values leading into Brand Personality, in turn leading into Brand Essence. Midway in the model, the metaphor switches, creating confusion on what to do with this information. What are Brand Values? How are they different than Brand Personality? Does Brand Personality support Brand Essence, or are they all individual parts unrelated to each other in a hierarchical way?

In my role as a Chief Creative Officer during the middle part of my career, I would sometimes be handed strategic documents such as the brand ladder and brand pyramids above and told to go create promotional concepts from them. My question was always the same: Which one should I pay attention to? When the answer came back frequently,

"All of them," it left me shaking my head. Implementing all of these strategies would obviously elicit multiple personality disorder in the form of too many different choices on what the brand aspired to be. Whether this was due to the suspicion that the marketing team couldn't make up their minds, or that "complicated" signified "rigorous" to them, or that they wanted to keep it vague so only they could then say that our resulting ideas were on strategy or not, their entire approach constituted a Rube Goldberg process for a very singular task. If you don't recall Rube Goldberg's unnecessarily complex machines, they involved a series of pulleys and levers and balls and mechanics to achieve a goal that was patently obvious and achievable in one small step. Below, you can see Mr. Goldberg's "Simple Alarm Clock," which of course, is everything but simple.

Simple Alarm Clock

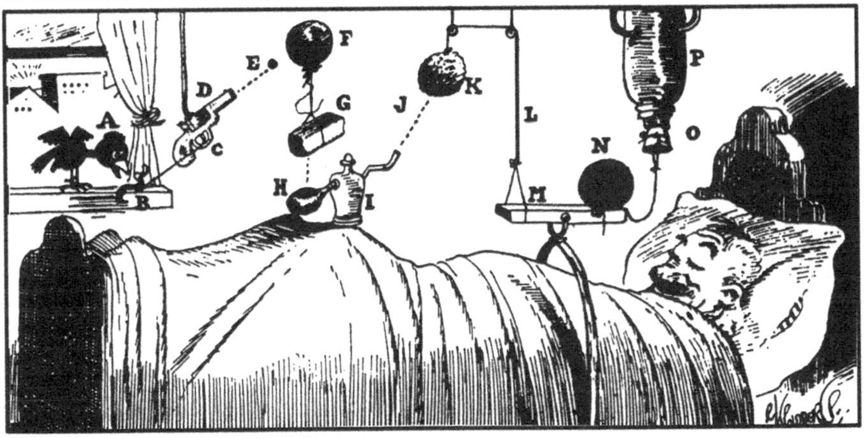

The early bird (**A**) arrives and catches worm (**B**), pulling string (**C**) and shooting off pistol (**D**). Bullet (**E**) busts balloon (**F**), dropping brick (**G**) on bulb (**H**) of atomizer (**I**) and shooting perfume (**J**) on sponge (**K**)–As sponge gains in weight, it lowers itself and pulls string (**L**), raising end of board (**M**)–Cannon ball (**N**) drops on nose of sleeping gentleman–String tied to cannon ball releases cork (**O**) of vacuum bottle (**P**) and ice water falls on sleeper's face to assist the cannon ball in its good work.

So, why do healthcare clients insist on an over-engineered brand identity strategy that precipitates identity crises, instead of the simple, elegant two-part model proven over decades? My guess is that it's in their nature. That is, healthcare clients are highly rational people who work in a life-and-death field where the very products they sell are rigorously tested in multiple trials with diverse populations to make sure that they haven't overlooked anything that could go wrong. When the focus is trying to prevent something from going wrong rather than focusing on trying to get things right, the inevitable result is an over-engineered process. They simply don't trust simplicity.

In the same way I'm often forced to prove to new clients that asking doctors to reveal things about themselves won't upset the doctors, I find that I must also validate the tactical outcomes for other successful brands in order to gain a client's trust in the simplicity and elegance of the two-part brand identity strategy. You'll undoubtedly run into this kind of resistance yourself, but stay the course and use the examples I've revealed in this book—a two-part brand identity strategy is the one sure path to effective results.

This leads us to the subject of my next chapter on how strategy directly impacts the visual and verbal assets of a healthcare brand.

9

The Goldilocks Process Part 3: Brand Experience Design: Dressing For the Job Your Brand Really Wants

This chapter deals with the third and final part of The Goldilocks Process, Brand Experience Design, the area of brand identity that agencies and clients often equate with Brand Identity itself: the primary design hallmarks—logo (or brand mark), color palette, iconography, typography—and the secondary branding system that brings together the whole outfit so that it is flexible and uniquely expresses the image the brand seeks to put forth. But before we go any further, let's get one thing straight: a logo is a tactic; a visual expression of a brand's identity, not to be confused with the brand identity itself. This may sound semantically trivial, but deeming a brand's logo or ad campaign to be its brand identity is a widespread misconception and another one of the main hidden causes of brand identity crises, especially in healthcare (more on this in a moment).

A logo and its appointed elements mean absolutely nothing by themselves, just as a closet full of clothes means nothing by itself. Identity is more than letters and colors and shapes. Identity is—as stated in the last chapter—the sum total of a unique set of values expressed by a Brand Promise and a Brand Personality, and delivered in a Brand Experience. And the role of branding hallmarks is to signal a brand's intentions—its claim to an image and identity to which it aspires. Over time, a brand's identity comes to mean the composite of what the brand says, does, and how it behaves (the Brand Experience). One can design a logo that projects the aspiration of Power or Reassurance, for example. But unless customers come to believe that the brand is powerful or reassuring, then the logo is just a sad reminder of a failed brand identity—an irony that's all dressed up with no place to go.

> A LOGO IS A TACTIC—A VISUAL EXPRESSION OF A BRAND'S IDENTITY, AND NOT THE IDENTITY ITSELF.

A logo is a fairly empty banner that, over time, will come to signify all the values of the Brand Experience not by virtue of them being crammed into the design, but rather by signifying its unique presence to the citizens who salute the values it has demonstrated through action. The role of a logo, therefore, is to act as a flag does for a country or official entity.

Like a flag, a logo should be simple so it can peacefully co-exist with the flamboyance of other branding assets and activities and absorb the values of the brand's behavior and performance over time. And it should be able to stand out next to other logos. (The French flag's colors have long been associated with French royalty. But the simplicity of design enables it to absorb other aspects of France's identity, such as the three guiding principles of the French Revolution: liberty, equality and fraternity.)

It should communicate a few key brand values, but not be overburdened by them. (The Japanese flag is intended to honor the role that the sun has played throughout Japan's history. Some argue that the symbol acclaims the primacy of its people, with the bare elegance of the red sun rising on its citizens first among all countries.)

It cannot be so literal that it can be construed as a therapeutic claim. (People often mistake the Swiss flag with that of an ambulance or hospital, signifying first aid.)

Unfortunately, many clients in healthcare ignore these elemental principles and instead prefer to have the logo shout and scream as much as possible.

[THE MOST COMMON IDENTITY CRISIS SYMPTOM IN HEALTHCARE LOGO DESIGN IS OVER-DESIGN.]

There's just too much going on, and design ultimately clashes with the qualities of the entity for which the flag is supposed to make room. Let's illustrate with one of the most over-designed flags in the world, the Stars and Stripes.

Here's what our founding branders intended: the strategy was "unity," a brilliantly simple brand promise that was then completely over-designed. There are the stars that represent the United States (a flawed design premise that forced the flag to be re-designed 26 times as new states joined the union), and the stripes that represent the original 13 British colonies. So far so good. We are still on the strategy of unity. There is deep blue for authority and legitimacy (the American flag has blue in common in British and French flags, two super-powers at the time), red for the blood that was spilled in pursuit of independence (we're straying pretty far from unity now), and white for the purity of the founders' intent (so now it's about purity?).

But what identity do people see when our flag is displayed? Unity? In these days of red and blue states, that's probably the opposite of what many people believe about America's brand. The most frequent answer among our citizens would arguably be Freedom, yet there is nothing in the current design that reflects this value (indeed, it's a pretty regimented design). Why? Because as I've argued above, the Brand Experience—the composite total of our country's actions toward its citizens and the people of the world—defines the brand, not the design intentions of its flag. As you can see in the following illustrations, this discrepancy gets played out in innumerable parodies, depending on how the individual sees the United States' brand identity.

Top and bottom left: the flag is draped around an attacking eagle, our national bird, signifying America's military might, which is echoed in the stealth bomber flag below. Middle top and bottom: the states' stars are replaced either by corporate logos (suggesting that our capitalism is what defines us), the President (the values of the party that's in power), or a shining beacon of freedom when paired with the Statue of Liberty. Right top and bottom: finally the flag can become a symbol of how we usurped and "stole" the country from native Americans, or an icon of romanticized patriotism for the cowboys that helped make it happen.

So if you are participating in an identity exploration, remember this first principle: the brand is less about appearances and more about actions, so let the logo play the unadorned, distinguishing role it can gracefully play, and then make sure your brand lives up to its simplest, most noble intentions with how it behaves. You are designing a flag to represent an identity, not a movie to tell its life story.

Everyone in healthcare marketing (and many more who are not) is comfortable discussing promotional tactics such as ads, online activities, and TV commercials. We are exposed to these media every day, and there are even columnists who critique and help us build our promotional literacy. Not so for discussions about logo selection. Very rarely do healthcare marketers get a chance to launch a brand identity. And since most people do not "speak logo," a logo presentation usually results in a brand team staring in silence, afraid to say anything that would make them feel diminished. Often, the dialogue devolves into what people "like" or "don't like," or what the logos remind them of, all of which would be fine if those preferences related to some strategic insight and not just to someone's preference for, say, purple, or their hatred of "swooshes."

This is normal. Learning a vocabulary and grammar about logos is not unlike learning Spanish or Chinese. It requires a willingness to expand one's horizons, educational opportunities and continued study. What follows are the top five best practices for learning about and discussing logos in a meaningful way. They don't cover every situation, but they are enough to get you on your way to fluency. If you are part of a marketing team and are in the process of creating a brand identity or refreshing an existing identity, it might be a good idea to copy this out and share it with your colleagues so that you are all, literally, on the same page.

How to speak Logo

1. **Know your logo anatomy**. As with learning any foreign language, the first step is to understand what things are called. See the illustrations below.

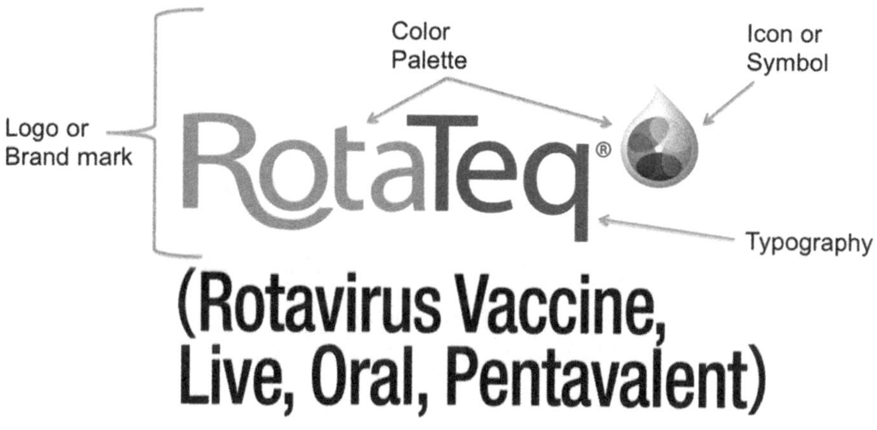

The basic components of this logo (or brand mark, as designers call it) are three-fold:

A. The brand name rendered in distinctive typography;
B. A symbol or icon; and
C. A color palette.

Here the symbol (a droplet) is representational: RotaTeq is an oral liquid vaccine for babies. (Often, the symbol is abstract, like a shape or a swoosh or some other graphic flourish to avoid making an overt claim.) RotaTeq is a vaccine for babies indicated to prevent the five most common strains of rotavirus, signified by the five different colors inside the droplet that form a pentagon shape at the hub: yellow, yellow-green, purple, blue, and teal. In conjunction with the dove gray of the "Rota" prefix, these colors constitute the Color Palette of the brand. The typography is customized for strategic reasons, which we'll get into in the next section. Taken together, these elements constitute what we call the logo. Further, the illustration is an example of a "logo lockup," meaning that the exact, relative proportions of the elements are fixed. The illustration above is called a horizontal lockup and is used in vertically narrow spaces. The illustration below is called a vertical lockup and is used in horizontally narrow spaces.

There are many different kinds of logos, but the formats that are most often used in healthcare are:

A. An Icon Mark—as in the RotaTeq example above—a brand name in distinctive typography that's accompanied by a symbol or icon as part of its lockup;
B. A Word Mark like the Lilly logo example below left, which does not use an icon; and
C. A Holding Shape like the Roche logo example below right, which has a geometric area in which the typography and color reside.

These three logos demonstrate proper respect for design elements and a good appreciation of the role of the logo as discussed above. A good branding expert can help you find the proper logo elements for your brand.

The color palette, as the name suggests, features approved colors for marketers and designers to use when creating promotional tactics (every color in the palette is not necessarily used in the logo). Some brands have many colors in their palette (e.g., RotaTeq); some have two or three; while others use only one (Lilly and Roche). (I'll take up color more thoroughly later on in this chapter.)

2. **Use the branding strategy as your north star**. Decisions about type, color, and icons are neither subjective nor accidental. As discussed in the previous chapter, they derive from a very specific branding strategy that has two components: the Brand

Promise—the promise the brand makes to customers—and the Brand Personality—the tone and style in which the promise gets delivered. For the RotaTeq logo, the Brand Promise is "Rest Assured," and the primary Brand Personality traits are Authoritative and Nurturing. You can see Authority in the plum (the color of royalty), and Nurturing in the dove gray. Nurturing is also brought out in the typography, as the initial capital "R" cradles the "O" like a mother holding a baby. As you can see, there's both a science and an art to converting brand identity strategy into design, but that's a topic for another book.

3. **ABC (Always Be Constructive)**. Start out any critique with what you like. This keeps the conversation on an upbeat note so that it doesn't become a Grinch session. By talking about what you don't like, you are not helping yourself or anyone arrive at a useful direction. Ever been with a friend when you are trying to figure out where to go to dinner and they say, "Well, I don't like Italian or French or Chinese food?" Big help, right? By starting out with what you like, others can join in your enthusiasm, and before you know it, you've picked a logo about which everyone is happy.

4. **Presume wise intentions**. Good designers know what they are doing, and they know more than you or me why they rendered a logo in one way versus another. Ask questions that help focus the designer and others on what your specific preferences or concerns are. "What's your thinking about the relative sizes of the logo type and symbol?" or "What's the reason behind not using crimson in the logo?" are good types of questions with which to start. The answers may prove very enlightening. (I've been doing this for decades and I continue to learn how to view the intentions behind logos more clearly.)

5. **Be part of the solution**. If you are going to criticize an idea, always contribute a way to make it better. "I like the symbol in logo concept number three, but I'm not crazy about the logo font. Can you explore different logo fonts that are still on strategy?" Criticism alone carves you out of the process—makes you an observer, not a participant. Do your part in helping to birth a wonderful idea or improve on an existing one.

With your newly found fluency, you may not speak Logo often, but when you do, you'll look and feel like a natural. And unlike French or German, you don't have to worry about nailing the accent.

Earlier in this chapter, I alluded to the reality that healthcare marketers are especially prone to asking for and approving logos that are over-designed. This has to do, in part, with the nature of when logo development begins for pharmaceutical or biotech brands. Unlike consumer goods brands, where the time to market launch is dependent on the marketer's abilities and resources, regulated healthcare brands are at the mercy of their own regulatory timetables and those of the FDA (USA) or EMEA (EU), which are out of the hands of the marketer. It routinely takes about three years between the time a drug enters its Phase III trials (final drug trials with fixed doses and efficacy/safety goals in humans), submits a new drug application (NDA), and then waits for the authorities to approve it for use. If you are in a brand director's role for a regulated healthcare product, you know that packaging is one of your earliest deadlines because of the long lead time required for producing and vetting government-sanctioned packaging. And if packaging is needed, then a logo is needed. Can you imagine naming a baby and selecting its outfits three years before it comes into the world? It puts undue pressure on the brand team and its branding agency to envision their baby's entire life based on a Brand Promise and a Brand Personality. Despite the absolute fact that these are the only two aspects one needs to develop a logo, some brand teams panic and feel that much, much more is called for. Let's look at the dynamic and some serious identity crises that can and do ensue.

Before a brand comes to market—before it has had a chance to deliver a Brand Experience through usage, marketing, and other forms of customer engagement—it has no value in and of itself. It will develop its values and equity through a comprehensive delivery of its Brand Experience once launched. There will be promotional and public relations campaigns, sales efforts and convention hoopla, speaker programs, and clinical trial presentations—all touting its uniqueness, superiority, and essential place in customers' lives. All the hopes the manufacturer has for its success in the market will be in play and hinge on this collective Brand Experience. Millions of dollars and years of development are on the line.

What happens in this dynamic? The crushing weight of all those hopes and expectations cited above—all the financial pressures, all the career plans—suddenly come crashing down on the feeble shoulders of a handful of letters, a symbol, and some colors. Despite the obvious impossibility of a logo being able to bear the burden of so many expectations, the marketing and agency teams often get so caught up in the frenzy that it blinds them to the more reasonable, experienced approach discussed above in this chapter. (While working on the logo of what would become one of the biggest pharmaceutical blockbusters of all time, Lipitor (atorvastatin), I had the client say to me and our team: "I just saw that *Mission Impossible* movie with Tom Cruise. I want our logo to feel like that!" Mission Impossible indeed.)

There are three common ways that brand teams default into bad behavior and produce an identity crisis when expectations overheat:

1. The client triples down on the strategy in the logo with over-designed results;

2. The client pays too much attention to the competition and forgets about its own strategy; or
3. The client ignores the branding strategy and focuses on some aspect of the brand that's more relevant to them than their customers.

Let's take them one at a time. One winner of the "Too Much Going On" award is Toprol-XL (metoprolol succinate), a very good drug used to treat hypertension and angina. Evaluating Toprol's logo above, we can conclude that the Brand Promise is 24-hour protection for hypertension and angina; the Brand Personality is Straightforward, Powerful and Friendly. The all-cap, black serif typography is an excellent and simple start to communicating Powerful. And it is common knowledge that the suffix, XL, usually means 24-hour (extra long) action in drug vernacular, thus making it fairly easy to deliver on the Brand Promise. Good logo, right?

Not so fast. With XL already in the logo, how do we explain the client's need to add the icon of a moon/sun to show that the drug lasts a full 24 hours? They've doubled down on the Brand Promise. Further—just in case you didn't get the point—they've added ONCE-A-DAY in all caps italic confirming once again that this brand is hard at work, all day and night. A rare triple-down on the Brand Promise. Not content to stop there, they put a square holding shape around the moon/sun icon like a tent on a circus, to what purpose I cannot say. This logo makes so much visual noise on a page that it outshouts the promotional concept that's trying to endorse it, creating an identity crisis that would have been easily prevented by adhering to the methods in this book.

Next, here's what can happen when the focus is too much on the competition and not enough on one's own branding strategy. The "I'll Have What He's Having" award goes to a mammoth hyperlipidemia therapy, Crestor (rosuvastatin), which came to market right after Lipitor. In pop music, the story goes that after Paul McCartney heard Pete Townsend's loud, raucous anthem *I Can See For Miles*, it compelled him to top that in gross overstatement, so Sir Paul wrote *Helter Skelter*. Crestor is hyperlipidemia's *Helter Skelter*. From the two logo illustrations above, we can see that Lipitor had fat, italic upper and lower case letters. Crestor topped that with all-cap typography. Lipitor was elegant teal, so Crestor went royal blue and Seville orange—colors so contrasting that our eyes vibrate trying to take in this optical assault. Lipitor had what are called the "lumen rings" icon, signifying clear arteries. Crestor dropped in a 40-ton icon that's half "sun cresting" and half "rest-room symbol cheering." It's brash, like Bozo the Clown, trying too hard to out-Lipitor Lipitor and embarrassing itself. Its Brand Promise? A bigger, better Lipitor. While sales were robust for Crestor, it never caught up to Lipitor's market share while the latter was still under patent. The old golf adage sums it up nicely: Don't play the competition; play the ball.

Lastly, the "Logo Sandwich" award goes to Caduet (amlodipine besylate/atorvastatin), a very effective combination agent that works on the reduction of hypertension and cholesterol respectively. (Please search for the Caduet logo online as Pfizer did not grant permission to reproduce it in this book.) The practice of graphically highlighting two different medications delivered in one agent is quite common in healthcare logo design as fixed-dose combinations become more prevalent. However, you will see that, in the Caduet logo, the mouthful of generic and dosing information—centered, to boot—compels the two red symbols above and below the logo and generic type to digest it like a giant set of lips chomping down on all the typography. The icon itself, conscripted to tell a "combination" story breaks into two parts rather than one integrated whole, thereby leaving the original strategic intent of "two-in-one" unfulfilled. This is an example where design is being shoe-horned into a strategy that may be vitally important to the marketers at the expense of being incommunicative to customers.

All of the above design failures—over-design, clunky design, and tortured design—are evidence that no cohesive branding strategy was faithfully guiding the design choices. Rather, the impetus for the designs came from putting too many expectations on the logo to tell the entire marketing story (Toprol-XL), or keeping one's eye on the competition instead of the ball (Crestor), or losing sight of design best practices by over-focusing on a strategic mandate that ended up blurring itself out (Caduet).

Aside from typography and iconography, decisions about color should also closely adhere to the brand strategy, especially the Brand Personality. But clients and agencies often treat color choice as an afterthought, or, worse, make color decisions without any link to the brand strategy at all. That's right: color is the first aspect the eye sees, but it is the Rodney Dangerfield of branding hallmarks—it gets no respect compared to typography and iconography in the development of healthcare brands. True, some healthcare marketers honor the role that colors play in brand building. But they are the exception rather than the rule. When it comes to a brand's color palette, a design element consumer marketers study and exploit with great care, healthcare marketers make only a token effort, one usually uninformed by the thousands of pages that have been written on color psychology. Why is that?

In all fairness, many of the pages written on color are goofy takes on the subject, doling out blatantly obvious observations that red is the color of passion or green the color of renewal. It's not so much that this is untrue, but rather that such reductivism isn't helpful or insightful. There is no red or green; there are thousands of reds and greens and other hues, of course. Just take a tour of the lipstick counter at Sephora or the swatches at a Benjamin Moore store and you'll get dizzy from all the options.

However, even considering the bad press out there, many healthcare marketers—and worse, their agency creatives—often try to come up with their own theory about color as if previous science on the subject hasn't existed for decades. In a recent analysis of healthcare branding, I asked the art director of an ad agency how she came up with the color palette for an antiviral vaccine. She said, "I took all the colors that the competition uses, eliminated them, and then chose from what was left over." (She is not alone in applying this "process.") The logotype was a bright orange, and the icon was rendered in lime green. Instead of a serious medicine, the brand looked like a Hi-C juice box. (And who can read orange type when it reduces?)

Imagine if a restaurant chef selected his/her menu items using this same approach—eliminating what everyone else was serving and then selecting from what was left over. You'd dine on Pancreas Tartar, Squirrel Chowder and Fricassee of Hen Wattle (OK, this last one may be a French delicacy, but still).

While this chapter cannot cover the body of learning on color psychology and color theory (please, people, go read *Pantone Guide to*

Communicating with Color!), here are the top five guidelines for honoring the role that color plays in branding:

1. **Color is informed by the branding strategy, not someone's spouse**. Tiffany, the retail brand, doesn't use its distinctive robin's-egg blue just because no one else does. It's intended to convey what color psychology has established as the following personality traits: elegant, hopeful, pure and cherished. Over the years, as the brand experience gained momentum like a snowball down a mountain, the color grew to mean luxurious and uncompromising as well. These are objective truths that can often elude healthcare marketers and their agencies. Never accept a color recommendation for your brand if it isn't objective (e.g., just because it's what the brand manager's spouse likes).

2. **Color in branding should be branded**. Stop using generic terms like yellow or green when evaluating color options. It dumbs down the dialogue and over-simplifies the complexity involved in selecting the right colors for your brand. Instead of presenting the branding colors for Propecia (finasteride), a hair-loss therapeutic identity on which I worked, as gray and blue-green, we proposed flannel and Caribbean. This was inspired by the branding strategy: a treatment for men that's as professional as a gray flannel suit and as serene and tranquil as a Caribbean pool. If this seems silly to you, consider this: one of the colors we proposed for the anti-depressant Effexor was an uplifting yellow. The brand director responded: "Yellow is the color of fear, and we cannot base our brand strategy on fear." We came back and presented the same color a week later, only, this time, we branded it as "marigold." "That's much, much better," said the same brand director. Still have doubts? Which lipstick do you believe will sell better: dark red or Vampire State Building?

3. **There is no "I" in color**. While my first two guidelines discussed individual colors for the sake of making my respective points, brand color habits in healthcare rarely trend to one color, but rather to a proprietary set of colors. (Nexium, the "purple pill," actually uses quite a lot of yellow in its palette. Ironically, it is a capsule and not a pill at all.) As we discussed before, this set of colors is called a color palette. In addition to having the primary colors that evoke the personality traits of the brand strategy, secondary or accent colors help customize how the brand appears on a surface (online, in print, on packaging, etc.) and can make the primary colors more expressive or muted. The reason? When juxtaposing colors, we see the individual colors differently than if they were isolated. Take a look at the illustration below. Thc red is exactly the same color on each background.

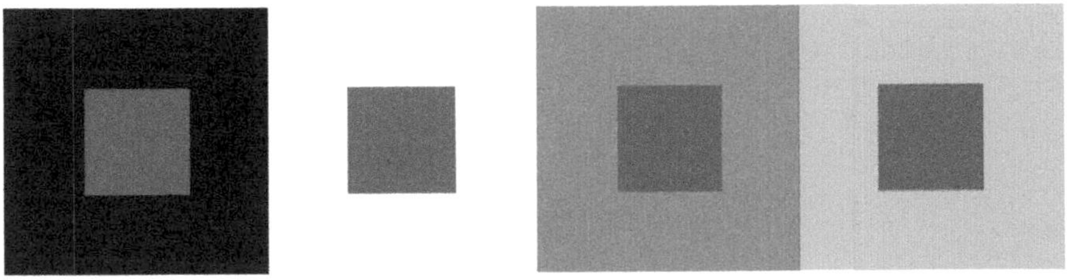

Against the black background, red pops more than it does when underlain with white. The red square also seems larger than it does on black than on the other color backgrounds. Surrounded by orange, and creating a low-contrast combination, red appears anemic. But red glows like a hot coal over blue. So avoid the conversational trap of "the competition owns blue" and come back with: "The competition uses a Windex blue always in combination with candy-apple red; we can own indigo and Lamborghini yellow."

4. **Black and white are colors, too**. And so are the 50 shades of gray in between. According to *Forbes Magazine*, the top three

best-selling colors for new cars are white, black, and silver (a sort of gray). Yet they get overlooked in healthcare. How many black healthcare brands can you recall? I know, I know. Black is the color of death, and we cannot have death as a brand identity. But black is also the color of tuxedoes and women's favorite little dress. And when paired with the right secondary color(s), black can be classic, sleek, and sophisticated, as rendered here in the Omacor identity.

OMACOR
Omega-3-acid ethyl esters

The same goes for white. Yes, white is the color of death in some cultures and in others evokes drained passion ("blood") from a romance. But look at how white and red make each other irresistibly watchable in this execution for Target.

If black and white scare you too much, then seek the refined presence of the grays. When you see gray alone, you may get "dull, drab, dispassion." But again, combine a soft dove gray with red or even yellow, and the results can be Authoritative, Inspiring, and Stately.

5. **There is such a thing as too many colors**. While there is no hard, fast rule on how many colors are too many, let common sense be your guide. Many colors hold the risk of making the palette difficult to manage when different vendors try to apply the brand guidelines, thereby threatening the integrity of the brand's

proprietary appearance. Further, many colors could prove to be a production nightmare when trying to match the exact color formulas in different venues. However, if one wishes to own a multi-colored palette, then one must commit to truly owning it, just as the fashion designer, Paul Smith, has done so memorably.

If you feel that a two- or three-color palette may limit the display of your brand's personality, then don't add another color; add different densities (or shades) of the existing colors, as shown below.

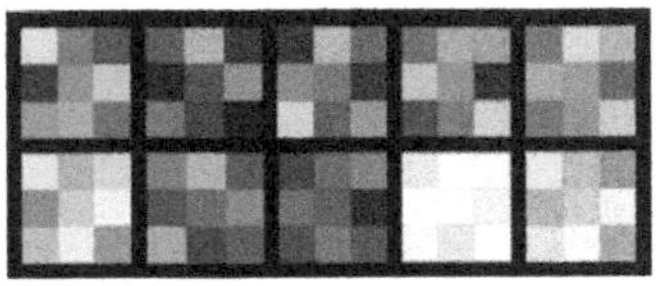

Each color in the palette may have two or more related shades that keep color on strategy and cohesive, yet offer flexibility when creating well-branded materials.

Again, use common sense: avoid the embarrassment of the "yellow is the color of fear" kind of comments I've mentioned above. Colors do not have absolute values, but rather a host of nuances. Concerns that red means stop, so people will quit reading; or sanitation uniforms are green, so people will think the brand is garbage; or purple equates your brand with Barney the Dinosaur are usually just irrational fears. This kind of talk takes a rich, fruitful exploration of how color can differentiate and deliver on the brand strategy and reduces it to the lowest denominator of human perception. And that just makes me blue.

Up until now I've restricted my comments to the primary branding hallmarks, but there are secondary hallmarks in a comprehensive system that are essential to your brand in graphic design. Holding shapes, rules, patterns, and other visual assets lend a proprietary look and feel that go beyond a mere logo. This gets back to the subject matter in Chapter 2: a logo is not a brand identity. Many agencies slap a logo on one of their concepts and feel that they've checked the box on making sure that concept has advanced the brand's identity. But one should be able to put one's thumb over a logo and still know the brand that is behind the promotional concept. See the illustration below for a well-branded look and feel using secondary elements and a branding system for Saflutan (tafluprost), a liquid glaucoma medication.

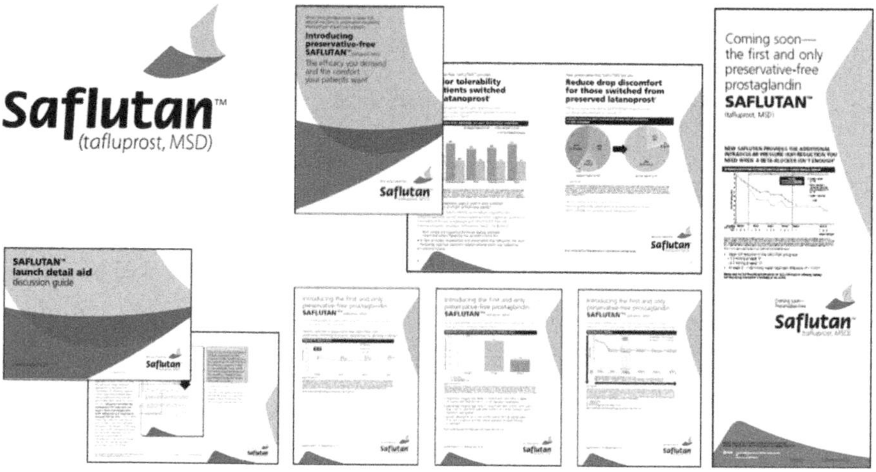

Even the charts have a consistent and proprietary appearance that tacitly reinforces the connection between the brand's data and the brand's visual identity. Without such secondary elements of a branding system in place, the brand identity erodes over time and enters into an identity crisis, where customers notice the promotion but do not give due credit to the specific brand.

The same is true for virtual brands: technologies that exist in the palm of your hand or on tablets and iPads. Here the need is to provide a branded look that flows with the navigation of an app or the delivery of a service. For Vree Health, a patient outcome technology licensed to hospitals, pharmacies, nursing homes, and private practices, we created branded icons and data displays so that even when a third party is using the technology, customers can see the fingerprints of the technology brand and know the values that such a brand brings to the initiative.

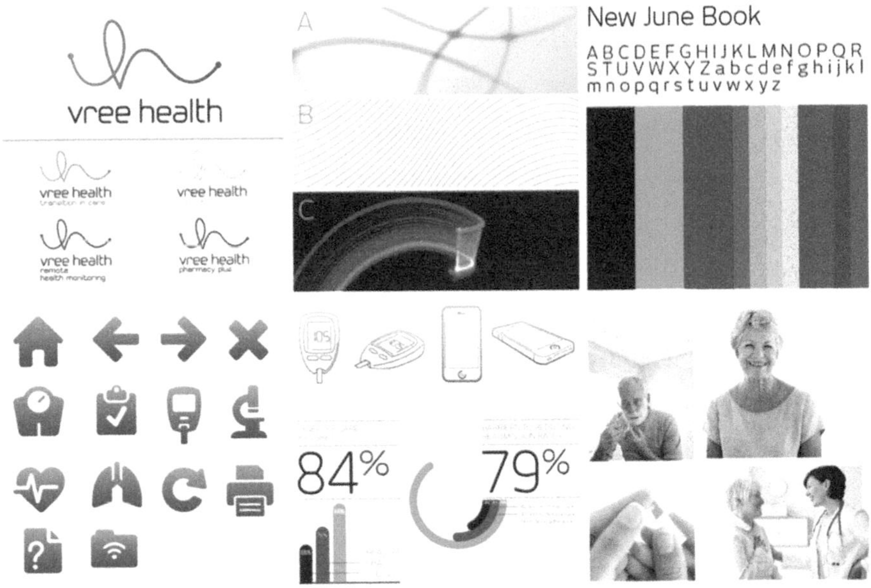

AT A LOSS FOR WORDS: WHY DON'T HEALTHCARE BRANDS USE TAG LINES?

My colleagues and I consider a tag line part of the primary branding hallmarks along with the logo, typography, iconography and color. So why is it that regulated healthcare brands almost never employ a tag line as part of their core brand identity?

First, let's settle the primary debate ensuing from my last question: is a tag line a branding asset or just part of the messaging? It depends on whom you ask. If one believes that a tag line should be considered an immutable part of the brand identity, only to be altered with considerable deliberation, then one would say it is a blood relative of the logo, icon, color palette and typography. If, on the other hand, one feels that its particular marketplace is so dynamic and volatile that the tag line should be up for grabs at any given moment (especially when a new agency comes aboard!), then it becomes just another phrase in the messaging platform. However, even those consumer brands that alter their tag lines do so infrequently and over the course of years. So I contend that this practice tips the balance of the argument in my favor: tag lines should be considered a primary branding asset.

When I ask marketers of healthcare brands why not a tag line, the usual answers are:

- **a.** It's a policy we have not to use tag lines,
- **b.** I don't think the FDA allows it,
- **c.** Whatever it would be, it wouldn't translate well around the world, or
- **d.** I don't know.

When I question further on "a" I get "d" as an answer. When I point out that "b" is not the case and ask the question again, "d" comes up! And as far as things not translating around the world, some very successful consumer brands have somehow figured out a way to consistently overcome that non-barrier. I believe that healthcare marketers are simply at a loss for words. That is, they've looked around the market, saw that nobody else seems to be doing it, conclude that it must be a bad practice, and keep quiet. First, do no harm, right?

Let's see if we can build a case. Before considering a tag line, one should consider its role in the brand identity. A tag line is supposed to reinforce the commitment to customers by the brand—the Brand Promise. It should not be a list of brand personality traits. Remember Nuprin's *Little. Yellow. Different.*? Neither does anyone who buys Advil, Aleve, Motrin, or any other pain reliever still on the market. A tag line should function neither as a wish for continued commercial success—*The number one glaucoma therapy in America*—nor as a stage for pathetic bragging—*The only hospital antibiotic that comes in pre-filled syringes.* Why not? Well, one reason is that a move by competitors can effectively take away the right to make such claims. Another better reason is that these tag lines should be working so much harder for the brands in ways that cannot be revoked.

Let's do a small exercise: think of your favorite tag lines for consumer goods. Here are some of mine:

Don't leave home without it
Because you're worth it
Drivers wanted
Come to where the flavor is
You can do it. We can help.

Now what do these memorable tag lines have in common? They are short and to the point, sure. But more importantly they speak *to* the customer and not *about* themselves. They are a careful warning (*Don't leave home without it*); an encouraging cheer (*You can do it. We can help.*); a seductive invitation (*Come to where the flavor is*). They connect with customers on deep emotional levels: on the road of life, there are passengers and there are drivers—*Drivers wanted.* Don't just use any beauty product; use the one that understands you deserve the very best. *Because you're worth it.* And if these tag lines were for healthcare brands, they do not constitute claims and therefore would pass muster with internal or governmental regulatory authorities.

As for working around the world, it is an issue every global brand faces every day. While certain aspects of color are universal—e.g., blue evokes calm and trustworthiness—some colors have extra meaning in different cultures. For example, in certain Eastern cultures, red is the sign of a married woman or the color of a wedding dress. However, red shares a number of positive associations across cultures: excitement, passion, prosperity, and so on. Likewise, differences in languages may result in tag lines being interpreted differently. So successful consumer goods companies don't translate tag lines, they trans-create them. That is, they go for consistency of strategic intent rather than a literal translation. In some cases, trans-creation and translation are one and the same. *Venga donde esta el sabor* is close enough: *Come to where the flavor is.* But McDonald's *I'm lovin' it* becomes *Me encanta* in Spanish (I really like it) and *I just like it* in China. Not the same, but strategically consistent.

So if just one major healthcare manufacturer decides to go first and embrace a full-spectrum branding practice, my guess is that many more will follow suit. If the first rule of medicine is *First, do no harm,* it seems that the second could be *Don't miss the bandwagon*. And that's my tag line for this whole matter.

In Chapters 7, 8 and 9 I have gone into great detail about The Goldilocks Process for building single-brand identities. This process is at the heart of good branding, and these three chapters are worth spending the time to re-read, not only to ensure you understand the process itself, but so that you're well aware of the hidden problems clients and agencies face when building brand identities.

My next chapter deals with the topic of brand families: corporate, franchise, and sibling brands that seek a Brand Architecture—a formal structure and hierarchy that guide the collective behaviors of a brand family. Brand Architecture is a growing trend among healthcare companies looking to consolidate their brand identity assets, so let's examine the hidden problems agencies and clients encounter with brand families and the best practices to avoid an identity crisis in this area of branding.

10

Brand Architecture and the Crisis of Delay

Brand Architecture is an omnibus term for the complementary ideas of a Brand Family—a series of brands that co-exist at the company, franchise, product, and sub-product levels—and Brand Hierarchy—the primacy of brands in relationship to each other. Brand Architecture lays out a series of rules for how brand families should position themselves *vis-à-vis* one another so that each entity in the family can leverage the equity of its parent and sister brands . . . or not. I say "not," because some brand families choose to pursue an "every brand for itself" architecture (commonly called a House of Brands), while others have very strict rules where a master brand has great sway over the family (Branded House).

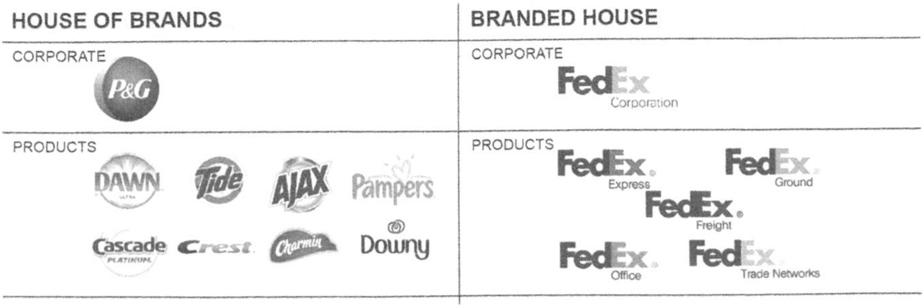

In the illustration above, we can see the polar extremes of a Brand Architecture paradigm. On the left, the parent brand, Procter & Gamble, has virtually no association with the product brands in its portfolio. In fact, certain brands in the house, such as Tide, Era, and Dynamo (the latter two not shown) actually compete against each other. On the flip side, the master brand, FedEx, exerts an ironclad control over how its sub-brand identities look and perform. It is clear to see that the FedEx master brand values dominate, while in the P&G architecture the product brands dominate without any acknowledgment to the parent brand. While there is no single right answer in terms of which architecture is right for any brand family, there is one big hidden problem for most brand families in healthcare: clients wait until they are too far along in their portfolio development before thinking about Brand Architecture. It's one thing to have a House of Brands, but to let it happen by accident is another of the most common causes of identity crisis in healthcare branding.

Before we get further into the haphazard ways in which many healthcare brand families manage (or not) their architecture, it's important to point out that in addition to the polar extremes cited above—House of Brands and Branded House—there are also several nuanced variations across the continuum from one to another. Here are four variations of a House of Brands architecture that illustrate how multidimensional the concept really is:

Here the General Motors example is as Detached as the P&G model. GM addresses the market situation by letting its strong franchises (Chevrolet, Buick, and Cadillac, to name a few) battle it out with similar lines of cars from competitors, as well as each other. The flip side in the auto industry would be BMW, which establishes values at the master brand level (BMW), and then has those values trickle down to each of its franchises, the 3-, 5- and 7- series, for example.

Then there is Disney, which takes somewhat of a "shepherd" approach—a bit less Detached than GM, yet exerting a stylistic Overbrand

aura so the sibling brands are clearly related to the parent in look and feel. Next, there's the Sky Team example, here called an Endorsed House of Brands because while each member of the Sky Team is permitted to have its own unique identity apart from the parent, these identities are all linked by the Sky Team logo endorsement. And finally, even in a House of Brands architecture there's room for a Nike master brand that's so strong it can allow its sub-brands to depart from a regimented look and feel to exist on their own, yet still have the blue eyes (i.e., the swoosh) of the parent brand on display.

As we can see from the illustration below, a Branded House architecture also has some flexibility.

With the Apple example top left, we notice a common typography that every sub-brand uses, as well as a nomenclature commonality (i.e., the "i" prefix or the "mac" prefix), even though the products have unique identities in diverse categories such as computing, music, and telecommunications. On the top right, the Microsoft Branded House exerts a slightly more regimented architecture over its sub-brands than its Disney Overbrand example in the previous illustration. The Endorsement example for United Technologies calls for not only the same typeface, but also the same icon associated with its brand family. And finally, the Intel example is similar to the FedEx House of Brands' master brand approach.

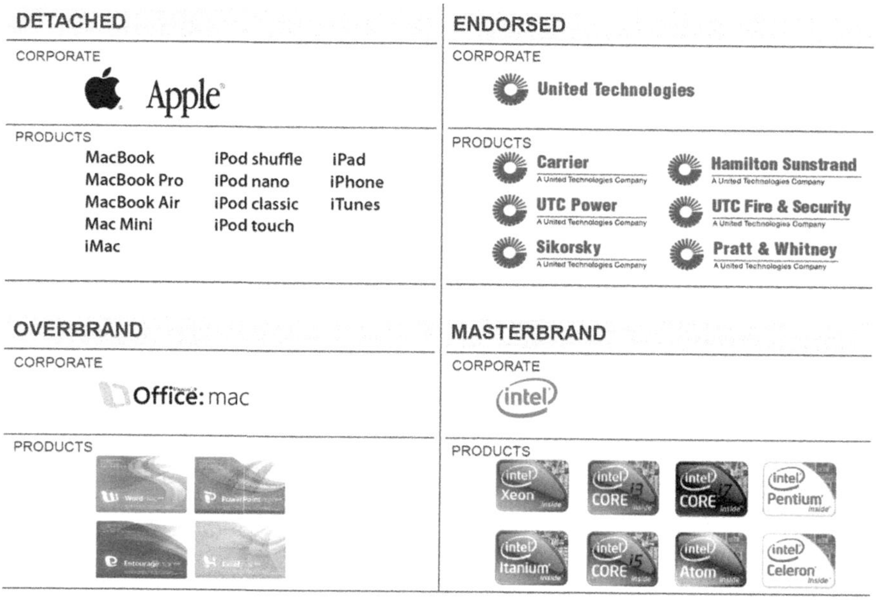

In pharmaceuticals and biotech, the trend has been moving toward more of a Branded House Architecture over the years. Some potential reasons responsible for the trend could be:

- The parent brand has more esteemed equity than the product brands, so the family members should remind customers of how closely they are tied to the accomplishments of their forebears;
- A Branded House architecture offers a more efficient way to manage all brand assets, since the branding guidelines are established for the family overall and then leveraged with each new sibling brand (rather than starting from scratch each time);

- Sometimes the sibling product lines are playing in a rather "me-too" commodity market, and differentiation is better at the parent (corporate) brand level (see Ethicon example below); and
- Sometimes the company brand is small and focuses on only one or two therapeutic categories. Having a Branded House architecture announces to the market that they are a dedicated niche player (see Novo Nordisk below).

Two of the most organized Branded House families with which I've worked are Ethicon Sutures and Novo Nordisk. With Ethicon Sutures, the reputation of J&J's flagship hospital-supply business is of such paramount importance to surgeons and their colleagues that it trumps the functionality and practical values associated with its different brand families of sutures, such as Sutures Plus and Sutures CV, as well as those at the product brand level Monocryl and PDS, and Ethibond and Prolene, respectively. The illustration below shows this brand family's architecture.

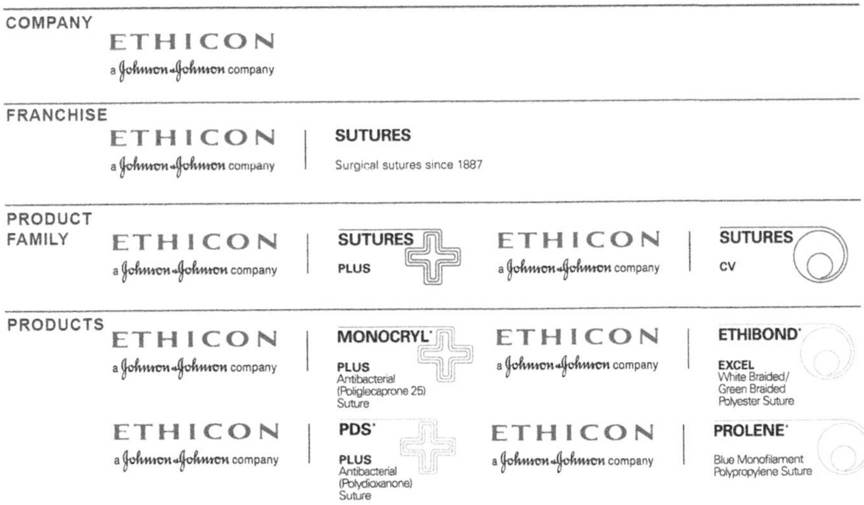

Whereas Ethicon's approach to a Branded House is a true Master Brand architecture, Novo Nordisk takes more of an Overbrand approach. We can readily see the nomenclature device at work as the "novo" prefix graces most of their brands. However, as we see in the illustration below, from a design point of view, each member of the product brand family is permitted to have its own stylistic look and feel, with different typography from the parent brand, as well as unique iconography and color palettes.

novo nordisk

NovoFine® Plus

NovoSeven®
Recombinant Factor VIIa

novoeight
Antihemophilic Factor (Recombinant)

NovoLog®
insulin aspart (rDNA origin) injection

NovoLog® Mix 70/30
70% insulin aspart protamine suspension and
30% insulin aspart injection, (rDNA origin)

For those companies that are fielding more of a House of Brands architecture, here are several reasons that model may work for them:

- They are a large pharma or biotech company where the corporate brand is associated with many different therapeutic categories, so the brand families and sibling brands have greater relevance and equity (see Lilly's Central Nervous System (CNS) Portfolio example below);

Lilly CNS Portfolio

Zyprexa
Olanzapine

strattera®
atomoxetine HCl

Cymbalta®
duloxetine HCl

Symbyax
Olanzapine and Fluoxetine HCl Capsules

- The corporate infrastructure is not set up so as to have management and budgets in place at a franchise (brand family) level, so the company has defaulted to a House of Brands model; and
- The product brands are blockbusters and have greater equity than that of the parent brand.

Looking back at the Lilly CNS Portfolio illustration above, ever since the company struck "anti-depression gold" with Prozac, Lilly has had a string of highly successful sibling brands. The blockbuster Zyprexa is a multi-billion dollar brand, while Cymbalta and Strattera are the most exciting medical advances to come out for the treatment of depression and ADHD, respectively, in years. My team has had the great fortune of working on all of these identities, not to mention the launch identity for Symbyax, a combination of the molecules found in both Prozac and Zyprexa. As you can see, each of these brands has a distinctive identity; and the CNS brand family functions well as a House of Brands, not only because of their individual successes, but also because Lilly maintains strong brand family presences in Oncology and Diabetes, to name two.

When Amgen first launched in the early 1990s, its corporate reputation soared, so it began as a Branded House with a Detached architecture similar to Apple, where the nomenclature (i.e., the "gen" suffix taken from the parent brand) were evident in both Epogen (epoetin alpha) and the previously discussed Neupogen (filgrastim). Today, Amgen's brands are such blockbusters (both Enbrel and Neulasta are among the top 20 best-selling bioengineered drugs in the world) that the company has evolved into a House of Brands approach. (Please seek out online the logos for all brands cited here as Amgen categorically refused to grant permission for inclusion in this book.)

Whether choosing a Branded House or House of Brands, the most successful companies actively cultivate from as early a stage as possible the five critical principles around which successful Brand Architectures are built:

1. **Companies must have the institutional will.** Companies that seek to use Branded Houses as part of the marketing mix must commit fully to operationalize this model. They must establish a franchise (portfolio or brand family) marketing team that has discretion over the marketing teams for the individual brands in the franchise. They must have a budget sizeable enough that the individual brand managers are incentivized to compete for the franchise's subsidies and cooperation. Without such resources in place at the franchise level, the individual brands will do whatever they please because the company doesn't have any mechanism for compelling compliance. Trying to "tax" the individual brands so that programs can be fielded at the franchise (portfolio) level will not only fail to generate results, it will also frustrate and anger the brand managers who will contend that they are receiving mixed messages about how their performance will be measured: product sales or company cooperation? These two incentives can often be at odds, especially for flagship brands that deliver hefty profits for the franchise and seek all the money they can "keep" from other, less successful brands in the franchise.

2. **Be smart enough to field brand equity research.** This may sound like a no-brainer, but many companies do not bother to do external research with customers about their plans for a Brand Architecture. Further, whatever research they do field too often is about the product brands themselves and not how the brand identities of the company and the individual products reflect customer esteem. Brands are like friendly mirrors: they embody values that are dear to customers so that customers see a flattering reflection

of themselves whenever they encounter the brand. Research that focuses on traditional marketing measurements—awareness, share of voice, ranking of product elements—may be helpful in building campaigns and messages, but they hardly scratch the surface of why grouping these brands into a franchise would be welcomed by customers. Discover if customers identify with your company values and which ones they esteem the most. Understand the equity of your product brands in customers' minds. Do they leverage any corporate values? Do they share a common value? If combined, is the sum greater than the collective parts? By conducting brand identity research, you can learn the value of each perceptual asset in the portfolio and use these as building blocks for your franchise. (See Chapter 7 for a greater discussion on Discovery research.)

3. **Dare to stand for more than just the products you sell**. Back in the 1980s, a relatively small company named Stuart Pharmaceuticals made a commitment to meet a market need in oncology. While chemotoxic brands (those that kill cancer) and chemostatic brands (those that keep cancer from growing), were the main subject of research and development for other companies, Stuart was among the first to realize the potential of hormonal therapies in breast and prostate cancer. (These are called adjuvant therapies, or therapies used to sustain remission achieved with other agents.) Their first drug brand, Nolvadex (tamoxifen), would go on to become one of the best-selling and paradigm-changing brands in the category. However, before its launch, no oncologist had ever heard of Stuart Pharmaceuticals. So their oncology franchise did something that the oncology community sorely needed: it committed to raise awareness about breast cancer, its devastating effect on the population, and the need for early screening. Working with their agencies, Burson-Marsteller for public relations, Young & Rubicam

for consumer awareness, and Sudler & Hennessey, where I was a key leader on the healthcare promotion side of the equation, they created and promoted Breast Cancer Awareness Day in conjunction with leading doctor and patient societies. Not only did the oncology community become immediately cognizant of Stuart, but they also applauded the fact that the company was investing in more than just promotion for their upcoming drug. Of course, today we all appreciate the phenomenon that has become Breast Cancer Awareness Month. The Stuart oncology franchise went on to launch their portfolio of brands, each with the franchise family suffix, "dex": Zoladex, Arimdex, Casodex, and Faslodex. Today, we know Stuart by a new company name, Astra-Zeneca, one of the world's leading pharmaceutical brands. And they can trace their franchise success to their sage wisdom of daring to stand for more than just the products they sell. They committed to a cause that rallied a nation and at the same time gave their brand the national visibility it needed for long-term success.

4. **Build the brand family around your customers, not your brands.** I started off this discussion by addressing the need to base the franchise (portfolio) identity around customers and their lives. If I had to name the single greatest error most companies commit in fielding a franchise, it would be failing to abide by this principle. Sure, companies create franchises for good internal reasons: better resource allocation across the portfolio, a better way to position the assets in the portfolio to maximize profits as a whole, a great way to energize and incentivize marketing and sales personnel. However, when it comes to creating an external promise to customers, the franchises that continue to look only inward will ultimately fail. Ethicon, discussed earlier in this chapter, learned this lesson well. The quality and reputation of Ethicon's

many brands are an acknowledged aspect of the company's equity among customers. But healthcare cost containment is perhaps the single greatest ongoing issue facing hospitals. So despite the high esteem hospitals and surgeons have for the Ethicon brand, circumstances compelled them to purchase cheaper brands from opportunistic competitors. Sales began to decline for each element in the Ethicon portfolio: sutures, needles, scalpels, and structural mesh used to strengthen tissue in certain procedures, and so on. Hospitals began awarding contracts for each item to the lowest bidder. But Ethicon knew their customers and used the principles we have discussed above to right the ship. They discovered that hospitals needed something more than just supplies; they needed to simplify supply management and streamline procedures. If hospitals could do this, they would save much more money than by pinching pennies on the supplies themselves. Ethicon reorganized the company franchise offerings not by the products, but rather by the procedures that surgeons performed: The Hernia Franchise, The Breast Augmentation Franchise, The Bariatric Surgery Franchise. By bundling products and services tailored toward how their customers used them in concert with each other, Ethicon sustained its dominance through a customer-centric Brand Architecture approach.

5. **Recognize that it is a marathon, not a sprint**. If ignoring principle number four is the most common error in franchise development, then my last principle here is decidedly the second most common. Don't start a Branded House architecture if your company cannot or will not sustain the effort for a long time. Too many companies have ruined their reputations by forming a franchise while they have brands to support it, only to fold the tent once the brands lose their patents. Customers will never forget such a betrayal.

> And the next time that the company tries to restart the Branded House approach, or tries to start a different one, customers will mistrust their intentions and avoid engaging with them or their brands. This behavior can be found in companies of all sizes. Large companies that focus on different revenue streams from different therapeutic categories can be distracted from one commitment as they try to foster too many others. Small companies may never amass the muscular resources needed to truly fulfill the promise that is in their hearts. They can all grow fatigued and drop out of the race by not recognizing that their customers are running a marathon, while they were in a sprint.

So if there are clear principles and such a broad continuum (eight shown at this chapter's outset) of Brand Architectures, what's the identity crisis in healthcare branding? Answer: The overwhelming majority of healthcare companies that create franchises—or branded portfolios of products and/or services—do so as an afterthought. That is, they launch a few product brands without ever thinking of their corporate or sibling brands in the pipeline, eventually run into conflicts about how to represent those products to customers, and then layer over the products with a portfolio approach that (more often than not) is based on what they have to sell rather than why customers are buying. Do you think that Coca-Cola would ever launch a sparkling beverage without a full review of how it could help or hurt their bedrock Coke franchise? Never. So why is this identity crisis so ever-present in regulated healthcare marketing? My only answer: sometimes, an embarrassment of riches blinds companies to the fact that such riches can earn them greater customer loyalty and esteem than they already have. "We're doing great. Why change?" They never ask themselves if things could get even better.

Back in 2010, one of the inVentiv Health advertising agencies with which I was affiliated as Chief Branding Officer for the corporation called me with a frantic question: "Botox wants to know what colors they should give to their new Chronic Migraine prevention indication." As I've written in the last chapter, if Allergan, Botox's parent brand, had planned out the Botox (Botulinum toxin type A) brand experience from the beginning, they would have already had this answer in hand. And the more I investigated the situation, the more I realized just how much of an identity crisis Botox was experiencing.

For those of you who know of Botox only in its Cosmetic brand identity, you will be surprised to discover that the brand actually makes roughly four times as much revenue from non-cosmetic indications. As it turns out, Botox is somewhat of a miracle drug: a nerve-paralyzing toxin (a poison) that in the hands of Allergan became a life-changing agent for many different medical conditions. In post-stroke spasticity (PSS), Botox injections calmed the random jerky motions to allow the sufferer to simply sit down in a chair comfortably and eat dinner or watch TV. For cervical dystonia (CD) (also called spasmodic torticollis), a painful condition in which your neck muscles contract involuntarily, causing your head to twist in all directions, Botox also calms the action, normalizing simple life functions for patients in great distress. And for certain people who sweat profusely under their arms—a condition called hyperhidrosis (HH)—Botox can also relieve the over-activity. One logo stood for each of Botox's indications:

BOTOX®
Botulinum Toxin Type A

But these conditions—PSS, CD and HH—are relatively unknown to the general public. No surprise, then, that when Botox suddenly became the age-defying treatment of aspiring divas, most of the world assumed it was Big Pharma's overnight answer to Paris Hilton: beautiful, famous, but essentially superficial. So some faction at Allergan, wary of the existing brand identity's ability to adequately express its more fashionable side of the family genealogy, decided to put out its own variation of the logo:

BOTOX®
—Cosmetic
onabotulinumtoxinA

Notice that the original Botox logo was put on a crash diet, resulting in its Size 2 typography and big "Cosmetic" indication—the first for Botox among any indications. Allergan even found a way to obscure the word "toxin" in the generic. Little did they suspect at the time that their seemingly small logo tweak would set in motion an identity crisis that would lead up to the phone call I received and well beyond for the next 18 months.

You see, Allergan continued aggressively to pursue new clinical indications for the non-cosmetic portfolio. However, unlike PSS, CD and HH, these new indications were going to help millions of people in a therapeutic way, thereby leveraging the brand's original identity of Essential, Enabling, and Compassionate. The only problem was that the brand now stood for Vain, Indulgent, and Superficial. Research showed that loyal neurologists and other professional Botox users were very upset that the therapy they relied upon to normalize their injured patients' lives had become a punch line on late-night talk shows. Back in 2010, Botox was looking at three horizon indications that would double its revenues and offer significantly unique relief for the major conditions of Chronic Migraine (CM), Overactive Bladder (OAB), and Benign Prostatic Hyperplasia (BPH or an enlarged prostate). Yet the original logo had been hijacked by the Hollywood and fashion elite. "Ring! Ring!" went my phone. "What should we do?"

It turned out that the rather simple question—what colors should the Chronic Migraine indication use in its palette?—turned out to be a much larger question: what is the desired Allergan/Botox brand architecture, and how does it guide the selection of design elements and market positioning? Had Allergan instituted a proper brand architecture strategy to begin with, they would have avoided this identity crisis.

Botox had violated Principle #1 above and precipitated a common brand identity crisis: they did not set up their corporate infrastructure with management and budgets in place at a franchise (brand family) level, so the company had defaulted to a House of Brands model. Instead of one central Botox brand manager, there were brand managers for each of the indications. And each indication manager would launch their indication somewhat in silos, creating micro-processes and idiosyncratic branding strategies that had little to do with the sibling indications. The most prominent example, as stated, was the Cosmetic indication, which established a precedent for putting the indication right into the logo, something that had never been done using the established Botox logo, and setting in motion an internal contest to reclaim the medical side of the brand by further trying to tweak the logo (e.g., what colors should I make the Chronic Migraine Botox logo?)

One ambitious and smart Allergan marketer quickly understood the situation as we explained it, and appealed to his management for a promotion of sorts to a Botox franchise level, where he could help shepherd the entire Botox Medical architecture as a centralized resource. Management gave him the elevated role, however, because they gave him no budget; his position was largely ceremonial as those with the money (the indication managers) could do whatever they wished to have their indication succeed in the market. Still, Allergan is a reasonable company populated by genuinely good people, and, with our help, our "acting" brand family manager was able to form a willing coalition of the Botox medical indication managers. We convened a Brand Architecture workshop, which follows the same format as the branding workshop outlined in Chapter 8, only with a few different exercises:

- We performed a brand family exercise in which the workshop teams each selected a famous family in real life or fiction, and then we used the family as an analogy to the Botox Medical family. (The Corleones and The Kennedys were the examples chosen);
- We examined the Brand Promises and Brand Personalities of the existing indications (PSS, CD, HH, and others) to look for commonalities; and
- We helped create Brand Promises and Personalities for the horizon indications (Chronic Migraine, OAB, and BPH) that leveraged those from the existing indications.

We also forged a Brand Family Promise for the Botox Medical franchise—*The source for life-changing results* (since Botox is injected directly into the "source" of the physical ailment and provides transformational relief)—as well as a Family Brand Personality: Enabling, Liberating, and Compassionate. Post workshop, we even explored the possibility of a Botox Medical look and feel:

BOTOX Botulinum Toxin Type A
OAB | over active bladder

BOTOX Botulinum Toxin Type A
CM | chronic migraine

BOTOX Botulinum Toxin Type A
PSS | post stroke spasticity

However, because Allergan never really instituted a well-resourced Medical Brand Family infrastructure, the initiative went back to the original two logos for Botox and Botox Cosmetic, and the company ended up defaulting to a unique type of brand architecture: the single-brand franchise.

Unlike the brand families discussed earlier with multiple brands in their architecture, Botox is a rare bird—a single-brand franchise: a brand with different indications for different conditions treated by different medical specialists. I have had the good fortune to work on a half dozen or so of these brands and have refined and repurposed some of my workshop techniques outlined in Chapter 8 to help clients understand their unique asset. Let's take the time to explore this unusual brand architecture.

SAME BRAND, MULTIPLE INDICATIONS: IS A SINGLE-BRAND FRANCHISE STRATEGY RIGHT FOR YOU?

Remember Deion Sanders, the pro athlete who played not only for National Football League teams (two of which won the Super Bowl), but also for several Major League Baseball teams, including the 1992 Atlanta Braves, which made it to the World Series? Many admired his gridiron skills and ability to play many different positions effectively: cornerback, kick returner, running back, and wide receiver. Most players would be happy excelling at one sport in one position. But not Deion. He was an athletic legend, like Jim Thorpe before him, and his ability to deliver value in multiple arenas helped foster the concept of the one-man (single-brand) franchise.

Bayer Aspirin was probably the first to market itself as a healthcare single-brand franchise. Renowned for its pain-relieving ability for sore joints and muscles, it gained a greater reputation as a preventative therapy for heart attack and stroke, as well as colon, lung, esophageal, and breast cancers. As such, generic aspirin, a.k.a. acetylsalicylic acid, or ASA, was rebranded as The Wonder Drug by Bayer, and The Miracle Drug by Dr. Mehmet Oz, the ubiquitous celebrity M.D.

Over the past 20 years, cultivating a single-brand franchise in healthcare has become a much more common practice primarily due to the proliferation of bioengineered therapies targeting key elements of the immune system in auto-immune disorders, which can vary from asthma to MS to psoriasis to cancer, each with differing patient types and different treating physicians. For example, having been approved for non-Hodgkin lymphoma in 1997 by the FDA, Rituxan (rituximab) made its mark early as an effective agent in boosting chemotherapy regimens and extending life. But the brand's long-term plans to explore many different indications in many diverse disease states had then-partners Genentech and Roche asking the all-important question: should the Rituxan brand bear the burden—and the glory—of being a single-brand superstar like Deion Sanders, or should different brand names be used when the time came to launch into new indications?

Rituxan®
Rituximab

The brand came to my team and me at this point, and on my advice, we carried out a brand architecture workshop to answer some important questions:

- Are there values for the existing indication that can benefit the horizon indications?
- Are those values to be found in a functional attribute? Practical application? Emotional benefit?
- Are there risks with the horizon indications that could harm the brand's stature for the existing indication?
- Do different, unrelated physician specialties care how a drug performs in indications other than the one they treat? And if so, can these perceptions be leveraged?

The brand's predictable knee-jerk response to this last question was, "Does it really matter?" If you use traditional research—e.g., one-on-one interviews or focus groups—specialists in one field will always default to the safe harbor of "It doesn't matter as long as there is data supporting that it will work in my specialty." But my experience shows that physicians make choices beyond statistics about the brand; they base their choices also on what they believe about themselves and on what they feel other people believe about them (see more on this in Chapter 5).

In the case of Botox, which was used for years as a life-altering treatment for neurologic conditions such as PSS and CD, it earned Botox a reputation among neurologists as a serious medical treatment, and established a track record of safety and tolerability (remember, it's a toxin), which mattered a great deal to those anticipating the OAB and BPH indications (urologists). When Botox made headlines for its non-medical use as a short-term wrinkle cure, medical specialists who had been brand loyalists for years suddenly began questioning their own use of the brand. So, yes, the brand perceptions of specialists in unrelated fields absolutely matter.

Creating a single-brand franchise is not always the right choice. Again, it depends on whether the equity of the existing indication can be leveraged and/or whether the horizon indications threaten the existing indication. I touched upon this briefly in Chapter 6, where fluoxetine branded as Prozac was inappropriate ("It's not all in my head!") for another of its indications, Pre-Menstrual Dysphoric Disorder, a severe form of PMS. In a similar example, Merck's Proscar (finasteride) earned a serious reputation in the treatment of enlarged prostate and later in prevention of prostate cancer. However, the additional indication of treating alopecia (hair loss) threatened Proscar's brand equity. Despite its proven efficacy and safety, physicians had trouble seeing themselves using Proscar ("I don't 'treat' baldness."), and insurance companies balked at the idea that they would never be certain if they were authorizing coverage for a medical therapy or a cosmetic improvement. Hence, Propecia (also finasteride) was born.

Propecia® (finasteride)
TYPE II 5 ALPHA-REDUCTASE INHIBITOR

PROSCAR® (finasteride)

With the exceptions of Bayer aspirin and Deion Sanders, my team and I have helped all of these brands and many more to research and strategize their options. As biotech development continues to introduce multi-talented monoclonal antibodies, and pro-drug technology gives new lives to existing molecules, more and more healthcare companies will be asking themselves if a single-brand franchise approach is right for them. If they start early enough and use branding protocols that have been proven in the past, there could be many more legends in the making.

For the final chapter in this book, I want to turn our attention to things beyond a product brand identity and branded conditions that can help avoid identity crises by building a better understanding about cause and effect in treatment and promoting better dialogues between healthcare professionals and their patients. Branding the Science is the term given to such initiatives, but even this is too narrow a term for all that branding can do to raise awareness and foster engagement among the healthcare constituencies beyond products and services. For our purposes, I call it Branding the Healthcare Landscape.

11

Branding and the Healthcare Landscape

I began this book with a call for a greater appreciation of how health and wellness have become paramount factors in how we craft our own identities, how we define who we are to ourselves, our family, our friends, and our co-workers. Mostly, I've concentrated on the central building blocks essential to avoiding a brand identity crisis for products and services: a correct definition of branding and how it functions; an intimate, insightful understanding of healthcare customers; The Goldilocks Process; debunking the idea that healthcare branding is anything like consumer goods branding; the cultivated approach to brand architecture; and the proactive willingness to connect branding design to insights, strategies, and even a coherent branding system. I've also touched on the branding of healthcare conditions, and tried to demonstrate that such a process, which is often maligned by critics who seek to profit by instigating fear, is actually a public service to publish "wanted posters" of the pathological enemies that beset our minds and bodies so that we may gain power over them and reduce their ability to shame, diminish, or defeat us. What I wish to do in this last chapter is close the loop on aspects of the healthcare landscape that, when branded effectively, can help in preventing our ongoing struggle against identity crises in which significant aspects of our lives are defined by wellness and/or illness.

The human mind has a fundamental affinity for branding. In order to mentally "file" the many concepts that bombard our minds each day, we naturally assign them unique identities—shorthand branding—because otherwise such concepts become overwhelming and unable to be assimilated. When my twin daughters were around five or six, I would invariably bring them back small gifts from the countries I visited on business travel to help them appreciate how vast and different the world was beyond their neighborhood frame of reference. I once came back from a trip to Germany having purchased two identical German Black Forest dolls in traditional dress. My gift-giving theory: don't show favoritism and give each of my twins the exact same doll. I handed one to each of my girls. They examined them with joy and then switched them, each preferring what I had given to the other. Here's the verbatim dialogue:

Me: Why did you switch them? They're both the same.
Lauren: No they're not. This one's the smart one.
Erika: And this one has better adventures.

The smart one   The one with better adventures

Perhaps because they are twins, my daughters may be more in need of distinguishing between one's own and one's sister's property. But it was a revelation to me. My daughters needed them to be different. They couldn't tolerate two things being exactly the same. And they branded the dolls on the spot with reflections of themselves: Lauren was usually deep in thought, while Erika was commonly involved in physical activity.

I began observing even the smallest ways that people selected between identical items just because they were searching for the one that best reflected who they were: the third copy of *The New York Times* in the stack (because he's discriminating?); the Diet Coke on the left (because she's left handed?); the isolated black car next to a sea of identical black cars on the dealer's lot (because it looks cooler?). The human mind cannot abide sameness. We've seen this principle in operation in healthcare when my physician father picked Zestril (more powerful) over Prinivil (less powerful) even though they were both brands of lisinopril (Chapter 5). Or when a mother of four selected Robitussin (trusted) over Mucinex (aggressive) even though they are both guaifenesin, a mucolytic (Chapter 4). And even in my opening chapter, where we witnessed how Advil was the serious "doctor-in-a-bottle" version of ibuprofen, which outsold the identical drug Nuprin (celebrity pain) 10-to-1, we can see how our minds welcome branding as a means of sorting the world into "me" and "not me" preferences. With these observations in mind, there is no concept in healthcare where branding cannot offer the differentiation human beings crave when contemplating how health and wellness influences their lives.

> THE HUMAN MIND HAS A FUNDAMENTAL AFFINITY FOR BRANDING. WE INSIST ON ASSIGNING ENTITIES UNIQUE IDENTITIES BECAUSE OTHERWISE SUCH ENTITIES BECOME OVERWHELMING AND UNABLE TO BE ASSIMILATED.

When we hear terms like Soccer Mom or Gym Rat, we understand that these are successful attempts to brand respectively a) young, responsible, middle-class housewives who are very involved with their children and shepherd them to sporting events and play dates; and b) physically active men who—no matter what their occupation or social status—spend an inordinate amount of time working out or playing sports. These branded terms are very helpful in succinctly conjuring up segments of the population for the purposes of self-identifying—or the opposite—self-distancing. The same concept can be branded in healthcare.

Back in the early '90s, when I was a Creative Director at Young & Rubicam's global healthcare agency Sudler & Hennessey, we were working on a campaign for a brand of oral contraceptive by Parke-Davis called Loestrin. Loestrin, as the name strongly implies, had very little estrogen (at the time estrogen was just beginning to be questioned for possible links to cancer and cardiovascular events). Women 18-35 were the largest customer segment for oral contraceptives, and Loestrin was trying to target this demographic successfully. But it had a problem: the low estrogen dosage in Loestrin created a side effect called "breakthrough bleeding," meaning bleeding from the uterus occurring between menstrual periods. The young women Loestrin was targeting have generally healthy, robust periods, yet little tolerance for breakthrough bleeding. Our client thought the brand was doomed . . . until we did some branding research. As it turned out, there was a different patient segment that needed oral contraceptives but had more tolerance for breakthrough bleeding: 40+ women who had had their families already or were divorced or never married but were still fertile. This patient segment had experienced more of what life could throw at them, so they were more likely to accept Loestrin's side effect in exchange for the lower exposure to estrogen in their bodies. "It's better for you . . . what's a little breakthrough bleeding?" Now that's a mouthful to say in promotion when trying to identify a patient type, so our team came up with a way to brand this patient segment much in the way the term Soccer Moms did its job. These were women who were not yet menopausal and still sexually active. We branded this person The Perimenopausal Woman, and the segment brand name has stuck ever since. Below is a recreation of the promotional concept that launched the patient segment branding and made Loestrin one of the top-selling oral contraceptives that's still in use today (the logo featured below is a contemporary one because the older one, along with the original ad, could not be found):

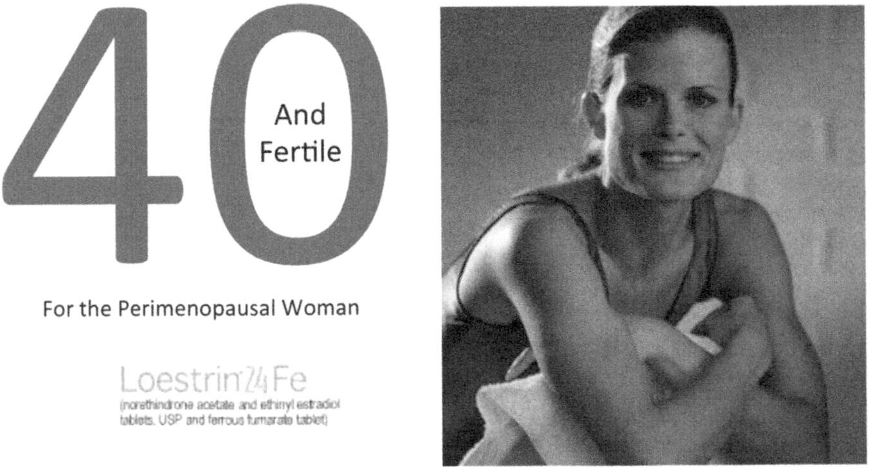

Other branded health segments also benefit society by giving people a well-defined group that they can choose to join or not, but at least people can view their choices as a society and make decisions that impact their self-image in regard to health and wellness. Consider the Weekend Warrior, a term we coined on behalf of Advil back in the 1980s: usually a man in his 30s-40s who in his spare time still engages in sports and really feels the pain the next day:

Or consider these: the Worried Well, a more flattering term for "hypochondriac"; the Treat and Street, a term we coined for ER physicians on the part of once-daily Rocephin, a blockbuster antibiotic discussed in Chapter 2, to brand patients who could be discharged on a single shot of the drug rather than requiring hospital admission and an overnight stay; or The Walking Wounded, the term used by psychiatrists to brand a type of patient who is in denial about their mental illness.

NB: If you are trying to enlighten the healthcare community about a branded patient segment, take great care not to make it unfairly cruel or pejorative as it will become a stereotype that will be used to hurt rather than help. Said a different way, when branding patient segments, always try to conjure a demographic or psychographic profile to enable more rapid recognition, more productive dialogues, and a consensus of action around the diagnosis and treatment of key sets of healthcare customers.

Another part of the healthcare landscape concerns the way we define how our therapies work. The mechanism of action (MOA) or the class designation for therapies are also open to be branded in ways that reveal a mode of attack or defense of our bodies and minds. Certain types of physician specialties—Neurologists, Oncologists, and Psychiatrists—crave branded MOAs just as my daughters craved their own "brand" of German doll.

When Prozac first came out, it worked in a very different way from typical tricyclic anti-depressants at the time, so the marketing team—in conjunction with leading psychiatrists—gave it a new class designation to highlight the difference. Prozac works by selectively blocking the re-uptake of serotonin, a mood-altering neurotransmitter. Because it worked differently from tricyclic anti-depressants, Prozac was able to explain scientifically why it managed mood, why it was not addictive and could not be used in volume to commit suicide (like tricyclics), and why there was no need for titration (a gradual increasing of dose so the body gets used to the therapy over time).

Psychiatrists are chemists at heart, and they listened intently to how Prozac offered a different pathway to address mood management. Prozac's new class brand of Selective Serotonin Receptor Inhibitor (SSRI) was a revolutionary way to think of a medical approach to depression and forever changed the way physicians and patients alike viewed depression therapy. With one pill once daily, SSRIs like Prozac (Zoloft and Paxil were two others that followed) completely changed the treatment paradigm by enabling primary care physicians safely and effectively to treat—and keep—their depressed patients without having to refer them to a psychiatrist. On the patient side, not having to go to a "shrink" removed the stigma that surrounded depression and encouraged a more de-stigmatized and frank dialogue about this mental illness. For their part, psychiatrists were relieved of much of their mild depression caseload and focused their attention on patients with more complex mental health issues. And all as a result of branding a new class of therapy that served as a lever that moved the world.

While working on the launch of the anti-depressant Effexor (venlafaxine) for Wyeth back in the 1990s, the client had a very potent drug, but it didn't happen to be the flavor of the day, an SSRI. Effexor worked on two neurotransmitters, just like the old tricyclics: serotonin and norepinephrine. Its double action made it potent for treating moderate-to-severe depression, often more effectively than the SSRIs. However, with an old class name, it didn't garner much attention from the chemically minded psychiatrists. So my team and I held a class branding workshop with the Wyeth marketing team and their academic physician advisors, and we came up with an accurate but more highly relevant class nomenclature of SNRI: a Serotonin Norepinephrine Reuptake Inhibitor. By co-opting the SSRI nomenclature format, yet staying true to how Effexor worked, we were able to brand a new class of therapy that helped Effexor get noticed and implemented to provide exceptional relief for tough depression.

On another front, while working with the inventor (Searle, now a part of Pfizer) of what would become Celebrex (celecoxib), and further following our pursuit of a new class of pain reliever with Vioxx (rofecoxib, discussed in Chapter 7), a multi-agency effort helped launch the first new class of anti-inflammatory in decades: Cox-II (now Cox-2) Inhibitors. Branding this new class of drugs would help establish a revolutionary treatment option for doctors and their patients with chronic pain management issues. Let's take a look at how we did it.

To simplify matters, let me illustrate the three different categories of class branding available to healthcare marketers.

- The site of the action: branding a class based on where it works in the mind or body;
- The action itself: branding a class based on what the drug actually does in the system; and
- The benefit of the action: what the customer gets out of the process in practical or emotional terms.

So this is the model for the anti-inflammatory pain category:

SITE OF ACTION	ACTION	BENEFIT OF ACTION
Cox-II Inhibition	Non-steroidal anti-inflammatory drugs (NSAIDs)	Disease-modifying anti-rheumatic drugs (DMARDs)

Here, the "Action" category is a catchall for any anti-inflammatory drug that isn't a steroid, including ibuprofen. As it turns out, both Celebrex and Vioxx are NSAIDs (just like all dogs and cats are mammals, but not all mammals are cats or dogs). To differentiate the true benefit of these more contemporary pain management agents—they block only the pathway to pain (Cox-II) and not the pathway to digestive distress that leads to ulcers (Cox-I)—we developed a class nomenclature and a visual diagram to help distinguish why these new entities could provide not only relief from pain, but also relief from gastrointestinal side effects typical of NSAIDs. In the workshop, our collective team coined the class name—Cox-II inhibitors—and developed the now famous wishbone diagram that simply shows why these drugs work to fight pain and inflammation yet spare the gut by leaving the Cox I pathway untouched (unlike other NSAIDs).

In the auto world, "four-wheel drive, all-terrain suspension" is a site-of-action mouthful that characterizes the class of transportation by its physical description, but Sports Utility Vehicle is much simpler and more evocative. Similarly, class branding can simplify and elucidate healthcare MOAs with new nomenclature that helps everyone understand things better. For doctors, the term Cox-2 Inhibitor quickly became shorthand for pain relief without stomach distress, and this is still a go-to class of pain reliever for patients with chronic pain.

As you consider this chapter and the other collective lessons of this book and begin to work them into your day-to-day practices, it's important to keep in mind that whenever you are asked as a healthcare marketer or agency strategist to help launch a new healthcare brand or to fix a problem with an existing healthcare brand, your job is not just

The COX-2 Hypothesis

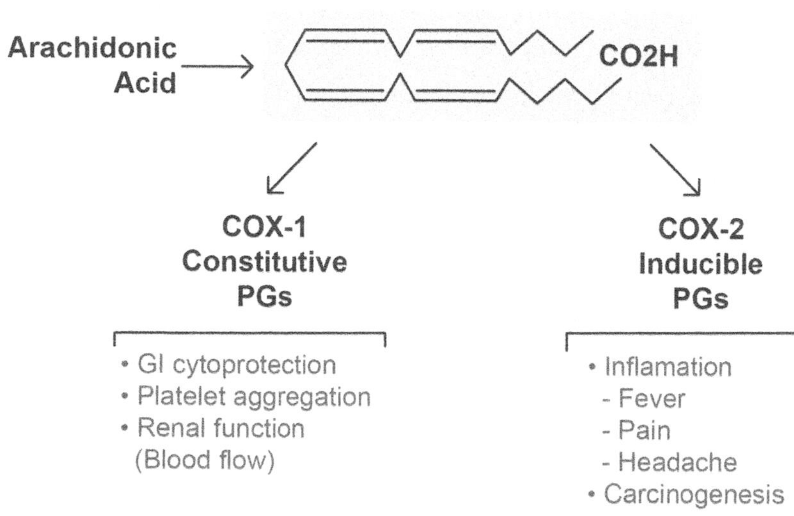

to focus on the messaging, the advertising, or even only the brand itself. Think about branding the entire healthcare landscape as part of your assessment. Ask yourself:

- Have HCPs' and patients' psychographic profiles been factored into the mix?
- Are there It, Me, and Them Beliefs that should be examined?
- Is the strategy Sustainable, Credible, Ownable, Relevant, and Exciting?
- Is the Brand Architecture being leveraged in a beneficial way?
- Can you draw a straight line between a Discovery insight, the strategy, and a design element or system?

- Is the disease or condition poorly branded?
- Is ineffective class branding holding you back?
- Does the patient segment need to be better branded?

Branding is so much more than words or images about a company, product, or service. It is a transfer of enthusiasm about the hope for a better life through health and wellness, and the possibilities that you are creating in the entire healthcare landscape that could make it a reality. The identity crisis plaguing healthcare is only as pathologic as we let it become. Shine a light on the hidden problems that hold back remedies from being as empowering as they can be. Let the proven processes and methodologies articulated in this book vanquish healthcare identity crises from our world so that healthcare branding can be the force for good to which it has always aspired. Let's exert our branding power over the concepts of health and wellness so that we can help define the kinds of selves we wish to be on our best days, and stop diminishing who we are by thinking of ourselves not as objects of our own illnesses, but rather as subjects of our own restoration. Be well, brand well, and the rest will follow.